Lecture Notes in Economics and Mathematical Systems

420

Lecture Notes in Economics and Mathematical Systems

420

Founding Editors:

M. Beckmann
H. P. Künzi

Editorial Board:

H. Albach, M. Beckmann, G. Feichtinger, W. Hildenbrand, W. Krelle
H. P. Künzi, K. Ritter, U. Schittko, P. Schönfeld, R. Selten

Managing Editors:

Prof. Dr. G. Fandel
Fachbereich Wirtschaftswissenschaften
Fernuniversität Hagen
Feithstr. 140/AVZ II, D-58097 Hagen, FRG

Prof. Dr. W. Trockel
Institut für Mathematische Wirtschaftsforschung (IMW)
Universität Bielefeld
Universitätsstr. 25, D-33615 Bielefeld, FRG

Marga Peeters

Time-To-Build

Interrelated Investment and
Labour Demand Modelling
With Applications to Six OECD Countries

 Springer

Author

Dr. Marga Peeters
Anjelienstraat 20
6002 TP Weert
The Netherlands

332.6
P37t

ISBN 3-540-58809-4 Springer-Verlag Berlin Heidelberg New York

Library of Congress Cataloging-in-Publication Data

Peeters, Marga, 1965- . Time-to-build: interrelated investments and labour demand modelling with applications to six OECD countries / Marga Peeters. p. cm. – (Lecture notes in economics and mathematical systems; 420) Includes bibliographical references (p.) and index. ISBN 3-540-58809-4 (Springer-Verlag Berlin Heidelberg New York: acid-free paper) – ISBN 0-387-58809-4 (Springer-Verlag New York Berlin Heidelberg: acid-free paper) 1. Investments–Mathematical models–Case studies. 2. Labor demand–Mathematical models–Case studies. I. Title. II. Series. HG4515.2.P44 1995 332.6–dc20 94-43958

© Springer-Verlag Berlin Heidelberg 1995
Printed in Germany

Typesetting: Camera ready by author
SPIN: 10486698   42/3140-543210 - Printed on acid-free paper

Acknowledgement

The research results presented in this monograph were obtained when I was a Ph.D. student, working at the University of Limburg (The Netherlands) and at the Centre de Recherche en Economie et Statistique in Paris (CREST, France). I gratefully acknowledge both institutions, the Netherlands Organisation for the Advancement of Pure Research (NWO, The Netherlands), Shell NL and the 'Stichting Organisatie van Effectenhandelaren te Rotterdam' for financial support.

Many people contributed to the realisation of this monograph. In particular, I owe a lot to Franz Palm. His constructive criticism has always stimulated me and improved my work considerably.

CONTENTS

1 PHYSICAL CAPITAL STOCK INVESTMENTS AND LABOUR DEMAND
Theoretical background on dynamic modelling

APPENDIX

2 INVESTMENT GESTATION LAGS
Construction lags, delivery lags and capital stock accumulation

OVERVIEW

0.1   Introduction

Investments are said to gestate because they bear potential utility or production possibilities. Examples of physical capital stock projects are housing investments that lead to (future) utility possibilities, and plant or machinery investments that lead to (future) productivity possibilities.

Many theories focus on the explanation of business investments. These investments contribute to the accumulation of physical capital stock which is an input for production. Especially in macroeconomics, a particular interest in business investments exists because the capital stock is a main determinant of economic growth. Interest in business investments also stems from their high fluctuations and the fact that these investments move in line with economic activity. They clearly replicate the different extremes of the business cycle.

While the gestation process of investment projects can be rather short or even negligible for small capital goods, the time of the process grows as the capital projects become larger. These large projects thus entail a gap between investment outlays and additions to the physical capital stock.

This is illustrated by Kalecki (1935). Graph 0.1, a copy of Kalecki (1935), shows the different phases of the business cycle. These phases comprise recovery, prosperity, recession, and depression. The curve of economic activity is represented by a solid line. Curves of investment orders and deliveries of capital goods are represented by a dashed and dotted line respectively. As can be expected, the investment orders precede the deliveries with a certain lag, being a gestation lag. Because of this gestation lag, whose length is here (theoretically) assumed to be constant over the business cycle, the moment where capital goods are demanded does not coincide with the moment where the capital good is delivered.

The growth of the capital stock is also given in graph 0.1, represented by a dotted-dashed, fainted line. This line shows that growth of capital stock can even be of increasing nature during periods in which the economic activity is decreasing, and vice versa. This is again due to the gestation lag.

Graph 0.1 Investment gestation

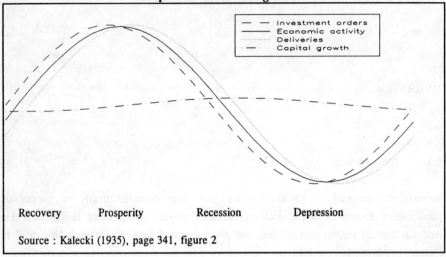

Source : Kalecki (1935), page 341, figure 2

The illustration of Kalecki[1] shows that the gestation lags are the reason for divergencies between increases (decreases) in gross investments and increases (decreases) in changes of physical capital stock and, consequently, productivity in the case of business capital stock investments. The theoretical reasonings of Kalecki on the consequences of gestation lags have been mentioned in the literature very often. Jorgenson (1963), for example, when modelling flexible accelerator investment models by long distributed lag functions, states that *the demand of capital is not the demand for investment* and is speaking of *the backlog of uncompleted projects* (page 248, 250). Jorgenson and Stephenson (1967) assume that *time is required for the completion of new investment projects*.

Kydland and Prescott (1982) concentrate on Real Business Cycle (RBC) models where fluctuations in macroeconomic variables are mainly explained by real shocks that may persist. Unlike most other RBC theory proponents, they emphasize the existence of gestation lags, which they christened 'time-to-build', as another important source of persistence in fluctuations besides the real shocks, as *the time required to complete investment projects is not short relative to the business cycle* (page 1348).

---

[1]   Kalecki (1935) in his theoretical study speaks in terms of capital equipment. As in the following chapters equipment is referred to as small capital projects, Kalecki's terminology is not adopted here. Also, the term 'delivery' of Kalecki refers to the completion and/or delivery of capital goods and their addition to the capital stock. This coincides with the end of the construction period and/or delivery lag discussed in chapter 2.

0.2   Main research aims

The chapters hereafter go into more detail concerning the 'gestation lag' concept. Primary questions that arise and are intended to be answered by empirical findings concern the projects for which gestation lags exist, the different phases of gestation, the length of the gestation periods and the importance of large projects within aggregate levels of capital projects. The theoretical reasonings of Kalecki that concern a fake aggregate capital stock are more well-founded as a result of gathering this kind of information.

One conclusion drawn quickly from these analyses is that a distinction is to be made between the different types of capital goods. A distinction between structures and equipment is made because all *structures* stock projects are built, thus the investments incorporate construction lags. The remainder of capital stock is then referred to as *equipment*, being relatively small capital projects (including for instance machinery) that are not constructed but may be subject to delivery lags.

Questions that arise and are subsequently answered have a more econometric nature. A formal specification, part of Kydland and Prescott (1982), is included in producer behavior models. In these models, a representative producer is assumed to maximize profits or minimize costs by choosing the optimal amount of labour and capital stock. The models are applied to data from the manufacturing industry of several industrial countries. Only time series are used in these econometric analyses.

One reason for using factor demand models is the fact that dynamics in this kind of models are usually specified as the result of adjustment costs. These costs are associated with changes in the work force and/or the actual capital stock of an entrepreneur. These dynamics imposed by adjustment costs might be not sufficient to explain the dynamics of investments. Investment gestation lags clearly have another signification and seem to be another source of dynamics. Therefore, the specification, identification, and estimation of both adjustment costs and gestation lags within factor demand models are research issues.

Another reason for using the factor demand models is the existence of interrelation between investments and labour. Business investments are closely associated with employment decisions. Many models concentrate only on investments *or* on labour. Examples of the former are Kalecki's model, the flexible accelerator models of Jorgenson (1963), and the q studies like Hayashi (1982). Examples of the latter are all factor demand studies that deny the importance of investments or assume a predetermined capital stock (see chapter 1). The econometric consequences of interrelated labour and investments together with the dynamics and persistence in the time series are also research issues.

Another issue which is finally investigated is the impact of inventories. Inventories may interrelate with labour as the possibility to keep inventories makes hoarding labour easier for producers. On the other hand, labour recruitment (temporarily) can be delayed if inventory stocks exist. Labour hoarding or delaying recruitment will certainly occur when adjustment costs of labour are high. An interrelation between physical capital stock and inventories may thereby exist, as more additional investments can be necessary to store the inventory stock. Decumulating or accumulating the stock of inventories may also be less expensive than extending or fully or partly utilizing the actual capital stock.

In many factor demand studies, the existence of a divergence between sales and production by entrepreneurs, by which inventory stocks must exist, is denied. Unlike the previous research issues, the investigation concerning inventories in factor demand models does not at the same time center on and test for the existence of gestation lags of physical capital stock investments. On the contrary, in these models, capital gestation lags will be imposed.

The framework of research can then be summarized as follows.

Dynamics in labour demand and investments in physical capital and inventories are investigated together with their interrelations. Manufacturing industries of several countries and several sectors in France, are used as an application. By carrying out investigations concerning different countries and sectors, the importance of gestation lags and interrelations of production factors in the models specified can be properly tested, and comparisons between the results can be made.

The reason for choosing only the manufacturing industry within this framework is due to the fact that this part of the economy can be considered to be 'an agent' that exhibits optimizing behaviour and is a driving force of economic growth. After all, this sector is the main supplier of goods on the domestic market. Along with this, and apart from the government and other industrial sectors, the manufacturing industry is a large economic agent that is considerably influenced by the economic climate. The economic activity is reflected by (industrial) employment decisions and investment possibilities.

The principle issue of research encompassed in this thesis is the extent to which investment delays, thus the (staggered) formation of physical capital stock, is of importance for production possibilities- hence economic growth, and employment decisions- hence income growth. Within the outlined framework, this subject can be properly investigated.

The methodology adopted in all econometric analyses is the following.

An econometric specification is chosen incorporating the issues to be investigated. Neoclassical assumptions, being rational expectations and profit maximizing or cost minimizing entrepreneurial behaviour, are made. The econometric optimization problem is 'solved', meaning first order conditions are obtained, or even a closed form solution is derived, and the models are estimated with time series for different countries. Thus, economic theory is used as a valuable vantage point and *structural models* result. Time series properties, like non-stationarities and serial correlation, are investigated using *non-structural* models. Information obtained by means of these analyses is incorporated into the structural models specified.

0.3   Outline

Chapter 1 provides background information on neoclassical modelling of factor demand. The *main aim* of this chapter is to make the reader familiar with the neoclassical factor demand models that are used in chapters 3, 4, and 5.

In *chapter 2*, data from the Dutch and French construction industry yield information on the construction of large investment projects, such as houses and plants. Since only the manufacturing industry is used as an application in the econometric analyses that follow, building of plants and delivery lags of equipment are the main focus. The model specification for construction lags by Kydland and Prescott (1982) is subsequently presented. This specification is incorporated into the models of chapters 3, 4 and 5.

The *main aim* of chapter 2 is to investigate whether it makes sense to assume that construction lags and/or delivery lags exist, and what length they have.

In *chapter 3*, a neoclassical factor demand model with structures, equipment and labour is specified including time-to-build for structures and adjustment costs for all production factors. A closed form solution is derived, and applied to both the manufacturing industry of the United States (1960.I-1988.IV) and the Netherlands (1971.I-1990.IV). This model relies on the main result of chapter 2, which is that gestation lags, in this case construction lags, exist for large structures investment projects. These construction lags are imposed and the economic interpretation of adjustment costs for structures besides the time-to-build dynamics is discussed. The existence of adjustment costs for structures, given time-to-build, is thereafter also empirically investigated.

The model in chapter 3 is an extension of a (closed form) model presented by Palm, Peeters and Pfann (1993). The main extension is that in chapter 3 an interrelation is assumed between the three production factors used: structures, equipment and labour. As a consequence of this interrelation, the closed form solution becomes more complicated and is more difficult to estimate. In Palm et al. the dynamics of both adjustment costs and time-to-build are estimated, while using a model without interrelations. With the model in chapter 3 it was not possible to obtain Full

Information Maximum Likelihood estimates. In principle, Maximum Likelihood is feasible. However, a dynamic, highly non-linear model results, with many high order moving average disturbance terms that hamper convergence. A conditional method is therefore used by which the dynamics resulting from time-to-build are imposed and not estimated. As interrelations clearly exists between the three production factors mentioned, the model in chapter 3 is more appealing economically than the model in Palm et al. (1993).

The *main aim* of chapter 3 is to investigate in a relatively simple, linear-quadratic framework whether or not the inclusion of construction lags for structures, of which the existence was made evident in chapter 2, can be identified from the very often used adjustment costs specification.

In *chapter 4*, a model equivalent to the one in chapter 3 is specified, with the addition of (more) interrelations in the production and adjustment costs function. For this model the derivation of a closed form is very complicated. Only the necessary conditions for the model are therefore estimated by an instrumental estimation method. In order to test the model specification, data from the manufacturing industry of the United States, Canada, the United Kingdom, West-Germany (all 1960.I-1988.IV), France (1970.I-1992.II) and the Netherlands (1971.I-1990.IV) are used.

The *main aim* of chapter 4 is to investigate the importance of, among other things, construction lags for structures in a model which is theoretically appealing but to be submitted to a less efficient estimation method. Because this model is less difficult to estimate than the model in chapter 3, the model is applied to manufacturing industry data from more countries. In this way, a more thorough validation of the model can be obtained.

Chapter 5 investigates the role of inventories in three different econometric models, including non-structural and structural models. The models or solutions of the models are estimated with aggregate data from five French industrial sectors (1970.I-1992.IV). The intention of these analyses is to compare the specification and the estimation results of the three models. The objectives of entrepreneurs concerning inventories and the interrelation with capital stock and labour is investigated. Time-to-build for capital stock is incorporated here.

The *main aim* of this model is to investigate if the inclusion of inventories, which is very appealing from an economic standpoint, turns out to be significant in factor demand models like those used in chapter 3 and 4. Here, however, a cost-minimizing approach is adopted. This implies that a direct comparison with the previous models is more difficult, though a way is found to concentrate more on the cost structures and to leave the specification of revenues aside.

In *chapter 6*, results are summarized and answers are presented to questions that were posed and empirically investigated. Drawbacks, unanswered questions, and new issues are discussed and left for future research.

The *main aims* of all analyses, being the questions whether or not gestation lags are economically appealing and important in econometric modelling, are finally answered. Finally, it is shortly discussed to what extent gestation lags might have implications for policies by management and governments.

CHAPTER 1
PHYSICAL CAPITAL STOCK INVESTMENTS AND LABOUR DEMAND
Theoretical background on dynamic modelling

1.1   Introduction

This chapter focuses on background information concerning the modelling of physical capital stock and labour demand. Attention is paid in particular to the dynamics of these production factors and the interrelation between them. Gross investments, being the flow of physical capital stock, are specifically taken into consideration.

Topics are presented as follows. Section 2 marks off the neoclassical modelling of the theory of the firm as described in literature. Some adjacent areas of literature are briefly mentioned. Section 3 describes in much more detail the dynamic modelling of labour, physical capital stock, and investment demand under neoclassical assumptions. The method of formal modelling adopted is comparable to that of Sargent (1987) among others, who uses model 2 described below, as a benchmark model to go into technical details about dynamic labour demand modelling. Section 4 discusses the background literature of dynamic modelling. Apart from the neoclassical theory, the q theory of investments exists. These two theories, in particular the dynamics or 'gestation lags' in business investments, will be discussed more elaborately. Section 5 summarizes the essentials and presents further extensions and possibilities for improving the neoclassical dynamic modelling of factor demand.

In the appendix, some statistics on the dynamics and interrelations in investments (disaggregated as structures and equipment) and labour are presented. The intention of these analyses is to confirm the importance of interrelation between investments and labour and their dynamics.

1.2   Entrepreneurial behaviour

In the theory of the firm, one firm or 'entrepreneur' is regarded as a representative of all the entrepreneurs in an economy. The entrepreneur is concerned with the acquisition of inputs in order to be able to produce commodities. Commodities, or 'output', are supplied on the output market at an appropriate price. As inputs physical capital stock, labour, energy, materials, and even inventories can be mentioned. Only the main determinants, physical capital stock and labour, will be taken into account hereafter. Labour is demanded on the labour market and a wage is paid in return. In a similar way, a physical capital good is demanded on the capital market and an investment price is the return.

In contradiction to labour, capital becomes a property of the entrepreneur. A market for used capital goods is often not taken into account. If a market exists, used capital goods might most realistically only be sold at a price below the paid investment price.

An entrepreneur can be assumed to determine (at least approximately) the potential output by the determination of necessary capital and labour inputs, thus the theory of the firm can be restricted to demand modelling of these production factors. This demand modelling is a partial modelling. Most often, no demand for output, no supply of labour, and no supply of capital goods (investments) is specified. To put it differently, it is assumed that the quantities are available or marketable at the market prices. In this way, the theory of the firm only analyses one group of agents within an economy. Further, the partial modelling only takes into account observable stocks and flows from outside the firm. Developments inside the firm, the production process and internal reasons for output supply, and labour and capital demand are a black box and are hardly or not at all taken into account. It is only assumed that the entrepreneur aims at maximizing profits or minimizing costs (a certain output level given).

In order to describe factor demand more formally, assumptions are needed with respect to the markets on which the entrepreneur is operating. Choosing the way of the least complications is to assume that the entrepreneur has to accept the market equilibrium prices as given on all three markets, i.e. the output, capital, and labour market. This assumption, implying that the product, investments and wage prices are not within influential reach of the entrepreneur, is a characteristic of the market structure 'perfect competition'. Allowing for different market structures, or even admitting the existence of price rationing or price rigidities, from which market disequilibria can result, would certainly be much closer to reality. Purely for reasons of convenience, but being aware of possible less than realistic assumptions made here, the assumption of exogenous prices will be maintained in the following sections.

1.3   Entrepreneurial behaviour under neoclassical assumptions

The neoclassical theory of the firm (or entrepreneur) has three main characteristics. As a first characteristic, the entrepreneur is assumed to behave optimally, in the sense that either profits (cash flows) are maximized or (the dual approach) costs are minimized given a production restriction. A second characteristic is that the entrepreneur operates on price clearing markets. This assumes that on each market a so called 'Walrasian auctioneer' exists who determines prices such that demand and supply always match instantaneously. As a third characteristic, the entrepreneur is not supposed to be 'myopic' or endowed with 'adaptive expectations'. Apart from past and current developments, forecasts of future developments are taken into account when making decisions. The available information given, optimal forecasts are then made. The entrepreneur is therefore said to be 'rational' (see Muth (1961)). This last characteristic however only applies to intertemporal models.

The neoclassical dynamic modelling of labour and capital demand are illustrated in this section using simple examples. The meaning of symbols can differ from example to example.

1.3.1   Model 1: Static labour demand

To formalize the behaviour of a profit maximizing entrepreneur the following model is introduced:

$$V_{1t} \equiv P_t^q Q_t - W_t^n N_t \quad \text{where} \quad Q_t \equiv f(N_t), \quad \frac{\partial f}{\partial N_t} > 0, \quad \frac{\partial^2 f}{\partial N_t^2} \leq 0. \tag{1.1}$$

The subscript t refers to period t. Only one production factor exists, N_t, which is referred to as labour. Q_t stands for the production, a function of labour at t, which is assumed to increase when more labour is employed until a saturation point is reached (the amount of N_t where $\partial f / \partial N_t = 0$). P_t^q is the nominal price of the product Q_t at t, thus the entrepreneur's revenues are $P_t^q Q_t$. The costs are represented by $W_t^n N_t$ where W_t^n is the nominal wage. The entrepreneur is further assumed to be a price taker at both the output and labour market, by which P_t^q and W_t^n are not within influential reach of the entrepreneur.

At period t the entrepreneur maximizes profits, i.e. V_{1t} (see (1.1)), by determining the optimal labour demand at t . As can be verified by differentiating V_{1t} with respect to N_t, the optimal labour choice for the entrepreneur is the amount of N_t where marginal profits equal marginal costs,

$$P_t^q \frac{\partial f_t}{\partial N_t} = W_t^n. \tag{1.2}$$

Further it will be assumed here that the production function is linear-quadratic,

$$Q_t \equiv \alpha_0 N_t - \frac{\alpha_1}{2} N_t^2 \quad \text{where} \quad \alpha_1 > 0, \tag{1.3}$$

and is an approximation of an underlying production function that better represents the true production process. α_0 and α_1 are unknown parameters to be estimated. It follows that the entrepreneur's optimal labour demand at each period t is given by

$$N_t = \frac{\alpha_0}{\alpha_1} - \frac{W_t^n}{\alpha_1 P_t^q}. \tag{1.4}$$

This equation states that the entrepreneur demands less (more) labour when real wages, that is W_t^n/P_t^q, increase (decrease). Labour demand also depends on the marginal productivity, that is influenced by α_0 and α_1.

1.3.2   Model 2: Dynamic labour demand

Apart from the negligence of many essential other factors that determine the entrepreneur's demand for labour, a major shortcoming of model 1 is its staticness. Labour demand equation (1.4) implies that an entrepreneur decides each period upon the demand for labour independently of the number of people currently employed by the entrepreneur. If this model were realistic, hiring and firing of persons would happen during each time period in such a way that the optimal N_t (see (1.4)) remained.

Obviously entrepreneurs can not immediately adjust their labour demand without costs. The costs of adjusting the work force have been introduced by Holt, Modigliani, Muth and Simon (1960). They associated costs with the changes in the size of the work force, ΔN_t where $\Delta N_t \equiv N_t - N_{t-1}$.

The adoption of a quadratic term $\gamma(\Delta N_t)^2$ changes model 1 into

$$V_{2t} \equiv E\{\sum_{i=0}^{\infty} \beta^i [Q_{t+i} - W_{t+i} N_{t+i} - \frac{1}{2}\gamma(\Delta N_{t+i})^2] \mid \Omega_t\} \quad \text{where } \beta \in (0,1), \gamma > 0. \tag{1.5}$$

As the entrepreneur is rational, not only profits at period t, but also forecasts (expectations) of profits at $t+1$, $t+2$.. now need to be taken into account. Profits are discounted with a discount factor β which is here assumed to be constant. The rational expectations are represented by the expectation operator, E, and are formed on the basis of the entrepreneur's knowledge at period t; Ω_t indicates the information set of the entrepreneur and contains past and current variables.

As prices are again assumed given to the entrepreneur, P_t^q can be chosen as a deflator, so $W_t \equiv W_t^n/P_t^q$ are real wages. The parameter γ is the adjustment costs parameter. If $\Delta N_t > 0$ ($\Delta N_t < 0$) the increase (decrease) in employment is higher than the decrease (increase), so more labour is hired (laid off) than laid off (hired).

The economic interpretation of the costs associated with $\Delta N_t > 0$ are hiring costs such as interviewing and selection, security and physical examinations, and training costs. As firing costs, associated with $\Delta N_t < 0$, prevail unemployment compensation insurances, contributions to guaranteed wage funds and employee transfer costs. Several other categories of costs are mentioned in Holt et al. (1960, page 68-69).

At period t the entrepreneur maximizes expected profits over an infinite horizon, V_{2t} (see (1.5)), by determining the optimal labour demand at t, t+1.. As can be verified by differentiating V_{2t} with respect to N_t and assuming the production function to be (1.3), the first order condition for model 2 is

$$\frac{\partial Q_t}{\partial N_t} = W_t + \gamma(\Delta N_t) - \beta\gamma E\{\Delta N_{t+1}|\Omega_t\} \quad \Leftrightarrow$$

$$E\{N_{t+1}|\Omega_t\} - (\frac{\alpha_1}{\beta\gamma} + \frac{1}{\beta} + 1)N_t + \frac{1}{\beta}N_{t-1} = \frac{1}{\beta\gamma}W_t - \frac{\alpha_0}{\beta\gamma}. \quad (1.6)$$

As a consequence of the adjustment costs specification, this equation is a stochastic second order linear difference equation. The equation can be solved for N_t and a unique solution is found, provided that a boundary condition[2], being a transversality condition, is also fulfilled. This transversality condition is

$$\lim_{T\to\infty} \beta^T[\frac{\partial Q_{t+T}}{\partial N_{t+T}} - W_{t+T} - \gamma\Delta N_{t+T}] N_{t+T} = 0, \quad (1.7)$$

certifying that at limiting conditions, t+T, either (discounted) labour demand or marginal profits minus marginal costs equal zero.

The characteristic equation associated with the left hand side deterministic second order difference equation in (1.6) is given by

$$f^2 - bf + \frac{1}{\beta} = 0 \quad \text{where} \quad b \equiv \frac{\alpha_1}{\beta\gamma} + \frac{1}{\beta} + 1,$$

and has the solutions

$$f_1 \equiv \frac{b}{2} - \frac{1}{2}\sqrt{b^2 - \frac{4}{\beta}} \quad \text{and} \quad f_2 \equiv \frac{b}{2} + \frac{1}{2}\sqrt{b^2 - \frac{4}{\beta}} \quad \text{where} \quad f_1, f_2 \in \mathbf{R}. \quad (1.8)$$

From the properties $f_1 f_2 = 1/\beta$ and $\beta \in (0,1)$, it can be concluded that the stability conditions $|f_1| < 1/\sqrt{\beta}$ and $|f_2| > 1/\sqrt{\beta}$ hold, provided that $|f_1| \neq 1/\sqrt{\beta}$. The solution of the Euler-equations (1.6)-(1.7) can then be written as

$$N_{t+1} = f_1 N_t - E\{\frac{(f_2 L)^{-1}}{[1-(f_2 L)^{-1}]}(\frac{1}{\beta\gamma}W_t - \frac{\alpha_0}{\beta\gamma}) \mid \Omega_t\} \quad \Leftrightarrow$$

$$N_t = c + f_1 N_{t-1} - \frac{1}{\beta\gamma}\sum_{k=0}^{\infty}(\beta f_1)^{k+1} E\{W_{t+k} \mid \Omega_t\}, \quad (1.9)$$

where the forward operator $(f_2 L)^{-1}/[1-(f_2 L)^{-1}]$ is applied, βf_1 for $1/f_2$ (resulting from

---

[2]   In fact two boundary conditions are necessary, the first being the initial level of N_{t-1} and the second the transversality condition in (1.7).

(1.8)) is substituted for $1/f_2$ after the second equality sign, and parameter c represents a constant.

The autoregressive term f_1 depends positively on the adjustment costs parameter (γ) and on the discount factor (β), and negatively on α_1, being a parameter that influences the marginal productivity. This confirms intuition as, for example, increases in γ make an entrepreneur less eager to change the number of employees unless marginal productivity increases or the discount factor decreases.

A feature of model (1.9) is that no higher moments than conditional means of real wages, W_t, appear. The 'certainty equivalence' or 'separation' principle holds in this case. It implies that the non-observed right hand notations W_{t+k} (k>0) in (1.9)) are separable from the terms N_t and N_{t-1} when solving the stochastic optimization problem (see Sargent (1987), page 396). The separation principle holds, due to the linear-quadratic criterium function (1.5).

The solution (1.9) boils down to a 'closed form' solution or an 'explicit' solution for N_t if and only if the rational expectations operator can be eliminated. Since it is possible to forecast W_{t+k} (k>0) by assuming a suitable stochastic process for W_t, a closed form from (1.9) can be obtained. It is worth emphasis here that this solution can not be achieved when the criterium function, either the production/revenues function or adjustment cost function, is of a higher degree than that of a quadratic. This closed form can also (in most cases) not be achieved if real wages depend on current or past numbers of employment. Otherwise stated, employment (N_t) may not Granger cause real wages (W_t).

Sargent (1987) pays detailed attention to the solution methods of stochastic difference equations such as (1.6). As a prototype model he uses the linear-quadratic profit maximizing model (1.5) to treat all technical problems involved in deriving the solution (1.9). By assuming autoregressive processes for wages, Sargent (1978) derives a closed form as a result of (1.9).

1.3.3 Model 3: Dynamic physical capital stock and investments demand

Like the demand for labour, the demand for physical capital stock (hereafter referred to as K_t) can be modelled dynamically as in (1.9). Representing gross investments and their real price as I_t and C_t respectively, the criterium function can be presented as

$$V_{3t} \equiv E\{\sum_{i=0}^{\infty} \beta^i [Q_{t+i} - C_{t+i}I_{t+i} - \frac{1}{2}\gamma(\Delta K_{t+i})^2] \mid \Omega_t\} \quad \text{where } Q_t \equiv f(K_t). \quad (1.10)$$

The production function here has the same properties as in (1.1). The (standard) capital accumulation rule is adopted here, that is

$$K_t = K_{t-1} - D_{t-1} + I_t. \quad (1.11)$$

This rule states that the change in physical capital stock in each period equals the difference between gross investments and the economic depreciation (or technical retirement) of capital, represented by D_{t-1}. In the following, depreciation will be assumed a constant percentage (κ) of physical capital stock, that is $D_{t-1} \equiv \kappa K_{t-1}$ with $\kappa \in [0,1]$, by which (1.11) becomes

$$I_t = \sum_{j=0}^{1} \varphi_j K_{t+j-1} \qquad \text{where} \qquad \varphi_0 \equiv \kappa - 1 \qquad \text{and} \qquad \varphi_1 \equiv 1. \qquad (1.11)^*$$

Maximizing function (1.10) with respect to K_t subject to $(1.11)^*$, then yields the Euler equation

$$K_t = c + f_1 K_{t-1} - \frac{1}{\gamma} \sum_{k=0}^{\infty} (\beta f_1)^{k+1} \sum_{j=0}^{1} \beta^{-j} \varphi_j \, E\{C_{t+k+1-j} | \Omega_t\} \qquad (1.12)$$

as $\partial I_{t+i} / \partial K_t = \varphi_{1-i}$ (i=0,1). The parameters f_1 and f_2 are defined as in (1.8).

As can be verified, the case without adjustment costs for capital stock gives the first order condition $P_t^q \partial f_t / \partial K_t = C_t + \beta (\kappa-1) C_{t+1}$. Since $\beta \equiv 1/(1+r)$ where r represents the interest rate, this can be approximated by $\partial f_t / \partial K_t = [r+\kappa-g_t] C_t / P_t^q$ if small cross products are neglected and $g_t \equiv C_{t+1} / C_t - 1$. The term between square brackets is called the 'user cost of capital' (see Jorgenson (1963)) and g_t represents an inflation indicator. Thus, marginal capital costs increase if the interest rate or depreciation increases or inflation decreases.

For this case without adjustment costs, the equality of the 'marginal efficiency of capital' and the interest rate follows since $\partial f_t / \partial K_t * P_t^q / C_t + g_t - \kappa = r$. See Keynes (1936, page 221-222) or Sargent (1987, page 94-95) where it is assumed that only one sector in an economy exists by which $P_t^q = C_t$. It is thus certified that the equality of the interest rate and the marginal efficiency of capital, the latter defined as the interest rate that associates the present stream of returns of a certain capital good with the purchase price of the good, is equivalent to the first order condition of present value maximization. Perfect markets, where capital stock can be sold and bought without restrictions, are here assumed throughout.

In (1.12) the dynamics in the autoregressive part result from the adjustment cost specification $\gamma (\Delta K_t)^2$. These adjustment costs of capital or investments were first mentioned by Eisner and Strotz (1963) who extended the capital demand modelling of Jorgenson (1963).

Two kinds of adjustment costs, being 'external' and 'internal', are distinguished in the literature. External costs are costs of imperfections on the capital goods market. An example is the situation where the entrepreneur is the only demander of capital goods (a monopsonist); a backward bending supply curve may in this case exist as the supply price can rise increasingly when more capital is purchased. Internal adjustment costs are costs that arise from technological frictions when the physical capital stock is changed. Examples are the set up costs of new product lines or costs of scrapping obsolete capital.

The case of external adjustment costs, referring to situations where investment prices are within influential reach by the entrepreneur (see Brechling (1975), page 83-95), will be ignored here. In the following, the internal costs, those associated with $\Delta K_t > 0$, and its counterpart, $\Delta K_t < 0$, will be referred to as installation and scrappage costs respectively.

Instead of $\gamma(\Delta K_t)^2$, literature mentions adjustment costs of capital to be sometimes modelled as γI_t^2. For example Treadway (1969) and Lucas (1967a) assume the first, whereas Gould (1968) and Lucas (1967b) stick to the latter specification. They all assume a one period construction time, in which case the difference between these two alternatives is only the depreciation because (see $(1.11)^*$)

$$\gamma I_t^2 = \gamma(\Delta K_t + \kappa K_{t-1})^2.$$

In the case of gross investments, equation (1.12) changes only in the way that

$$f_1 \equiv \frac{b}{2} - \frac{1}{2}\sqrt{b^2 - \frac{4*(1-\kappa)}{\beta}} \quad \text{and} \quad f_2 \equiv \frac{b}{2} + \frac{1}{2}\sqrt{b^2 - \frac{4*(1-\kappa)}{\beta}} \quad \text{where} \quad b \equiv \frac{\alpha_1}{\gamma\beta} + \frac{1}{\beta} + (\kappa-1)^2.$$

If replacement investments incur the costs like net investments do, specification of gross investment adjustment costs is advisable. The assumption of gross adjustment costs (γI_t^2) implies that net investments (changes in net stocks, ΔK_t) brings about the same costs as the replacement investments, κK_{t-1}. The situation where $I_t < 0$, the 'disinvestment' case, is often neglected under these circumstances. A market for used capital stock, the reversibility of investments (that is receiving a price C_t for extracted I_t, see (1.10)), is then not taken into account. This is known as the 'irreversibility' of investments.

The demand for gross investments can easily be derived from the demand for capital stock. By using the standard capital accumulation equation $(1.11)^*$, equation (1.12) can be transformed into

$$I_t = \kappa c + f_1 I_{t-1} - \frac{1}{\gamma}\sum_{k=0}^{\infty}(\beta f_1)^{k+1}\sum_{j=0}^{1}\beta^{-j}\varphi_j\sum_{i=0}^{1}\varphi_{1-i}E\{C_{t+k+1-j-i}|\Omega_t\}. \tag{1.13}$$

1.3.4 Model 4: Interrelation in physical capital stock and labour demand

As decision rules for capital stock and labour demand can be regarded together instead of being looked upon as two separate decisions, a simultaneous model will be specified here. If $X_t \equiv [K_t \ N_t]'$ and $P_t \equiv [C_t \ W_t]'$ are referred to as the vector of production factors and the vector of accompanying real factor prices, and $Y_t \equiv [I_t \ N_t]'$ is defined, the criterium function of the entrepreneur can be specified as

$$V_{4t} \equiv E\{\sum_{i=0}^{\infty} \beta^i [Q_{t+i} - P'_{t+i} Y_{t+i} - AC_{t+i}] \mid \Omega_t\}. \tag{1.14}$$

Q_t and AC_t are, respectively, the production and adjustment cost function, where again (linear-) quadratic order is assumed,

$$Q_t \equiv \alpha' X_t - \frac{1}{2} X'_t A X_t \quad \text{where} \quad \alpha := \begin{bmatrix} \alpha_1 \\ \alpha_2 \end{bmatrix} \quad \text{and} \quad A := \begin{bmatrix} a_{11} & a_{12} \\ a_{21} & a_{22} \end{bmatrix},$$

$$AC_t \equiv \frac{1}{2} \Delta X'_t \Gamma \Delta X_t \quad \text{where} \quad \Gamma := \begin{bmatrix} \gamma_{11} & \gamma_{12} \\ \gamma_{21} & \gamma_{22} \end{bmatrix}. \tag{1.15}$$

If A and Γ are both positive definite, function Q_t is strictly concave in X_t and function AC_t is strictly convex in ΔX_t.

The entrepreneur is assumed to maximize V_{4t} by choosing the optimal combination of K_t and N_t. The system of first order conditions for X_t is then given by

$$X_t = C + F_1 X_{t-1} + F_3 \sum_{k=0}^{\infty} F_2^{k+1} F_3^{-1} F_4 E\{[C_{t+1} \ C_t \ W_t]' \mid \Omega_t\}. \tag{1.16}$$

In this equation C is a (2x1)-matrix, F_1, F_2 and F_3 are (2x2)-matrices and F_4 is a (2x3)-matrix. They are functions of β, α, A and Γ.

If no interrelation in (1.14) exists, so if both off-diagonal elements of A and Γ are zero (see 1.15), decision rules for capital and labour equal the individual decision rules (1.9) and (1.12). Thus F_1, F_2 and F_3 are diagonal in this case.

F_1, F_2 and F_3 are non-diagonal if and only if one of the off-diagonal elements of A or Γ is non-zero. This interrelation in (1.16) gives rise to the dependence of capital (K_t) on one lagged labour (N_{t-1}) in the first equation and dependence of labour (N_t) on one lagged value of capital (K_{t-1}) in the second equation. Kollintzas (1985), among others, pays attention to these multivariate rational expectation models and their solution.

1.4 Dynamics and the literature

In this section some background information on dynamic factor demand modelling described in literature is given. In the first part, the economic interpretation of the dynamics that are presumed by choosing capital stock, investments and labour adjustment costs modelling are discussed. In the second part an investment theory, having an origin different from the neoclassical theory with adjustment costs, is discussed. Differences in both investment theories are summarized. The third part concludes with the treatment of studies that establish models with more extensive dynamic specifications for investments.

1.4.1 Dynamics in the neoclassical framework

The modelling of labour or capital demand with adjustment costs induces dynamics in the autoregressive part of factor demand, though only of a first order (see (1.9) and (1.12)). The same is true for gross investments demand (see (1.13)). As follows from (1.16), interrelation in labour and capital (in the production and/or adjustment cost function) causes cross dynamics, but also not of a higher degree than a first autoregressive order in the factor demand vector $X_t \equiv [K_t \ N_t]'$ (or similarly $Y_t \equiv [I_t \ N_t]'$). The underlying economic specification for the dynamics, the quadratic adjustment cost function, has a quite different economic interpretation for labour on the one hand and physical capital stock on the other; hiring and firing costs of labour have no similarities with installation and scrappage costs of capital. Costs with increases in labour and capital, hiring and installation costs respectively, thereby also differ widely from the costs concerned with the decreases, the firing and scrappage costs. The functional form of the adjustment costs specification, a symmetric and marginally increasing function, can therefore be regarded as conceived for reason of analytical convenience rather than out of economic sense. In, for example, Nickell (1986) and Nickell (1978) the limitations of the convex adjustment costs specification for labour and investments respectively, is critically brought up for discussion.

Nevertheless, the existence of labour adjustment costs was first confirmed by Oi (1962). He used detailed information on hiring costs, training costs (the major costs) and unemployment compensations of one American company in 1951. Labour is thereby referred to as a quasi-fixed production factor in the short run where the degree of fixity depends, among others, on the labour adjustment costs. Also Barron and Bishop (1985) found evidence from survey data concerning search and screening/interviewing costs in the United States. Unlike the adjustment costs of labour, (to the best of my knowledge) no clear statistical evidence exists for capital installation or capital scrappage costs.

The literature of econometric studies in which dynamic factor demand equations are estimated is broad. The pioneering work on the derivation and estimation of a closed form for dynamic models under rational expectations was carried out by Sargent (1978). He estimated the dynamic labour demand equations for two types of labour with aggregated United States employment and real wage series. His methodology was followed and elaborated upon by Meese (1980), Hansen and Sargent (1980b) and Pfann (1990), among others.

A problem that arises in these rational expectations models is the interpretation of the estimated coefficients. Reduced form parameters (like f_1 in (1.9)) can depend non-linearly on the structural parameters in the original model, by which they are not easily interpretable. In closed form solutions they depend on the parameters of the assumed marginal processes. If these processes were to be different, the decision rules would be different. The Lucas' critique (1976) thus applies because the identification of structural parameters is essential for drawing final conclusions.

If interrelations in production and/or adjustment cost functions exist, more structure is imposed in the model. Taking into account this structure in estimations can become difficult as (non-linear) restrictions across equations result (see for example Hansen and Sargent (1980a)). It is worth emphasizing here that the way of modelling- for example the taking into account of production factors interrelations when these interrelations exist- plays a crucial role in obtaining the correct conclusions concerning the dynamics in factor demand.

In studies that are in the tradition of the Sargent study, see for example Pindyck and Rotemberg (1983a, 1983b), no closed form is derived but Euler equations (like (1.6)) are estimated immediately. A possible reason for this methodology is the adoption of a non-quadratic production function or an asymmetric adjustment costs function, thus the abandoning of the linear-quadratic framework. For estimation, an instrumental method is then used that estimates the Euler equations directly, which is in contrast to the full information methods that are applicable when all information (concerning among others the factor price process) is taken into account.

1.4.2   q theory of investments

Common in almost all empirical factor demand studies is the statistical endorsement of the dynamics in labour and capital. Beside these dynamics, in the neoclassical framework capital and/or labour demand is explained by factor prices. As previously emphasized in the univariate derivation (1.13), investment demand is explained in this framework by only its past, and above this, past, current, and future real investment prices.

Apart from this neoclassical investment theory, another investment theory, the q theory of Tobin (1969), exists. The q theory was derived in a general equilibrium balance sheet framework, where the physical capital stock side or the 'real' side within an economy is confronted with the assets markets or 'financial' side.

The ratio of the market value of capital goods to their replacement value became thereby known as Tobin's q (later referred to as the 'average q'). According to Tobin, investments should be related positively to this q. If the market value exceeds (falls below) the replacement value, it is advantageous (disadvantageous) for the entrepreneur to increase (decrease) investments. In the optimal case there are no discrepancies between the asset market and the reproduction costs of the capital stock, by which q is equal to one. Thus the q theory suggests that all profit sources are tapped and disinvestments occur when a firm's market value falls below the replacement value of the capital goods. An equivalence with the (intertemporal) neoclassical theory of investments thus exists because this theory also assumes that an entrepreneur wants to have the value of capital stock at a level where profits are optimal.

Previously, Keynes (1936, in the 'General Theory' page 150-151) referred to this relationship between the market value and the replacement value of 'marketable' firms. In his view the existence of security markets, where a company's shares are revalued each day, inevitably has a decisive influence on the rate of investments. *For there is no sense in building up a new enterprise at a cost greater than that at which a similar existing enterprise can be purchased; whilst there is an inducement to spend on a new project what may seem an extravagant sum, if it can be floated off on the Stock Exchange at an immediate profit* (Keynes, 1936, page 151). He even states that a high quotation for existing equities involves an increase in the marginal efficiency of capital, thus having the same effect as a fall in the interest rate.

While the average q (with respect to the existing capital) is easy to calculate, the rate of investments is recognized to be related to the marginal q, being the market value of new additional investment goods divided by their replacement costs. Lucas and Prescott (1971) were the first to notice this, whereas Mussa (1977) in a deterministic model and Abel (1983) in a stochastic model confirmed it.

Although Tobin (1969) did not present an entrepreneur who shows optimizing behaviour by thinking in terms of production and adjustment costs functions, the neoclassical investment theory with adjustment costs and the q theory are not in contradiction with each other. In the neoclassical theory where adjustment costs of investments cause the staggering (or smoothing) of investment demand, in the best case the marginal costs equal the marginal value of installed capital. These marginal values are identified as being the marginal q (see for example Hayashi (1982))[3].

As the marginal q (in contrast to the average q) is not directly measurable, bridges were

---

[3]   Speaking in the language of the previous section, let $\sum_{i=0}^{\infty} \beta^i [f(K_{t+i}) - g(I_{t+i}, K_{t+i}) - C_{t+i} I_{t+i}]$ be the criterium function where $f(K_t)$ is the production function and $g(I_t, K_t)$ is the adjustment costs function. Optimizing this function under the restriction $I_t = \varphi_0 K_{t-1} + \varphi_1 K_t$ (see (1.11)*) gives as Euler equations for K_t and I_t, $\partial f / \partial K_t - \partial g / \partial K_t - \mu_t \varphi_1 - \beta \mu_{t+1} \varphi_0 = 0$, and $-\partial g / \partial I_t - C_t + \mu_t = 0$ where μ_t is the shadow price or Lagrange multiplier. μ_t / C_t is called the 'marginal' q_t, q_t^{marg}. From the last equation follows that $\partial g / \partial I_t = C_t [q_t^{marg} - 1]$ or $I_t = h_1(q_t^{marg} - 1, K_t)$, by which gross investments is a function, h_1, that is increasing in its first argument if and only if the adjustment costs function is strictly convex.

were necessary to make the q theory operational. One bridge was given by Hayashi (1982). Starting from a profit maximizing framework, he derived theoretically that the marginal q and average q are equal. This perfect equivalence is however only found when both the production and adjustment cost function are linearly homogeneous in capital, the entrepreneur is a price taker, and depreciation or taxes do not exist[4]. Another bridge for constructing the appropriate marginal q has been (for example) found by Abel and Blanchard (1986). They do not reason within a profit stream criterium function framework but start with a difference equation based on the value of the firm.

The transition of Hayashi (1982) from the intertemporal neoclassical model to the q model points at first in the direction of a direct link between both investment theories, but is only a one way transition. The q model is a model that may result from different theoretical settings; marginal q is the expectation of a present value of the marginal profit stream and can be defined in several ways. A sufficient setting is given by Hayashi. Starting with the intertemporal model, rather strong sufficient conditions are thereby made in order to derive the equivalence of the marginal and average q.

Although the q theory and the intertemporal neoclassical theory of investments are not in contradiction with each other, the following main differences concerning the theoretical assumptions can be mentioned.

Within the neoclassical framework, a production and adjustment cost specification, and a demand equation for the firm's output and potential tax and depreciation credits are required. These specifications all influence the form of the final investment demand equation. On the contrary, the investment demand equation is relatively invariable in the q theory. In this theory only the two economic variables, gross investments and the q, exist. Expectations about future courses of variables as well as functional forms are incorporated in the q, but the functional form of the investment demand equation is quite insensitive to slight specification changes.

In studies with the q theory, main attention is paid to the explanation of investment demand by the calculated q. Neoclassical studies concentrate on the estimation of reduced form or structural parameters and often pay more attention to the interrelation of capital and labour. Differences between both investment theories in empirical results are discussed in the following section.

---

[4]   If the criterium function in the previous note is defined as

$$V_t = \sum_{i=0} \beta^i [f(K_{t+i}) - g(\Delta K_{t+i} + \kappa K_{t+i-1}, K_{t+i}) - C_{t+i}(\Delta K_{t+i} + \kappa K_{t+i-1})], \text{ then } q_t^{marg} = \partial V_t / \partial K_t \text{ equals the average } q_t,$$

$q_t^{aver} = V_t / K_t$ if and only if V_t is linearly homogeneous in K_t. For this reason it is often assumed that $g(I_t, K_t) = K_t (I_t / K_t)^\gamma$ with $\gamma > 0$ by which $I_t / K_t = h_2(q_t^{marg} - 1)$. In empirical analyses function h_2 is often assumed to be linear.

1.4.3   Gestation lags

As the two theories of investments lead to different final equations for investment demand, most empirical studies concentrate on one of the two theories. The model that results from taking the neoclassical theory with adjustment costs as a vantage point is dynamic in investments (see (1.12) or (1.13)). On the contrary, the q theory gives rise to equations that are not dynamic in investments (see footnote 4). The q that has to be calculated before estimation, represents the expected infinite future marginal profit stream.

An empirical static q analysis is for example carried out by Hayashi (1982), who uses average q (modified for taxes). Abel and Blanchard (1986) estimate a q model with a calculated marginal q. In both studies one of the conclusions is that q is a significant signal of business investments, although a large, serially correlated, residual is left unexplained.

In order to find a dynamic specification for investment demand, Schiantarelli and Georgoutsos (1990) tried to improve the conventional q model assuming monopolistic competition. The investment equation they derive depends on expected future investments and above this, actual and expected output. Another attempt was made by Sensenbrenner (1991), who induces dynamics in the q model using the assumption of a more general adjustment costs function. Both Schiantarelli et al. and Sensenbrenner proxy the marginal q and find a significant evidence for their dynamic q equations. A convincing empirical foundation for the assumptions of monopolistic competition or adjustment costs in second difference investments is however not given.

Schaller (1990) who, in the line of Schiantarelli and Georgoutsos (1990), also assumes monopolistic competition, estimates a univariate q model with investment data (including inventory investments) from 188 individual firms. In this way he takes into account the heterogeneity in investments of firms. His estimation results indicate that much less autocorrelation is left in comparison to results obtained through aggregation, results that are more often found (in general) since aggregate data are found to contain more 'noise'.

Contrary to most q theory studies, empirical studies based on the dynamic neoclassical theory seem to perform better. In for example Nadiri and Rosen (1969), Brechling (1975, page 75-79), Meese (1980), Pindyck and Rotemberg (1983a,1983b), Pfann (1990, section VI.4) and Shapiro (1986), capital equations are estimated using adjustment costs of capital stock. No significant residual autocorrelation is found, although both Brechling, page 75-76, and Nadiri et al. reduce autocorrelation in the capital equations by corrections.

One major difference with q theory studies is that in these studies capital stock series are used[5], not investment series. Another major difference is that these studies include the interrelation between (at least) labour and their adjustment costs, an interrelation that turns out to be significant. The importance of interrelation between and dynamics in investments and labour in the manufacturing industry is also shown in appendix 1.A by some non-structural analyses.

Although a comparison between the empirical results of q studies and intertemporal neoclassical studies is hard to make due to the different model specifications, the latter seem to be favoured. Measurement of the marginal q remains poorly defined and seems to have gained most attention from Abel and Blanchard (1986). In their calculations, they remarkably find that the costs, rather than the marginal profits of capital, account for the major part of the variability of the marginal q. Their empirical analyses however show that investments do not strongly depend on this calculated q, indicating a misspecification, though its origin is unclear. The negligence of interrelations with at least labour and its dynamics, together with the fact that a reduced form is estimated, whereas intertemporal neoclassical models allow for a direct verification of estimated structural parameters with theoretical assumptions made (that are not often rejected), reinforce hence this impression that q studies are empirically less appealing.

The dynamic factor demand studies indicate that capital adjustment costs are at least as significant as the adjustment costs of labour. The result of the statistical endorsement of dynamics in capital stock might however not be a confirmation concerning the existence of capital adjustment costs. After all, an empirical endorsement for the adjustment costs was not found since installation and/or scrappage costs have never been shown.

For example, Malinvaud (1989) refers to the use of capital adjustment costs as the 'deus ex machina' and doubts its significance, particularly in the medium term. In his

---

[5]   It should be noticed that these factor demand studies could transform capital stock in investments like the transition from (1.12) to (1.13), and estimate (1.13) by means of investments data. This is done here in subsequent chapters. To the best of my knowledge, this has never been done elsewhere in neoclassical factor demand studies.

The volatility of capital stock and investments series is rather different (see for example the graphs in Jorgenson and Stephenson (1967)). Gross investment series are much more erratic, and macroeconomically even found to be one of the most erratic components of GNP. Capital stock series are often not observed but constructed by the rule $K_t=K_{t-1}-D_{t-1}+I_t$ (the 'Perpetual Inventory Method'). A benchmark is then used for K_0. The depreciation or obsolescence (D_{t-1}) is often assumed to be a constant percentage of K_{t-1} since practual depreciation (or even more needed, the practual obsolescence) is not observed. Resulting capital stock series, indicators of the growth of economies or sectors, therefore are in comparison with investments relatively smooth trending series.

view, production takes place at full capacity only in the long term[6]. This implies that the irreversibility of productive capital entails the making of two decisions concerning new investments; new investment goods (i.e. new production techniques) need to chosen, along with determining the level of production. According to Malinvaud the irreversibility of investment and uncertainty of future demand must be the main determinants of investment demand.

In earlier studies regarding the theory of investments, in particular the explanation of business investments, 'gestation lags' were often discussed. Investments are said to gestate because they bear potential productivity possibilities through the creation of capital stock. This gestation can last for a certain period.

In Jorgenson (1971), for example, studies are summarized that focus on objective functions forecasting the 'desired' capital stock (flexible accelerator functions). These flexible accelerator models belong to a different category of investment models than the q models of investments and the intertemporal neoclassical investment models. As explained in Jorgenson's article, these studies provide an explanation for the change in capital stock -determined by the real output, internal funds or liquidity, external funds or costs of capital- of net investments but not of gross investments. Out of the objective function, geometrically distributed lag structures of investments are derived. Studies with finite and rationally distributed lag functions are also reviewed.

The estimated time structure of the investments process is found to be rather long in several studies (see Jorgenson (1971), page 1134-1138). Jorgenson (1971, page 1135) refers to the studies of Mayer (1960) and Mayer and Sonenblum (1955). In their articles, evidence is shown for the existence of investment lags of plants, which are due to lags between decisions to invest and the start of construction. And above this, the lags between the start of construction and completion of projects.

Jorgenson (1963) in his model without adjustment costs also took these 'construction lags' into account by speaking in terms of investments in initiated new projects and the backlog of uncompleted projects (Jorgenson (1963), page 249-250). He confirms that the demand for capital is not the demand for investments because the short run demand of the latter depends on lagged responses in capital demand changes[7].

Much earlier, Kalecki (1935) more concretely paid attention to the 'gestation' of

---

[6]   In Malinvaud's view Tobin's q (used exogenously in q studies) is endogenous; q depends on the current and expected future capacity intensities that vary with the productive capacity, and hence with investments.

[7]   It should be noted here that this contradicts the rule $K_t=(1-\kappa)K_{t-1}+I_t$ since gross investments, I_t, do not immediately contribute fully to the productive capital stock, K_t.

investments (in 'equipment' in his terms). In a theoretical (general equilibrium) model he analyses different phases of the business cycle according to the supply and demand for capital. In the overview in this manuscript his presentation of the gestation lag is illustrated in graph 0.1. This graph clearly shows that changes in investment orders and changes in capital- capital deliveries minus depreciation, move together over the business cycle with a lag that is due to the gestation period[8].

Kydland and Prescott (1982) are obviously reasoning in the same way. They cast doubt on both the q theory and the adjustment costs theory of investments, because *the time required to complete investment projects is not short relative to the business cycle* (page 1348). In contrast to the previous investment studies, they give a structural foundation by formalizing the construction process of capital stock, along with an empirical foundation referring to the survey study of Mayer (1960) on lead times of plants.

Their specification for gestation lags is called 'time-to-build', and allows for a construction time for physical capital stock which is longer than one period. During the construction period a capital good (for example a plant, see Mayer (1960)) is constructed in stages. Investments are thereby made, but no returns exist yet. It is only after the construction process that the capital project can be used for production. The schedule of investments during construction as well as the construction period are assumed not to change over time.

A main distinction between time-to-build and 'delivery' lags is found in the timing of investment expenditures. Time-to-build allows for investments to take place during the whole gestation period. Delivery lags imply a waiting period for capital goods and a full payment takes place at the beginning *or* end of this period. There is also no confusion between the theory of time-to-build and the vintage theory of capital stock (see for example Broer (1987), chapter IV). Time-to-build assumes a capital stock that consists of productive capital stock and all current projects under construction. The vintage models only distinguish the different 'vintages' of productive capital stock to indicate the relatively higher productivity potentials of the most recent ones[9].

Kydland and Prescott (1982) adopt their time-to-build specification in a general equilibrium model (without adjustment costs). Their purpose is to improve the benchmark neoclassical model of capital accumulation which prevails in the Real Business Cycle (RBC) theory. This theory concentrates on the characteristics of dynamic (general) market equilibria. The existence of fluctuations, and even persistence or serial correlation in economic aggregates are thought to be caused by pure real shocks, such as technology and productivity shocks (see Plosser (1989)).

---

[8]   See also the overview in this manuscript.

[9]   See also chapter 2 on these issues.

Kydland and Prescott use calibration methods, and calculate and evaluate the co-movements for several macro-economic United States variables. The significance of the multi-period time-to-build for physical capital stock is thereby confirmed to be a main cause of fluctuations.

Park (1984) extends the time-to-build specification of Kydland and Prescott by allowing for changes in projects under construction ('a flexible investment plan'). A price needs to be paid for these changes, specified as the 'multi-period adjustment cost specification'. Within an Arrow-Debreu economy, a multi-sector economy where prices are endogenous and clear markets, both adjustment costs and time-to-build are adopted and empirically confirmed.

The time-to-build specification of Kydland and Prescott is further used by Taylor (1982), Kydland and Prescott (1988), Rossi (1988), Altug (1989) and Rouwenhorst (1991). The studies of Taylor and Rossi are factor demand studies and confirm the good performance of a multi-period time-to-build for capital stock in the United States and Swedish manufacturing industry. Rossi finds even more evidence for time-to-build than for the adjustment costs specification. Altug and Rouwenhorst follow the general equilibrium modelling of Kydland and Prescott, not making comparisons with the adjustment costs specification. Only Rouwenhorst concludes that the significance of time-to-build is not proved.

1.5   Short summary and extensions

The essentials of the previous sections can be summarized as follows.

The neoclassical theory of the firm, together with the assumption of adjustment costs, gives rise to dynamic models for labour and/or physical capital stock demand. Completely in line with this, gross investment dynamics are found to have dynamics, apart from investments prices, that only concern a first autoregressive order. On the contrary, Tobin's q theory (1969) of investments, derived in its standard form, is a static investment demand equation.

Empirical standard q theory studies show a poor behaviour of the q model of investments. Dynamic neoclassical models with labour and physical capital stock (instead of investments) seem to perform better.

The economic adjustment costs interpretation of physical capital stock or investments in comparison to labour is however much less evident. Even if capital adjustment costs exist, the question can be raised whether the dynamics in capital stock might not have a different major origin. Investments often have an irreversible character that influences the undertaking of investment projects. Furthermore, especially large capital projects are not built within short time periods (Mayer (1960), Kydland and Prescott (1982)).

Kuper and Visser (1993) give a survey of investment theories that concentrates less on neoclassical modelling, but is more comprehensive on other investment areas. A survey of flexible accelerator models is presented by Jorgenson (1971). This category of models is indicated by Chirinko (1993) as 'implicit' models. Contrary to 'explicit' models, these implicit models do not rely on underlying technology and expectation parameters. Chirinko extensively reviews the literature on these two categories of models and also goes into detail concerning the dynamics. Elaborate details on investment decisions under conditions of uncertainty concerning mainly individual capital projects, in a very broad context, are given by Dixit and Pindyck (1993). They review and summarize all kinds of concepts that are associated with an investment decision, such as the consequences of the irreversibility of a particular decision, the possibility of waiting, and the path dependence or 'hysteresis' for a certain firm.

The neoclassical factor demand modelling as presented in the framework described in this chapter remains simple, and can be extended in many ways.
One extension is possible by including technology phenomena. Technological developments influence the production possibilities (see for example Solow (1957)). It seems unrealistic to assume their independence of capital or labour in the production process. In the Real Business Cycle theory, technology shocks that occur are even proposed to be one of the main causes for fluctuations in macro-economic variables. These shocks are often assumed to be persistent, thus lasting longer than one period (see for example King, Plosser and Rebelo (1988)). By maintaining this assumption in factor demand studies, the interaction of technology shocks with production factors entails that technology shocks may induce dynamics in (interrelated) factor demand.
Another extension in modelling factor demand is the allowance of more general specification forms for the production and adjustment costs functions. As explained previously, a closed form is then not easily within reach. Instrumental estimation methods are in this case needed to estimate the first order conditions, being implicit forms of the demand equations for production factors. Unlike the closed form solutions, these instrumental methods do not incorporate transversality conditions, and consequently are less efficient. The question whether simple specification forms and full information estimation methods are preferred above more realistic specification forms and less efficient methods, or vice versa, seems still not answered in the literature[10].
Further extensions or improvements can be achieved by the inclusion of relevant

---

[10]   West (1986b) compares both estimation methods, that is the Full and Limited Information method, and finds that the first is slightly more efficient. A comparison of a more and a less general model by Limited and Full Information estimation respectively (like the models here in chapter 4 and 3 respectively) is more difficult to carry out.

production factors or the disaggregation of heterogeneous production factors into groups with homogeneous features. On a micro-economic level, technology and other differences between firms can even be revealed, leading to more insights.

An important feature that is often not at all accounted for in factor demand studies is the demand side on the output market. Factor demand studies assume that all products that are produced can be sold, barring the existence of output or demand restrictions. As the difference between supply and demand of goods is represented by inventory stocks that certainly exist in industries that do not produce to order (see for example Blinder (1986) or Christiano (1988)) and may interrelate with capital and labour demand, their influence might be important. Another option in accounting for the fluctuations in demand is to incorporate the utilization of capital stock[11]. This indicator of fluctuations of demand and supply over the business cycle is often not included.

Although abandoning price clearing assumptions and modelling disequilibria situations seems realistic, it is known to be of a much harder nature for applications. Literature in this direction is Licandro (1990), Meijdam (1991), De la Croix (1992) and Smolny (1993). In these theses it is assumed that output prices and wages are not perfectly flexible (thus a Walrasian auctioneer does not exist), by which supply and demand at least in the short run do not coincide. De la Croix and Licandro pay attention to the existence of demand uncertainty and the role of physical capital stock investments. As a consequence of demand uncertainty, capital stock may not always be fully utilized[12]. More in line of the manuscript subject here, being the gestation of investments, Smolny concentrates on slow capital stock and employment quantity adjustments that are not *only* due to the rigidity of prices.

---

[11]   Also in q studies the endogenous utilization of capital is not often mentioned. Motahar (1992) derives however from the intertemporal factor demand model with endogenous capital utilization the marginal q. According to the derivations, investments are biased upward by the assumption of a full capital utilization, since investments depend positively on capital utilization.

[12]   Because of the demand uncertainty and thus possible non-utilization, the marginal q is equal to or smaller than the average q. See also Motahar (1992).

APPENDIX 1.A

Dynamics and interrelation in structures, equipment and labour in six OECD countries

In this appendix some statistics on investments and employment time series are given in order to confirm the importance of interrelations between investments and employment series and the dynamics. Only univariate and trivariate reduced form systems are estimated. No factor prices are used or more structural restrictions (discussed in the previous sections) resulting from economic theory are imposed. Thus all analyses in this appendix are *non-structural*.

Annual time series of investments and labour from the manufacturing industry of six countries are taken into account. Total investments (in volumes) are separated here into structures (buildings and other 'large' physical capital stock projects) and equipment (machinery or 'small' projects) investments. Labour is measured in hours, that is the number of employed persons multiplied by the average number of weekly working hours. The sample period and countries under investigation are shown in the bottom part of table 1A.1. Further details about the data can be found in the data appendix.

As all time series are trending, each series is detrended to obtain a stationary series by which standard estimation techniques can be used. Detrended series are here obtained by regression of each original series on a constant and a polynomial deterministic trend of third order[13]. The residuals are normalized at 1985 and used in the further analyses.

Some results are presented by Table 1A.1.

The first step is the calculation of the standard deviation of each production factor, being structures, I^s, equipment, I^e, or labour, N. The statistics show that the variances of structures, equipment, and labour are, in general, in decreasing order. This indicates the flexibility and magnitude of the production factors. Usually, structures investments may be thought of as occurring less frequently and in larger volumes than equipment investments. The same may hold for the relation between equipment and labour.

---

[13] In subsequent *structural* analyses (chapter 3, 4 and 5) no deterministic detrend methods are applied but cointegration among the variables in the models is assumed. Detrend methods are used here in order to calculate some simple (univariate) statistics with the data under investigation.

Table 1A.1 Interrelation in structures, equipment and labour

i		St.dev.	AR(i) 1	2	3	4	Trivariate AR(i) 1	2	3	4	SC1	SC2	DW
US	I^s	0.171	0.38	**0.45**	0.42	0.41	0.42	**0.52**	0.43	0.50	1	1	1.57
	I^e	0.070	0.20	**0.34**	0.30	0.31	0.41	0.54	**0.57**	0.51	2		1.29
	N	0.039	0.12	**0.30**	0.27	0.28	0.09	0.40	**0.44**	0.37	2		1.56
CN	I^s	0.131	0.03	**0.40**	0.38	0.38	0.22	**0.50**	0.53	0.49	2	1	1.81
	I^e	0.125	0.23	**0.51**	0.50	0.48	0.45	0.71	0.82	**0.84**	2		1.45
	N	0.042	0.25	0.31	**0.46**	0.42	0.37	0.33	**0.47**	0.47	1		1.93
UK	I^s	0.175	0.12	0.47	0.49	**0.50**	0.30	0.69	**0.74**	0.70	2	2	1.40
	I^e	0.094	0.31	0.54	**0.56**	0.55	0.40	**0.74**	0.72	0.66	2		1.22
	N	0.041	0.28	**0.50**	0.49	0.47	0.35	**0.65**	0.62	0.59	2		1.41
WG	I^s	0.198	0.32	0.59	0.62	**0.65**	0.77	**0.83**	0.81	0.80	2	1	1.63
	I^e	0.082	0.38	**0.66**	0.64	0.64	0.59	**0.66**	0.60	0.62	2		2.00
	N	0.053	0.33	**0.49**	0.47	0.48	**0.61**	0.58	0.55	0.48	2		1.83
FR	I^s	0.093	0.23	0.46	0.46	**0.56**	0.51	0.50	0.52	**0.71**	2	1	2.14
	I^e	0.057	0.06	0.18	0.16	**0.28**	0.59	0.50	0.59	**0.60**	1		2.46
	N	0.015	0.01	0.23	0.19	**0.30**	0.54	0.60	0.74	**0.79**	2		2.08
NL	I^s	0.153	0.24	0.53	0.60	**0.65**	**0.50**	0.40	0.28	0.04	2	2	2.19
	I^e	0.103	0.04	0.11	**0.24**	0.21	0.48	0.73	0.67	**0.75**	3		1.54
	N	0.017	0.16	0.45	0.55	**0.58**	0.20	0.76	0.68	**0.80**	2		1.42

US = United States 1960-1988
CN = Canada 1960-1988
UK = United Kingdom 1960-1988
WG = West-Germany 1960-1988
FR = France 1970-1992
NL = The Netherlands 1971-1990

St.dev. is the standard deviation (of the detrended series). The columns under 'AR(i)' and 'trivariate AR(i)' contain the adjusted R^2 for each production factor by estimation of the system of production factors with a 1,2,3 and 4th order lag respectively. 'SC1' and 'SC2' are the lag orders according the Schwarz criterium for the univariate and the trivariate analyses respectively. DW is the Durbin-Watson statistic for the trivariate analyses with a first lag.

Table 1A.1 furthermore contains statistics per country of univariate autoregressions for each production factor and vector autoregressions for the system of factors. For both the univariate and trivariate analyses, up to the fourth order, lags are taken into account. The adjusted R^2's are shown in order to make a comparison of the models across columns possible. The order lag where the highest adjusted R^2 is found is indicated with bold print. Another selection criterium is given, the Schwarz-criterium (see Schwarz (1978)), which in contrast to the adjusted R^2 severely punishes the addition of lags. From these analyses some conclusions can be drawn.

Despite the relatively short and low frequency of the time series, already a high explanatory power is found in the univariate series as measured by the adjusted R^2 ranging from 0.24 to 0.66. The interrelation between structures, equipment and labour adds clearly to the explanation, as follows from the increases in adjusted R^2 when a trivariate system is estimated. The importance of interrelation between physical capital stock[14] (instead of investments) and labour series was already found by Brechling (1975) and Nadiri and Rosen (1969), for example.

A similar lag order for the three production factors can not be selected. According to the adjusted R^2's of the trivariate systems, structures and labour differ obviously in lag order, while the equipment dynamics in most cases equals one of these lags. The Schwarz criterium, when choosing the order for the whole system, refers in four cases to a first lag, and in two cases to a second lag.

In order to obtain more insights in the autocorrelation structures, graph 1A.1 gives the first ten partial autocorrelations of the individual (detrended) series. Graph 1A.2 gives these partial autocorrelations with the residual series from the trivariate AR(1) system. The i-th partial autocorrelation coefficient measures the correlation not accounted for by an AR(i-1) and consequently must be zero if the series under investigation is an AR(i-1). Thus if the production factors follow an autoregressive process of first order, as suggested by the neoclassical modelling with adjustment costs (see section 1.3), the partial correlations above one should be close to zero. As a very rough critical value for 'close to zero', 0.30 is used for the first four countries, 0.35 is used for France, and 0.37 is used for the Netherlands (since the partial correlations are approximately normally distributed with zero expectation and variance $1/\sqrt{T}$, where T is the sample size).

As follows from graph 1A.1, a turning point exists after the first correlation but high partial correlations are found at the second and sometimes even at much higher lags. As

---

[14]   The difference between investments series used here and physical capital stock series is the treatment of depreciation/obsolescence (see footnote 5) and the capital stock in comparison with investments demand timing (see footnote 7).

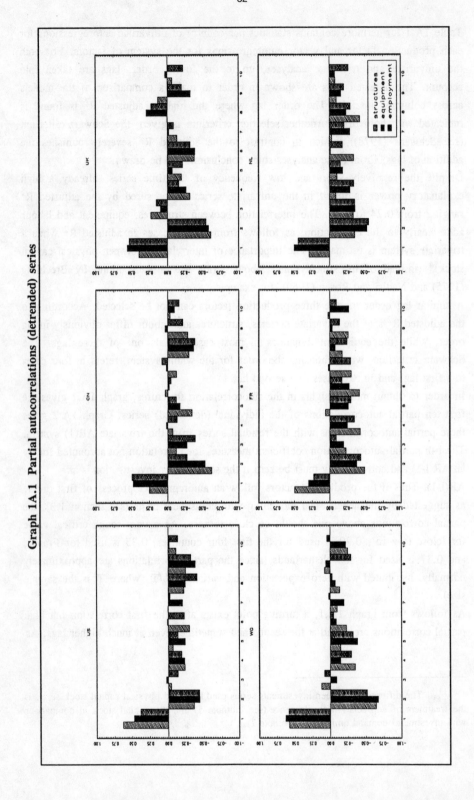

Graph 1A.1 Partial autocorrelations (detrended) series

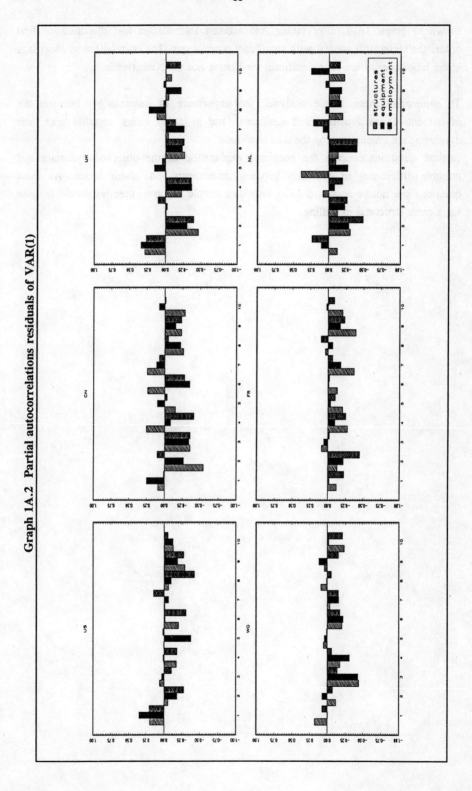

Graph 1A.2 Partial autocorrelations residuals of VAR(1)

shown in graph 1A.2, after taking into account interrelation and dynamics of first order, the series still are left with significant correlations. The correlations at short lags in the labour series are only significant for France and the Netherlands.

To summarize these simple analyses, the importance of interrelations between the investments series structures and equipment, and in labour series, together with their dynamics, are emphasized by the data used here.

Logical questions concern the economic explanation of the observed dynamics and possible differences in dynamics between investments and labour series. As these questions can not be answered using only data simple analyses, theories should be used for a more structural modelling.

CHAPTER 2
INVESTMENT GESTATION LAGS
Construction lags, delivery lags and capital stock accumulation

2.1   Introduction

Large investment projects are usually not carried out within short time periods.
Investment plans and decisions are made, and necessary financial and/or legal
permissions have to be obtained before the execution of plans can start. The period
between the start and the completion of the project, the construction period, can be
rather long. During this whole gestation process of an investment project (initial) plans
can be revised and even be withdrawn. For both small and large investment projects
delivery lags may exist that also hamper fast accumulations of the capital stock and,
thus fast production or consumption enlargements.

One objective of this chapter is to pay attention to the construction process of physical
capital goods and the existence of delivery lags. Issues addressed concern the capital
projects that are submitted to a considerable construction or delivery period and their
'average' lead time. Another objective is to pay attention to the difference between both
kinds of gestation lags and, associated with this, the difference in the accumulation of
capital stock submitted to construction lags or delivery lags.

The outline is as follows.
In section 2 data from the Dutch and French construction industry are used to illustrate
the construction lags of houses and plants. In section 3 the formalization for time-to-
build by Kydland and Prescott (1982) is given. Section 4 clarifies the difference
between construction and delivery lags. Section 5 summarizes studies that are
concerned with lead times. Section 6 illustrates the divergences between the calculation
of capital stock series by assuming a one period construction, a multi-period construction, and a multi-period delivery lag. In section 7 a summary is made and
conclusions are drawn.

36

Graph 2.1 Construction of houses in the Netherlands

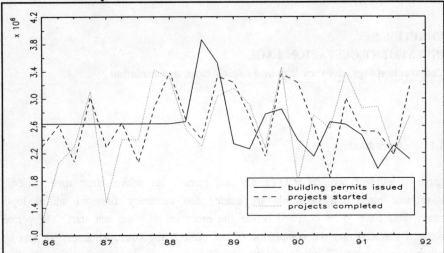

Source: 'Monthly bulletin of construction statistics', Netherlands Central Bureau of Statistics
Unity: Gross investments in volumes

Graph 2.2 Construction of plants in the Netherlands

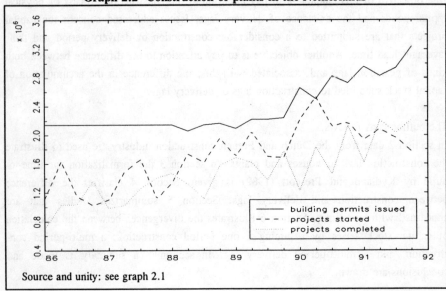

Source and unity: see graph 2.1

Graph 2.3 Construction of houses in France

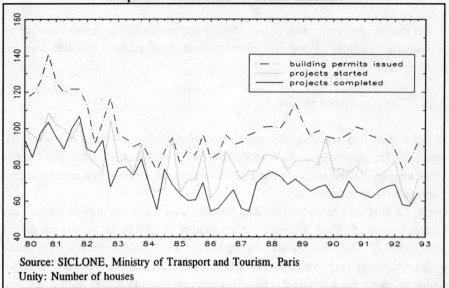

Source: SICLONE, Ministry of Transport and Tourism, Paris
Unity: Number of houses

Graph 2.4 Construction of manufacturing industry plants in France

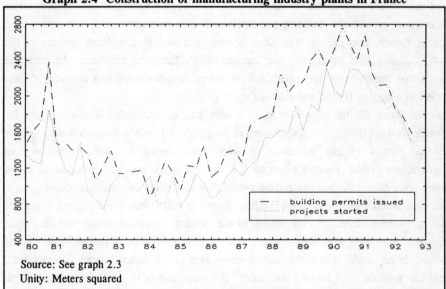

Source: See graph 2.3
Unity: Meters squared

2.2 Construction lags

In this section, the construction phases, the average construction time and cancellations of investment projects are consecutively considered. Data available and used here are on an aggregate level.

2.2.1 The construction process

In this section data regarding the construction of residential buildings and plants are presented. The gestation process is subdivided into two consecutive stages: the stage in which designers' plans are made and building permits are obtained (the preconstruction stage) and the construction stage.

Graph 2.1 shows the series for 'building permits issued', housing 'projects started' and housing 'projects finished' in constant Dutch guilders of 1980 in the Netherlands during 1986.I-1991.IV. The series for housing projects for which building permits were issued is (unfortunately) only available from 1988.I onwards, quarterly. Graph 2.2 shows similar series for reconstructions, expansions and new plants in the agriculture, industry and transport sector.

The graphs show the precedence of the 'building permits' series before the 'started', and the 'started' before the 'finished' series. The lagging behind of the 'started' series in comparison with the 'building permits issued' is to be interpreted a lead time during the preconstruction period. The time between started and completed projects is the construction period or literally the 'time-to-build'. The level differences between the series may thereby refer to projects not yet started or cancellations. A crossing of lines refers to a lagging behind and catching up of projects.

Similar series for the construction of houses and manufacturing industry plants for France during 1980.I-1992.IV, presented in graph 2.3 and 2.4 respectively, give a clearer picture of the existence of lead times during the preconstruction *and* construction period. From the graphs 2.1 and 2.3 it follows that cancellations occur more often during the preconstruction period than during the construction period.

An even better example of the existence of time-to-build, that is the lagging behind of the 'completed' series in comparison to the 'started' series, is found in Lee (1992, figure 1, page 422), who uses monthly data for the construction of houses in the United States. In his study, where the multi-cointegration of the series 'started', 'completed', and the 'housing stock under construction' is investigated, it is calculated that about 2% of all projects that start in the United States are not finished.

Table 2.1 Value-put-in-place of plants on the building site in the Dutch industry 1988.I-1990.IV

	≥10	≥11	11	12	13	≥15	≥16	≥17	≥14	≥15	≥16	≥17
Before '86	2,320	1,200	0	0	0	678	531	284	0	0	0	0
86.I	3,165	1,570	458	692	543	586	447	522	0	0	0	0
86.II	3,321	2,862	2,242	3,511	1,800	0	0	0	0	0	0	0
86.III	12,393	10,453	7,610	10,602	7,140	2,295	0	0	0	0	0	0
86.IV	4,863	0	0	0	0	0	0	0	522*	575*	415*	554*
87.I	20,872	15,358	9,965	7,717	5,136	1,926	1,188	0	0	0	0	0
87.II	60,371	29,172	13,809	10,499	1,803	1,426	748	0	0	0	0	0
87.III	112,914	44,612	15,184	13,590	10,680	5,700	1,510	0	0	0	0	0
87.IV	149,078	91,279	28,101	13,560	8,262	6,920	3,237	2,193	1,972	2,233	1,624	2,146
88.I	80,187	148,394	73,194	38,915	16,696	10,117	4,673	1,787	0	5,110	0	0
88.II	0	121,988	171,493	136,780	59,398	29,848	17,426	13,696	7,609	7,144	2,615	2,590
88.III	0	0	82,667	177,399	110,659	44,844	15,617	10,957	9,061	4,344	4,800	6,300
88.IV	0	0	0	116,572	201,053	141,527	44,993	19,660	5,408	12,238	3,139	3,449
89.I	0	0	0	0	95,965	183,876	92,957	51,241	20,817	41,644	6,216	5,938
89.II	0	0	0	0	0	127,755	185,175	147,622	66,427	76,218	18,056	14,936
89.III	0	0	0	0	0	0	91,475	188,797	115,604	134,962	30,230	24,037
89.IV	0	0	0	0	0	0	0	109,606	157,075	216,133	55,854	43,054
90.I	0	0	0	0	0	0	0	0	152,175	149,556	101,379	64,716
90.II	0	0	0	0	0	0	0	0	0	0	196,778	188,201
90.III	0	0	0	0	0	0	0	0	0	0	88,915	212,297
90.IV	0	0	0	0	0	0	0	0	0	0	0	113,068
Total	449,484	466,888	404,723	529,837	519,135	557,498	459,977	546,365	536,670	650,157	510,021	681,286
Construction time in quarters	≥10	≥11	11	12	13	≥15	≥16	≥17	≥14	≥15	≥16	≥17

* Value before 1987. All figures are in thousand Dfl, projects from 50,000 Dfl onwards.

Source: Netherlands Central Bureau of Statistics (unpublished data)

Graph 2.5 The distribution of plants investments 1989.II-1990.IV

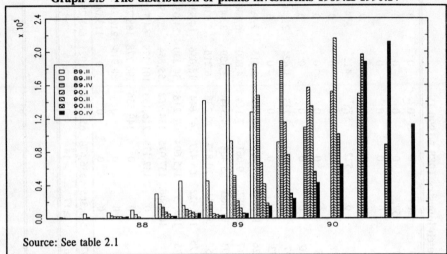

Source: See table 2.1

2.2.2 The length of the construction period

Information regarding the time-to-build period becomes clearer from studying table 2.1[15]. This table contains only data from the Netherlands that were, because of the fact that they are very detailed, not easy to obtain. Unfortunately, data from France were not at all obtained.

The figures in table 2.1 are in Dfl (Dutch guilders, in thousands) and concern reconstructions, expansions, and new plant projects in the Dutch industry from Dfl 50,000 upwards. The table shows for the 1988.I-1990.IV the value-put-in-place on the building site of projects per quarter in which the project was initiated. For example, the first column in table 2.1 and shows that in the first quarter of 1988, Dfl 449,484,000 were spent on the building of plants of which Dfl 2,320,000 on plant projects that were started before 1986, Dfl 3,165,000 on projects started in the first quarter of 1986 etc. The many zeros in 1986.IV and 1988.I indicate that in those periods no large projects were started.

The last row in table 2.1 yields the calculated construction time from this category of plant projects. This construction time ranges from 10 to 17 quarters. The same figures (not given here) on the restoration and rebuilding of plant projects for the same period and also for projects from 50,000 Dfl onwards, indicate that this category of plant

---

[15] These data are in a way 'vintage data' since they distinguish the different vintages of the construction projects.

projects has a construction time ranging from 4 to 9 quarters.

Graph 2.5 that is based on the data of table 2.1 shows the investment schedule during construction of these reconstructions, expansions, and new plants. For example, the investments of 1990.IV are represented in full black bars. They mainly concern projects that were started in 1990.III. But, they also contain projects that were started in 1987.IV (see table 2.1). Hence, the time-to-build is more than two years. A comparison of the different distributions shows that the investments schedule is always skewed to the left; most investments occur in projects that were just started or were begun one quarter earlier. The investment schedule changes over the sample period since the time-to-build differs (see the construction time in quarters in table 2.1 below) and along with this, the distribution's weights around the mode.

For the modelling of housing construction, Alphen and Merkies (1976) used similar 'vintage' data (1965.I-1972.III). With these data they find that the Pascal distribution is best suited to estimating the investment distribution during gestation. Later, Merkies and Steyn (1994) pay attention to the contractionary and expansionary effect of the time-to-build period during recession and recovery periods, respectively. They refer to these movements as the 'accordion effect'.

Table 2.2 Plants in the Dutch industry 1979-1989

Building sum (Dfl x 1000)	Number of projects of which building permits are issued									
	1979	1980	1982	1983	1984	1985	1986	1987	1988	1989
20-50	725	876	663	601	670	688	768	809	*	*
50-100	737	815	544	488	503	594	694	713	686	708
100-200	791	760	460	387	460	563	696	759	755	833
200-500	1092	1067	515	447	510	666	826	902	896	985
500-1,000	486	492	217	211	209	283	367	390	445	486
1,000-2,000	243	276	106	79	113	153	182	197	244	251
2,000-5,000	120	141	76	60	77	105	117	127	156	178
5,000-10,000	25	39	20	18	16	20	28	31	42	41
10,000-20,000	10	10	7	11	14	12	12	9	11	16
>20,000	3	4	2	7	3	3	5	6	0	7
Total	4232	4480	2610	2309	2575	3087	3695	3943	3235	3505

* Figures missing. The year 1981 is also missing.

Source: "Monthly bulletin of construction", Netherlands Central Bureau of Statistics

A considerable construction time is apparent but the statistics sofar do not reveal the variation among projects under construction. For example, the projects that were started before 1986 and still need to be finished in 1988.I, 1988.II, 1989.II-1989.IV (see table 2.1) may concern just a few plants, while many other projects are finished within a short time. As a consequence, an average time-to-build is not derived yet.

Therefore, a classification of plants according to their individual building sum (total expenditures during construction) for 1979-1989 is given in table 2.2. This table shows that between 1/4 and 1/5 of all reconstructions, expansions, and new plant projects for which a building permit was issued, consisted of small projects of Dfl 20,000-50,000.

A weighting of the ratios of values and production per building sum class, by the amount of projects per class in 1985, renders an average 'time-to-build' of 13.8 months. These statistics apply to 1986, 1988 and 1989, for 12.6, 12.4 and 13.2 months respectively.

2.2.3   Cancellations

In publications of the Central Bureau of Statistics ('Monthly bulletin of construction statistics') some information about cancellations of intended projects during the gestation time is presented. During 1979-1986, 22% of all orders received by architects and 4.5% of all projects for which building permits were issued within the industry, were withdrawn. Facts about changes in investment plans during the construction time are not known.

Alterations of started projects also follow from graphs 2.1-2.4 but are not easy to calculate. Alterations seem, however, to become less likely as the gestation process proceeds and may even be negligibly small in view of the withdrawal rates (of 4,5% during preconstruction) mentioned here.

To summarize sections 2.2.1-2.2.3, in regards to all of these simple calculations, it can be concluded that time-to-build of new plants within the industry seems considerable; about 10 to 17 quarters construction time is found for new plant projects (reconstructions, expansions, and new plants) whereas 4 to 9 quarters are used for the restoration and rebuilding of plants. As no projects of less than Dfl 50,000 were included in these calculations, the average time-to-build of construction will be less when projects of that smaller size are taken into account. By averaging data of building permits that were issued, and taking into account the variations among projects, a time-to-build of 12 to 14 months during 1985-1989 is found.

From a producer's point of view, the construction time of a project depends only on the plan of the total project, and the production speed of the construction industry. Many small projects and possible cancellations (that are not accounted for here) will decrease the average time-to-build within the industry unless the production speed of large projects is relatively fast. As individual data are not available, the question about the 'real' average time-to-build remains unanswered.

2.3 Time-to-build specification

Kydland and Prescott (1982) model the accumulation process of capital stock as

$$K_t = K_{t-1} - D_{t-1} + S_{1,t} \tag{2.1a}$$

$$I_t = \sum_{j=1}^{J} \delta_j S_{j,t} \tag{2.1b}$$

$$\sum_{j=1}^{J} \delta_j = 1 \quad \text{where} \quad 0 \le \delta_j \le 1 \tag{2.1c}$$

and

$$S_{j,t} = S_{j+1,t-1} \quad \text{for} \quad j=1,2..J-1. \tag{2.1d}$$

They call this specification 'time-to-build'. Productive capital at the end of period t is represented by K_t and obsolescence or depreciation by D_{t-1}. The expenditures of the capital project that is j periods from completion during period t is represented by $S_{j,t}$. The total construction time or time-to-build equals J. According to (2.1b), at each moment (at most) J current capital projects $S_{j,t}$ (j=1,2..J) exist that can be characterized by their production stage j . The capital project which is finished at the end of period t, $S_{1,t}$, is added to the productive capital stock K_t (equation (2.1a)). Gross investments during period t, I_t, consist of the sum of the 'values-put-in-place' $\delta_j S_{j,t}$ (j=1,2..J) of current projects during period t^{16}. Both the time-to-build and the distribution of the investments during the time-to-build (see (2.1c)) are assumed to be fixed. The last equality (2.1d) states that the total expenditures of the projects that are j periods from completion at time t, are the same as the total expenditures of the projects that needed j+1 periods to be built during the previous period. As a consequence, investment projects that are once started, are not changed during construction. For this reason this specification is called a 'fixed investments plan specification'.

---

[16] As should be noticed, no confusion among vintage models and time-to-build models can arise. Vintage models are concerned with a heterogeneous capital stock, K_t, to distinguish between productivity potentials of capital goods from different vintages. Time-to-build concentrates on the capital stock projects under construction $S_{1,t}, S_{2,t}.. S_{J,t}$.

Park (1984) generalises Kydland and Prescott's time-to-build modelling; a 'flexible investment plan specification' is specified by modifying equation (2.1d) into

$$S_{j,t} = S_{j+1,t-1} + \Delta_{j,t} \quad \text{for} \quad j=1,2..J-1. \tag{2.1d}^*$$

The revisions of current projects during period t, $S_{j,t}$, are represented by $\Delta_{j,t}$. If $\Delta_{j,t}<0$, the current project which is j periods from completion is decreased in size and possibly cancelled. This project is increased in size if $\Delta_{j,t}>0$. As each moment during the construction time further from the initial decision moment gives more information about the final product market conditions at the time the capital project becomes productive, longer construction times seem to make alterations more likely. Alterations in a downward direction ($\Delta_{j,t}<0$) could certainly occur whereas changes in an upward direction ($\Delta_{j,t}>0$) can only occur provided that additions to current projects are possible and permitted during the construction period. For example, in the latter case and in regards to the building of plants, new building permits have to be obtained. Therefore, a high price probably has to be paid to change investment plans.

Not much evidence for changes during the construction period was found from the descriptive statistics (see the preceding part 2.2.3). The probability that plans are withdrawn seems, however, to decline as the gestation process proceeds. And although the assumption $\Delta_{j,t} \neq 0$, (j=1,2..J-1) seems realistic, the assumption $\Delta_{j,t}=0$ will be maintained hereafter in light of the small and declining withdrawal rates found during gestation.

As can be verified easily, the time-to-build specification (2.1) boils down to the very often used capital accumulation equation,

$$K_t = K_{t-1} - D_{t-1} + I_t, \tag{2.2}$$

if J=1 and as a consequence $\delta_1=1$. In this equation gross investments, I_t, instantaneously add to the productive capital stock, K_t.

By rewriting (2.1d),

$$S_{j,t} = S_{1,t+j-1} \quad \text{for} \quad j=1,2..J-1, \tag{2.1d}$$

and rewriting (2.1a),

$$S_{1,t+j-1} = K_{t+j-1} - K_{t+j-2} + D_{t+j-2} \quad \text{for} \quad j=1,2..J-1, \tag{2.1a}$$

and assuming depreciation to be a constant percentage (κ) of capital stock, thus being $D_{t-1}=\kappa K_{t-1}$, it follows by substitution of (2.1d) and (2.1a) in (2.1b) that,

$$I_t = \sum_{j=0}^{J} \varphi_j K_{t+j-1} \quad \text{where} \quad \begin{aligned} &\varphi_0 \equiv \delta_1(\kappa-1), \\ &\varphi_j \equiv \delta_j + \delta_{j+1}(\kappa-1) \quad \text{for} \quad j=1,2..J-1, \\ &\varphi_J \equiv \delta_J. \end{aligned} \tag{2.3}$$

The multi-period time-to-build $(J>1)$ totals retirement and net changes weighted by the time-to-build parameters, that is $\delta_j \kappa K_{t+j-2}$ and $\delta_j(K_{t+j-1}-K_{t+j-2})$. As in the one period time-to-build case (see (2.2)), the sum of the weights in (2.3) still equals the retirement rate since

$$\sum_{j=0}^{J} \varphi_j = \kappa. \tag{2.4}$$

2.4 The difference between construction and delivery lags

Delivery lags for capital stock exist if a capital good can not be delivered immediately. For example, if it takes L periods to have new capital delivered, and the investment outlays need to be done at the beginning of L periods, the accumulation process of capital is to be specified as

$$K_t = K_{t-1} - D_{t-1} + I_{t-L+1}. \tag{2.5}$$

If instead, investment outlays occur at the moment of delivery, specification (2.2) holds, and the delivery lag becomes observationally equivalent to time-to-build lags with $J=1$.

For example Maccini (1973), who pays attention to delivery lags, investigates the role of additional costs (adjustment costs) such as research and planning costs of the recently placed orders. He assumes that payments to the supplier of the capital good occur at the delivery moment. Therefore, investment outlays immediately improve production capacities. The influence of the delivery lags is by him only reflected in the adjustment cost structure.

As follows from comparing (2.1) with (2.5), both specifications coincide if and only if $\delta_J=1$ and $J=L$ and consequently $\delta_j=0$ for $j=1,2..J-1$. The major specification difference of construction lags with delivery lags concerns the stagewise investment outlays that occur during the whole gestation period (so $\delta_j \neq 0$ for $j=1,2..J-1$)

From an investors point of view, it may not seem to matter whether lags are due to time-to-build (see (2.1)) or to delivery (according to (2.5)); in both cases investments are irreversible because sunk costs exist at the beginning of the lead time. The fact that the existence of lead times as illustrated in graph 2.6 are highly important, especially in cases where uncertainty and opportunity costs of delay are great, is emphasized in Majd and Pindyck (1987). They pay attention to the net present value rules for (individual) investment decisions that dramatically change when lead times exist. Bar-Ilan, Sulem and Zanello (1993) also emphasize that the presence of uncertainty, in particularly demand uncertainty, in case of construction or delivery lags may increase the costs of 'waiting to invest' and hence induce investors to invest more quickly as lead times lengthen. The building of an electric utility industry, and the aircraft and mining industries, are examples mentioned in these studies.

The difference between both types of lead times (see graph 2.6) becomes, on the other hand, apparent in econometric modelling and estimation because more serial correlation is assumed in (2.1) than (2.5). The richer dynamics in gross investments resulting from time-to-build become apparent from identity (2.3) since I_t depends on I_{t-1}, $I_{t-2}..I_{t-J+1}$ if $\delta_j \neq 0$ for all $j \in \{1,2..J\}$.

Graph 2.6 A delivery lag or a construction lag for a capital good

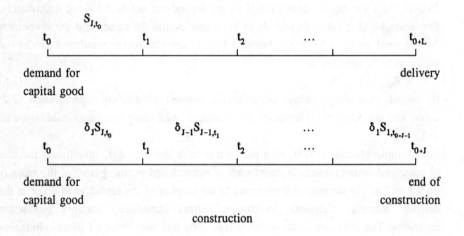

2.5   Statistical evidence on lead times

The existence of lead times of capital projects, induced by construction or delivery lags, is endorsed by information from actual practice by Mayer and Sonenblum (1955). They give evidence for construction and equipment of 108 sectors in the United States during World War II and the Korean period. For each sector the average estimated and actual lead time is given and a total lead time for a plant, including its equipment, is calculated.

Evidence for lead times for plants as a whole is also found in Mayer (1960). He surveyed 110 companies in 1954-1955. Averages are calculated by summing individual project lead times weighted by the costs of the projects. The construction period of both new plants and large additions to existing operating plants is found to be eleven months on average (unweighted).

The survey findings about the time lags before construction starts are confirmed by U.S. econometric analyses with quarterly data (1947-1960) by Jorgenson and Stephenson (1967), among others. They estimated average lags between the determinants of investment behaviour and actual investments.

Although these U.S. findings date from the fifties and sixties, they are quite well in line with the plants' construction time calculations for the Dutch industry. They indicate that the assumption of an average time-to-build of about one year seems probable.

Unfortunately these previous studies do not mention the investment outlays moment, by which the identification of the lead time as a delivery lag or time-to-build lag is not possible.

Some statistical evidence for delivery lags for different types of capital goods is given by Abel and Blanchard (1988). With annual data of 1967 and 1972 from the United States, they calculate delivery lags of on average of 2, 2, 3 and 0 quarters for the delivery of fabricated metals, nonelectrical machinery, electrical machinery, and motor vehicles, respectively[17]. These averages are calculated using data on the unfilled orders and mean shipments of the supplying industry. Along with this, they calculated construction lags of 3-5, 3-6 and 4-8 quarters for industrial structures, commercial structures, and other structures respectively with direct evidence of the nature of structures projects.

Most naturally seem to be delivery lags for equipment. After all, custom made machineries, installations that are not often demanded, or equipment that needs to be transported long distances will be subject to delivery lags. The lead times for construction, given by Mayer and Sonenblum (1955) and Mayer (1960), may thereby presumably be a time-to-build according to (2.1) like the statistical evidence for time-to-build available for structures projects (see section 2.2.1-2.2.2).

In the case where different lead times are aggregated, the average lead time is less evident. For example, by using aggregate manufacturing industry or macroeconomic investment series, construction lead times of large investment projects (i.e. 'structures') are averaged with the lead times resulting from delivery lags (i.e. 'equipment'). Abel and Blanchard find that for industrial sectors the average lead time of construction and delivery lags is 3.2 to 3.5 quarters.

---

[17]   Abel and Blanchard (1988), who investigate if differences in sales of industrial sectors are caused by delivery lags during 1958.I-1979.III (a question that is by their econometric analyses not confirmed), specify delivery lags with a stagewise payment of the investments like the time-to-build specification (2.1) (see Abel and Blanchard, equation (4), page 271). The calculation of the delivery lags of equipment, however, is carried out according to the goods (in volumes) that are delivered, by which delivery lags are calculated correctly. Whether the moment of payment is the investment order placement moment (according (2.5)), the delivery moment, or several moments during the delivery period (according (2.1)) is not revealed.

Table 2.3 Ratios structures/equipment investments

Year	National	Manufacturing
1970	0.86	0.38
1980	0.85	0.28
1990	0.64	0.20
Source: Netherlands Central Planning Bureau, unpublished data		

Table 2.3 shows the quotients of structures and equipment in the Netherlands for three years. It follows that macroeconomically structures are more relevant than in the manufacturing industry, due to the large proportion of residential buildings in national investments. Hence, in macroeconomic investment studies (Kydland and Prescott (1982), for example) the construction lead times deserve more weight than equipment lead times that may on average be much lower.

2.6   The calculation of physical capital stock series

Physical capital stock series are often used in econometric analyses. As the value or volume of capital stock is difficult to measure, Central Bureaus of Statistics mostly compute capital stock series from gross investments and on the basis of depreciation assumptions.

The method that is everywhere used by Central Bureaus of Statistics is known as the Perpetual Inventory Method (PIM); a benchmark is used for capital stock K_0, gross investments are added and depreciation (often assumed a constant percentage of the existing capital stock) is subtracted. More information on this method is found in Ward (1976), where this rule and slight variations are used to compute the capital stocks of OECD countries. By this rule, a one period time-to-build is assumed according to (2.2). The capital stock series does thus not account for time-to-build according to (2.1) or delivery lags according to (2.5).

The divergence in capital stock series consistent with the three possible methods is illustrated in graph 2.7. A benchmark of Dutch national physical capital stock for 1970, a depreciation rate of 2.5% ($\kappa = 0.025$) and Dutch quarterly national investment series are used, 1971.I-1990.IV, in constant prices of 1980 and seasonally adjusted. The first capital stock series is then calculated according to (2.2). The second series is according to (2.1) where it is assumed that $J=4$, $\delta_1=0.1$, $\delta_2=0.2$, $\delta_3=0.3$, $\delta_4=0.4$ and $S_{1971.I,1} = S_{1971.I,2} = S_{1971.I,3} = S_{1971.I,4} = I_{1971.I}$. The third series is according to (2.3) with a delivery lag of four quarters, hence $L=4$. The growth rate of these three constructed capital stock series are given in graph 2.7.

Graph 2.7 Growth physical capital stock

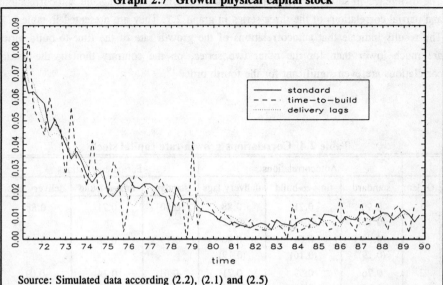

Source: Simulated data according (2.2), (2.1) and (2.5)

The graph shows that the fluctuations in the first and third capital series are similar, except for the delivery lag of four quarters. The time-to-build series does not replicate fluctuations of one of these series and is much more erratic. This is of course due to the investment scheme that was assumed here to be declining during a period of four quarters. In this case most investments occur in the period four quarters before the period where the capital good is added to the productive capital stock. Because of the investment scheme, the time-to-build series falls always 'in between' the standard series and the delivery lags series; see for example the fall of the standard series in 1978.I, the fall of the delivery lags series in 1979.I and the fall of the time-to-build series in 1978.III[18].

---

[18]   From this it follows that the Real Business Cycle study of Kydland and Prescott (1982) is not consistent. In their study they intend to use the time-to-build specification (2.1), but use capital stock series according to (2.2) instead. This inconsistency by Kydland and Prescott (1982) is, among others, also committed in Rouwenhorst (1991, see footnote 4 page 246) and Wolfson (1993). Rouwenhorst uses the same national capital stock series as Kydland and Prescott and analyses the importance of time-to-build in describing fluctuations. As the distribution of investments during gestation (δ_j, j=1,2..J) is calibrated instead of estimated and a significant serial correlation is neglected by using data according to (2.2) instead of (2.1), his main result, that time-to-build does not cause persistence can be cast much doubt. Wolfson (1993), disaggregating manufacturing capital stock as structures and equipment, is in his study also confusing. He speaks

The difference in serial correlation becomes clear after calculating the autocorrelations and partial correlations of the three series in graph 2.7. They are presented in table 2.4. The results indicate that autocorrelations of the growth rate of the time-to-build series are much lower than for the other two series, on the contrary though, the partial correlations are even significant for the fourth order [19].

Table 2.4 Correlations growth rate capital stock

	Autocorrelations			Partial correlations		
Order	standard	time-to-build	delivery lags	standard	time-to-build	delivery lags
1	0.90 (0.12)	0.71 (0.12)	0.88 (0.12)	0.90	0.71	0.88
2	0.83 (0.19)	0.64 (0.16)	0.80 (0.19)	0.13	0.28	0.13
3	0.76 (0.23)	0.59 (0.19)	0.71 (0.22)	-0.01	0.14	-0.03
4	0.70 (0.26)	0.65 (0.22)	0.65 (0.25)	-0.001	0.32	0.06

Values between brackets are standard errors. The standard error for the partial autocorrelations is 0.11 (1.96/$\sqrt{T}$ where T is the sample size).
Source: Simulated data (see text)

in terms of time-to-build while modelling delivery lags as in (2.3) for both types of capital and above this, using (almost surely) capital stock data according (2.2).

[19] From time series theory, it follows that the findings of non-significant second order partial autocorrelations for the first and third series imply that these series, i.e. the growth rate, is autoregressive of the first order. The growth rate of the series with time-to-build has different dynamics, which is a result confirmed in chapter 3.

2.7   Summary and conclusions

The main points can be summarized as follows.

Two kinds of gestation can be distinguished, being construction and delivery lags. Structures are obviously subject to time-to-build with a stagewise payment of investments during construction. Equipment seems most probably subject to delivery lags.

According to the quarterly Dutch data used in this section, plant projects need on average one year to be built although some caution in this 'average' time-to-build calculation should be taken. Statistical evidence for average equipment delivery lags and construction lags was found by Abel and Blanchard (in 1967 and 1972) to be about 1-2 and 3-6 quarters respectively. So construction lags are evidently longer than delivery lags.

Macroeconomically, taking account of time-to-build seems important, as a large proportion of national investments concern structures projects. These projects, mainly consisting of residential buildings, need long construction periods and entail a high serial correlation. For the manufacturing industry the aggregation problem of structures and equipment and their different lead times may lead to much lower average gestation lags as the major part consists of equipment.

The specification of Kydland and Prescott (1982) seems suitable to formalizing the construction process of capital projects and also nests the delivery lags specification. As shown here, existing capital stock series are inconsistent with this time-to-build specification. To be consistent and in order to identify lead times, gross investments instead of capital stock data are to be used.

CHAPTER 3
A CLOSED FORM SOLUTION FOR
A MODEL WITH TIME-TO-BUILD AND ADJUSTMENT COSTS
An application to the United States and Dutch manufacturing industry

3.1   Introduction

The realization of a physical capital stock investment plan can typically be characterized as an investment project that needs a period to be built, consumes (often irreversible) investment expenditures during the whole gestation, and is only useful to the investor when it is complete. Therefore, for the producer, who has to decide on new investment plans, events in a distant future (like product and/or factor markets and technological developments) are important. The irreversibility and non-productiveness during gestation of investment projects that need time-to-build, entail that longer lead times lead to more uncertainty.

As shown in chapter 2, Kydland and Prescott (1982) with the assumptions of 'time-to-build', are emphasizing these investment lags. In their view, fluctuations of macroeconomic variables are caused by persistent pure real shocks, like technology and productivity shocks, and the existence of time-to-build induces much more serial correlation. Dynamics in their general equilibrium model are described by persistent (stochastic) shocks and time-to-build.

In factor demand studies dynamics are mostly described by adjustment costs. Cost incurred when hiring or firing labour, which are labour adjustment costs, are modelled according Holt et al. (1960). In a similar way scrappage and installation costs of capital stock are modelled according Eisner and Strotz (1963). See also chapter 1, section 1.3.2-1.3.3.

These adjustment costs specifications for capital, assume that the capital stock can be adjusted within one period. The adoption of time-to-build in a factor demand model raises, however, the question whether additional costs to change the capital stock occur and are important. The chapter intends to answer this question.

The methodology to answer this question is as follows.

A factor demand model with time-to-build and adjustment costs is specified. The neoclassical assumptions of a profit maximizing and rational entrepreneur are adopted. As a linear-quadratic framework is chosen and additional assumptions (concerning production factor prices and technology shocks) are made, a closed form solution is obtained. The implications of adjustment costs in addition to time-to-build, are analyzed by estimating the solution with quarterly manufacturing industry data from the United States (1960.I-1988.IV) and the Netherlands (1971.I-1990.IV).

The outline is as follows.

In section 2, the linear-quadratic model is presented for structures, equipment, and labour. Adjustment costs for all production factors and a multi-period time-to-build for structures are adopted. Attention is paid to the economic interpretation of adjustment costs in the way the literature proposes. The demand for structures that have on average more than one quarter time-to-build according to the findings in chapter 2, is scrutinized in section 3. Three models for structures investment are thereby derived; one without adjustment costs, one with adjustment costs of net capital stock and one with adjustment costs of gross investments. In section 4 the closed form solution of the multivariate model is given. Section 5 summarizes the theoretical results and gives the goals of estimation. Empirical results are presented in section 6. Maximum Likelihood estimates are presented for the closed form data from the United States and Dutch manufacturing industry. The implications of the model are tested. The necessity of modelling adjustment costs for a multi-period time-to-build for structures is further investigated. Section 7 summarizes and concludes.

3.2   The model

In the first part of this section the contingency plan of an entrepreneur is specified. In the second part attention is paid to the economic interpretation of adjustment costs in comparison with time-to-build.

3.2.1   A neoclassical factor demand model with time-to-build

An entrepreneur is assumed to be a representative of firms within the industry. The entrepreneur is rational in the sense that at each moment of decision, information available is used to forecast future events in order to make the optimal decision.

Production can be increased by utilizing more physical capital stock and/or labour. The capital stock is disaggregated as a (productive) plant or structures stock and a (productive) equipment stock. Structures, equipment and labour are represented by K_t^s, K_t^e, N_t respectively. The production function is assumed to be an approximation of an underlying economic production function that is more interpretable and is linear quadratically specified as,

$$Q_t \equiv (\alpha + \lambda_t)'X_t - \frac{1}{2} X_t'AX_t \quad \text{where} \quad \alpha := [\alpha_1, \alpha_2, \alpha_3]', \quad A := \text{diag}\{a_1, a_2, a_3\}, \qquad (3.1)$$

where $X_t \equiv [K_t^s \ K_t^e \ N_t]'$ is the vector of production factors and $\text{diag}\{a_1, a_2, a_3\}$ denotes a diagonal matrix with diagonal elements a_1, a_2, a_3. The term $\lambda_t := [\lambda_{1t} \ \lambda_{2t} \ \lambda_{3t}]'$ represents a stochastic technology shock that, in addition to physical capital stock and labour, influences the level of production. Their accumulated effect is often called the Solow residual.

Concavity assumptions of the production function are satisfied, that is

$$\partial Q_t / \partial X_t > 0 \quad \text{and} \quad \partial^2 Q_t / \partial X_t^2 \leq 0, \qquad (3.2)$$

if and only if matrix A is positive.

Variable costs are given by VC_t. Let $Y_t \equiv [I_t^s \ I_t^e \ N_t]'$ represent the vector of structures and equipment investments and labour, and let $P_t \equiv [C_t^s \ C_t^e \ W_t]'$ represent the vector of the real investment price of structures and equipment, and the real wage. Then the variable costs are

$$VC_t \equiv P_t'Y_t. \qquad (3.3)$$

Additional costs that are incurred when changing capital or labour are given by

$$AC_t \equiv \frac{1}{2} Z_t' \Gamma Z_t \quad \text{where} \quad \Gamma := \text{diag}\{\gamma_1, \gamma_2, \gamma_3\}, \quad \gamma_i > 0, \ i = 1, 2, 3,$$

$$\text{and} \quad Z_t \equiv \Delta X_t \quad \text{or} \quad Z_t \equiv [I_t^s \ I_t^e \ \Delta N_t]'. \qquad (3.4)$$

Z_t is assumed here to be either ΔX_t *or* $[I_t^s, I_t^e, \Delta N_t]'$. The entrepreneur's objective is to maximize the present value of profits over an infinite horizon,

$$\underset{\{X_{t+h}^d\}_{h=0}^{\infty}}{\text{Max}} \ E\{\sum_{h=0}^{\infty} \beta^h \ [Q_{t+h} - VC_{t+h} - AC_{t+h}] \mid \Omega_t\} \quad \text{with} \quad \beta \in (0,1), \qquad (3.5)$$

where $X_t^d \equiv [K_{t+J-1}^s \ K_t^e \ N_t]'$ is the decision vector and Ω_t represents the available information set at time t. β represents the discount factor that is assumed to be constant. The product price is used as a numéraire here, which means that all factor prices are deflated by the product price, and puts the profit stream in real terms.

Structures are assumed to need more than one period to be built whereas equipment gestates only one period. According to the time-to-build specification of Kydland and Prescott (see chapter 2, (2.1) and (2.2)) it then holds that

$$I_t^s = \sum_{j=0}^{J} \varphi_j^s K_{t+j-1}^s \qquad \text{where} \qquad \varphi_1^s \equiv \delta_1(\kappa^s-1)$$

$$\varphi_j^s \equiv \delta_j + \delta_{j+1}(\kappa^s-1) \quad \text{for} \quad j=1,2..J-1$$

$$\varphi_J^s \equiv \delta_J \qquad\qquad\qquad (3.6a)/(2.3)$$

and

$$I_t^e = \Delta K_t^e + \kappa^e K_{t-1}^e. \qquad\qquad\qquad\qquad (3.6b)/(2.2)$$

κ^i represents the constant depreciation rate of structures (i=s) and equipment (i=e). $\delta_J, \delta_{J-1}..\delta_1$ is the investment scheme during the construction period and J is the total time-to-build of structures. As a consequence, investment in structures consist of past, current, and future structures stocks, whereas gross investments do not depend on future stocks of equipment.

The crucial feature[20] of this model is that due to the structures' time-to-build (see (3.6a)), the entrepreneur is forced to make decisions at time t about new structures projects, $S_{J,t}$ or K_{t+J-1}^s. As started projects can not be changed during construction, the end of the period structures stocks from t until t+J-1, i.e. $K_t^s, K_{t+1}^s..K_{t+J-1}^s$, (instead of only K_t^s) are already determined at the beginning of period t. The decisions of equipment and labour concern time t, so the decision variables are K_{t+J-1}^s, K_t^e, N_t (see (3.5)).

For the technology shocks in (3.1) and for the process of determining prices, the assumptions of autoregressive processes are made. That is,

$$\lambda_t = R\lambda_{t-1} + e_t^\lambda, \qquad\qquad R:=\{\rho_{ij}\} \quad i,j=1,2,3,$$

$$e_t^\lambda := \left[e_{1t}^\lambda \ e_{2t}^\lambda \ e_{3t}^\lambda\right]' \sim N_3(0,\Sigma^\lambda), \qquad E\{e_t^\lambda e_s^{\lambda'}|\Omega_t\}=0, \quad s\neq t, \ (3.7)$$

$$P_t = \sum_{k=1}^{p} M_k P_{t-k} + e_t^P, \qquad M_k:=\{\mu_{ijk}\} \quad i,j=1,2,3,$$

$$e_t^P := \left[e_{1t}^P \ e_{2t}^P \ e_{3t}^P\right]' \sim N_3(0,\Sigma^P), \qquad E\{e_t^P e_s^{P'}|\Omega_t\}=0, \quad s\neq t. \ (3.8)$$

---

[20] This is also the reason to assume both A in (3.1) and Γ in (3.4) diagonal for the time being; non-diagonal matrices A and Γ entail a first order condition for plants that contains future values of both labour and equipment. As a consequence, the derivation of the closed form solution is more difficult.

The assumption of an autoregressive[21] process for technology is in line with, for example, the model of Kydland and Prescott (1982). The assumption of an autoregressive process of prices implies that the entrepreneur is a price taker in the output and input markets. Hence, (Granger) causality from production factors to real prices is assumed to be absent.

3.2.2 Economic interpretation of adjustment costs and time-to-build

Adjustment costs are specified in (3.4) as a convex function in the flows of the production factors. It is assumed that net changes in labour demand incur additional costs (hiring and firing costs) at an increasing rate, so the last term of Z_t in (3.4) equals ΔN_t.

The literature on adjustment costs of physical capital stock is twofold. Sometimes adjustment costs of net changes in capital stock (ΔK_t), and other times gross investments (I_t) are taken into account. Usually a one period construction time is accounted for, such as the specification for equipment in (3.6b), in which case the difference between these two alternatives is the depreciation. See subsection 1.3.3 on this issue.

A multi-period construction time, like the specification for structures in (3.6a), changes the economic interpretation of adjustment costs. The adjustment costs (of structures) specifications, ACP_{1t} and ACP_{2t}, defined as

$$ACP_{1t} \equiv \frac{1}{2}\gamma_1(\Delta K_t^s)^2 \quad \text{and} \quad ACP_{2t} \equiv \frac{1}{2}\gamma_1(\sum_{j=0}^{J} \varphi_j^s K_{t+j-1}^s)^2, \qquad (3.9)$$

are not equal, even if there is no depreciation $(\kappa^s=0)$.

The assumption ACP_{1t} implies that adjustment costs are incurred if $S_{1,t} \neq \kappa^s K_{t-1}^s$. If the value of retirement exceeds the value of currently completed structures $(\kappa^s K_{t-1}^s > S_{1,t})$ the ACP_{1t} can be interpreted as scrappage costs. The interpretation of the costs when more structures are completed than retired $(\kappa^s K_{t-1}^s < S_{1,t})$ is however far less clear. At the moment of structures' completion, costs to install equipment and other costs to make structures usable for production are incurred. But these costs could mainly be contained in the adjustment costs of equipment.

Obviously, designers' costs and costs for building permits are incurred before the start of or possibly during the construction period. The specification ACP_{2t} specifies the

---

[21] The stationarity of ϵ_t^λ is confirmed by cointegration results in the empirical part and point estimates of $\{\rho_{ij}\}$, i,j=1,2,3 (see the empirical part).

costs during construction that are directly connected with the amount of investment expenditures. Scrappage costs are, by this specification, not explicitly modelled.

The main principle of the adjustment costs theory is to penalize quick adjustments (see subsection 1.3.2-1.3.4). The assumption of instantaneous and costless adjustment of production factor changes is usually dropped by the specification of a *convex* adjustment cost function, like $Z_t' \, \Gamma \, Z_t$ in (3.5). The convexity assumption implies that one unit adjustment is more costly than twice half this unit.

As the time-to-build investment plan specification already contains the issue of expense, not in the way that adjustment costs have to be paid but in the way that no profits are obtained during construction, the combination of adjustment costs and time-to-build is a double expense. This cost is questionable because of the unclear economic interpretation of adjustment costs other than time-to-build. In the model presented here, one might thus expect that $\gamma_1 = 0$.

The assumption of adjustment costs that are increasing at the margin and are marginally equivalent (only for the ACP_{1t}-specification because the ACP_{2t}-function contains only positive arguments) are other questionable and more difficult issues[22].

3.3 Three univariate models for structures

If no interrelation existed in the technology shock process (that is $R=\text{diag}\{\rho_1, \rho_2, \rho_3\}$ in (3.1)), the final closed form solution would consist of a structures, an equipment, and a labour equation that are only related by contemporaneously correlated disturbances. If only these correlations hold, each equation can be estimated (at the loss of some efficiency) consistent univariately.

In this section the structures equation is singled out from (3.5). This allows the opportunity to pay close attention to the differences that occur in a closed form solution when adjustment cost functions, in either net capital stock or gross investments, are considered. The model without adjustment costs is given first in order to emphasize the implications of adjustment costs.

The derived equations, referred to as model 1, 2, 3, in this section are used for estimation in the section 3.6. These models 1-3 resemble the model in section 1.3.3.

As the main results of this section are summarized in section 3.4 (table 3.1), reading this section 3.3 is not strictly necessary to understand the subsequent sections.

---

[22]   The point of marginally increasing adjustment costs for capital stock investments with a one period construction time was already addressed elaborately by Nickell (1978).

3.3.1 Model 1: Time-to-build with no adjustment costs

The assumption $Z_t' \, \Gamma \, Z_t = 0$ gives the Euler equation for structures as

$$K_{t+J-1}^s = \frac{\alpha_1}{a_1} + \frac{1}{a_1} E\{\lambda_{1,t+J-1} - \sum_{i=0}^{J} \beta^{i-J+1} \varphi_{J-i}^s C_{t+i}^s \mid \Omega_t\} \qquad (3.10)$$

and the transversality or end-point conditions are satisfied if all variables have an exponential order less than $1/\sqrt{\beta}$. The demand for new structures projects at the beginning of period t depends positively on the expectations of technology shocks at $t+J-1$[23]. Expected prices of structures investment from t until $t+J-1$ influence the demand negatively, because during the time-to-build period these prices have to be paid for structures projects that are initiated at the beginning of period t. The entrepreneur forecasts $\lambda_{1,t+J-1}$ and $C_{t+1}^s, C_{t+2}^s..C_{t+J}^s$ in the belief that their processes are given as in (3.7)-(3.8).

It is here assumed that there is no interrelation in the persistent part of the technology process, $R:=\text{diag}\{\rho_1,\rho_2,\rho_3\}$, and a first order autoregressive process of prices is assumed (i.e. p=1 in (3.8) and take $M \equiv M_1$). As a consequence,

$$E\{\lambda_{1,t+J-1} \mid \Omega_t\} = \rho_1^{J-1}\lambda_{1t} \quad , \quad E\{C_{t+i}^s \mid \Omega_t\} = [M^i]_1 P_t, \quad i=1,2..J, \qquad (3.11)$$

where $[.]_1$ equals the first row of the matrix in square brackets. It then follows that

$$K_{t+J-1}^s = \frac{\alpha_1}{a_1} + \frac{\rho^{J-1}}{a_1}\lambda_{1,t} - m^*P_t \quad \text{where} \quad m^* \equiv \frac{1}{a_1}\sum_{i=0}^{J} \beta^{i-J+1}\varphi_{J-i}^s[M^i]_1 . \qquad (3.12)$$

In regards to the estimations, this equation will be rewritten in terms of gross investments[24]. Equation (3.12) is pre-multiplied by φ_J^s on both sides, added to $\sum_{j=0}^{J-1} \varphi_j^s K_{t+j-1}^s$ and because of (3.7) and (2.5) it then follows that

$$I_t^s = \frac{\kappa^s \alpha_1}{a_1} + \frac{\rho^{J-1}}{a_1}\sum_{j=0}^{J} \varphi_j^s\lambda_{1,t-J+j} - \sum_{j=0}^{J} \varphi_j^s m^*P_{t-J+j}. \qquad (3.13)$$

Gross investments are a weighted sum of past, current, and future capital stock and therefore depend (contrary to capital stock) on lagged technology shocks *and* lagged

---

[23] The interaction of technology shocks (λ_t) and productive plant stock (K_t^s) are, among others, assumed to influence production. Alternatively, technology shocks could be specified as influencing current projects $(S_{j,t}$ for $j=1,2..J)$ that shift the marginal (plant) productivity, see for example Greenwood, Hercowitz and Huffman (1988).

[24] In the empirical analyses gross investment series are used. The estimation of (3.12) with physical capital stock series is preferable, but is not in consistence with the specification (3.6a). After all, physical capital stock series that exist are calculated assuming a one period time-to-build which is not in agreement with the theoretical model here (see also section 2.6).

prices in the recent past.

In order to estimate, the unobserved technology shocks are to be eliminated. A Koyck transformation can here be applied that gives

$$I_t^s = c + \rho_1 I_{t-1}^s - \sum_{j=0}^{J+1} m_j P_{t-j} + \sum_{j=0}^{J} \varphi_{J-j}^s e_{1,t-j} \qquad (Model\ 1\ (3.14))$$

where
$$m_0 \equiv \varphi_J m^*$$
$$m_j \equiv (\varphi_{J-j} - \rho_1 \varphi_{J-j+1}^s) m^* \qquad j=1,2..J$$
$$m_{J+1} \equiv -\rho_1 \varphi_0^s m^*,$$

where c is the constant term and $e_{1,t}$ is $e_{1,t}^{\lambda}$ multiplied by ρ_1^{J-1}/a_1.

This reduced form equation for gross investments (referred to as model 1) is an ARMAX(1,J,J+1) process, where the X-part refers to prices P_{t-J-1}, P_{t-J} up to and including P_t. If no persistent part in technology shocks is assumed ($\rho_1 = 0$), lagged prices up to only J periods, and a moving average of a J-th order remains.

The transitory part of the technology process ($e_{1,t}^{\lambda}$) causes the moving average. At the beginning of t, investment project $S_{J,t}$ is initiated. This influences gross investment at the beginning of t with the amount φ_J^s. During the construction time, at the beginning of period t+1, t+2..t+J, it influences I_{t+1}^s, $I_{t+2}^s..I_{t+J}^s$ by φ_{J-1}^s, $\varphi_{J-2}^s..\varphi_0^s$ respectively. As gross investments during t are a weighted sum of K_{t-1}^s, $K_t^s..K_{t+J-1}^s$, they are influenced by $\varphi_J^s e_{1,t}^{\lambda}$, $\varphi_{J-1}^s e_{1,t-1}^{\lambda}..\varphi_0^s e_{1,t-J}^{\lambda}$ which is the moving average part in model 1 (see (3.14)).

The lagged prices are weighted in a similar way with the time-to-build weights φ_j^s (j=0,1..J). m^* represents the forecasted part of prices that are at most J periods in the future.

If prices and technology shocks are not contemporaneously correlated, $E\{e_{1,t}^{\lambda} e_{1,t}^{p} | \Omega_t\} = 0$, the exogenous variables and disturbance e_{1t}^{λ} in (3.14) are uncorrelated and model 1 can be estimated consistently by Maximum Likelihood. This assumption will be made in the further analyses.

3.3.2 Model 2: Time-to-build and adjustment costs of net capital stock

If the assumption $Z_t \equiv \Delta X_t$ is made, the Euler equations for structures can be written as

$$E\{K_{t+J}^s - (\frac{a_1}{\beta\gamma_1} + \frac{1}{\beta} + 1)K_{t+J-1}^s + \frac{1}{\beta}K_{t+J-2}^s \mid \Omega_t\} =$$

$$E\{-\frac{\alpha_1}{\beta\gamma_1} - \frac{1}{\beta\gamma_1}\lambda_{1,t+J-1} + \frac{1}{\gamma_1}\sum_{i=0}^{J}\beta^{i-J}\varphi_{J-i}^s C_{t+i}^s \mid \Omega_t\}. \qquad (3.15)$$

The characteristic equation associated with the left hand side deterministic second order difference equation is given in chapter 1 (see subsections 1-3.2-1.3.3). The stability of the solution is guaranteed, among others, by the value of the discount factor (that is between 0 and 1). Similarly as in subsection 1.3.3, the solution of the (3.15) is then given by

$$K^s_{t+J-1} = f_1 K^s_{t+J-2} + E\{\sum_{k=0}^{\infty} (\beta f_1)^{k+1}[\frac{\alpha_1}{\beta\gamma_1} + \frac{1}{\beta\gamma_1}\lambda_{1,t+k+J-1} - \frac{1}{\gamma_1}\sum_{i=0}^{J}\beta^{i-J}\varphi^s_{J-i}C^s_{t+k+i}] \mid \Omega_t\} \quad (3.16)$$

where f_1 is the stable root of the difference equation in (3.15).

After substitution of (3.11), transformation to gross investments like in (3.13) and application of a Koyck transformation the reduced form (model 2) results,

$$I^s_t = c + (f_1+\rho_1)I^s_{t-1} - f_1\rho_1 I^s_{t-2} - \sum_{j=0}^{J+1} m_j P_{t-j} + \sum_{j=0}^{J} \varphi^s_{J-j}e_{1,t-j}, \qquad (\textit{Model 2 (3.17)})$$

where c is a constant term, $e_{1,t}$ is $e^\lambda_{1,t}$ multiplied by a constant, and m_j is defined as in (3.14). However, it should be noted that in this model m^* contains more future price forecasts than m^* in model 1 (see (3.14)).

Model 2 is an ARMAX(2,J,J+1) process that because of the adjustment cost assumption, is derived from forecasted factor prices and technology shocks in a distant future (see (3.16)).

Instead of assuming adjustment costs of net capital stock at period t, $\gamma_1(\Delta K^s_t)^2$, adjustment costs at period t+J-1, $\gamma_1(\Delta K^s_{t+J-1})^2$, could be assumed. In the case of adjustment costs at t+J-1 of the project that is initiated at period t, $S_{J,t}$, adjustment costs are already paid at period t. Hence, before the construction starts. As no interrelation effects are implied in the model, the reduced form of this specification resembles the reduced form of model 2. The only difference in structural form is the division by β^{J-1} in stead of β in (3.15).

3.3.3 Model 3: Time-to-build with adjustment costs of gross investments

If the assumption $Z_t \equiv [I^s_t \ I^c_t \ \Delta N_t]'$ is made, the Euler equation for structures equals

$$E\{K_{t+2J-1}^s + \sum_{i=1}^{J-1} \beta^i b_{J-i} K_{t+J+i-1}^s + \sum_{i=0}^{J} b_i K_{t+i-1}^s \mid \Omega_t\} =$$

$$E\{\frac{\alpha_1}{\beta \varphi_0^s \varphi_J^s \gamma_1} + \frac{\lambda_{1,t+J-1}}{\beta \varphi_0^s \varphi_J^s \gamma_1} - \frac{1}{\varphi_0^s \varphi_J^s \gamma_1} \sum_{i=0}^{J} \beta^{i-J} \varphi_{J-i}^s C_{t+i}^s \mid \Omega_t\} \qquad (3.18)$$

where $b_0 \equiv \beta^J$

$$b_i \equiv \sum_{n=0}^{i} (\beta^{n-J} \varphi_{J-n}^s \varphi_{i-n}^s)/(\varphi_0^s \varphi_J^s), \qquad i=1,2..J-1,$$

$$b_J \equiv (a_1/(\gamma_1 \beta)) + \sum_{i=0}^{J} \beta^{i-J} (\varphi_{J-i}^s)^2)/(\varphi_0^s \varphi_J^s).$$

The equalities $\partial I_{t+i}^s/\partial K_{t+J-1}^s = \varphi_{J-i}^s$ and $I_t^s = \sum_{j=0}^{J} \varphi_j^s K_{t+j-1}^s$ are used in the first equation. Here the assumptions $\delta_1 \neq 0$, $\delta_J \neq 0$ and $\kappa^s \neq 1$ are made and therefore $\varphi_0^s \neq 0$ and $\varphi_J^s \neq 0$. If these regularity conditions do not hold, a lower order difference equation results.

The characteristic equation associated with the left hand side deterministic $2J$-th order difference equation is given by

$$f^{2J} + \sum_{i=1}^{J-1} \beta^i b_{J-i} f^{J+i} + \sum_{i=0}^{J} b_i f^i = 0. \qquad (3.19)$$

If a decomposition is possible in J polynomials of second order, i.e. $\prod_{i=1}^{J} f^2 + b_i^* f + \beta^{-1}$, where the b_i^* $(i=1,2..J)$ are functions of b_i $(i=1,2..J)$ and β, the J solutions $f_j = -0.5 b_i^* - 0.5\sqrt{(b_i^* - 4/\beta)}$, in (3.19) for each of the second order difference equations have the accompanying solutions $f_{J+j} = 1/(\beta f_j)$, $(j=1,2..J)$ where $f_j \in \mathbb{C}$. Therefore the stability conditions $|f_j| < 1/\sqrt{\beta}$ $(|f_{J+j}| > 1/\sqrt{\beta})$ is upheld, provided that $|f_j| \neq 1/\sqrt{\beta}$ and f_j $(j=1,2..J)$ are all different.

Like the solution in (3.16), it then follows that

$$K_{t+J-1}^s = \sum_{j=1}^{J} f_j K_{t+J-1-j}^s +$$

$$E\{\sum_{k=0}^{\infty} \prod_{j=1}^{J} (\beta f_j)^{k+1} [\frac{\alpha_1}{\beta \varphi_0^s \varphi_J^s \gamma_1} + \frac{\lambda_{1t+k+J-1}}{\beta \varphi_0^s \varphi_J^s \gamma_1} - \frac{1}{\gamma_1 \varphi_0^s \varphi_J^s} \sum_{i=0}^{J} \beta^{i-J} \varphi_{J-i}^s C_{t+k+i}^s] \mid \Omega_t\}. \qquad (3.20)$$

Rewriting the equation into gross investment (like (3.17)) gives

$$I_t^s = c + \sum_{j=1}^{J+1} r_j I_{t-j}^s - \sum_{j=0}^{J+1} m_j P_{t-j} + \sum_{j=0}^{J} \varphi_{J-j}^s e_{1,t-j} \qquad (Model\ 3\ (3.21))$$

where $r_1 \equiv f_1 + \rho_1$

$$r_j \equiv f_j - \rho_1 f_{j-1}, \qquad j=2,3..J$$

$$r_{J+1} \equiv -\rho_1 f_J$$

and where c is a constant, $\epsilon_{1,t}$ is $\epsilon_{1,t}^{\lambda}$ multiplied by a constant, and m_j is defined as in (3.14) with m^* in this model representing a term that contains (much) information on future prices.

Model 3 is an ARMAX($J+1,J,J+1$) model. The assumption of adjustment costs of gross investments together with the fixed investment plan assumption, is the explanation for the autoregressive part of J-th order. The investment projects that are started at the beginning of period t need investments during the construction time and incur (adjustment) costs during the construction period. The fixedness of the investment plan entails that at a certain point in time, adjustment costs are already determined for the part $(\sum_{j=1}^{J-1} \varphi_j^s K_{t+j-1}^s)^2/(I_t^s)^2$. So even if no new projects are initiated, $(S_{J,t}=0)$, current investments are influenced by lagged investments.

In this case, the characteristic roots of the difference equation, the f_j ($j=1,2..J$) in the autoregressive part, are also functions of the time-to-build parameters. The time-to-build parameters imply that $\varphi_0 \leq 0$ and $\varphi_J \geq 0$ (because $\kappa^s \in [0,1)$, $\delta_j \in [0,1]$, $j=1,2..J$), whereas the sign of φ_j ($j=1,2..J-1$) is unknown. Thus, contrary to the values of f_1 and f_2 in (3.17), the eigenvalues f_j ($j=1,2..2J$) in (3.21) can contain imaginary parts.

The case of complex eigenvalues, where $|f_j| < 1$ ($|f_{J+j}| > 1$) ($j=1,2..J$), is referred to as 'endogenous cycling' by Cassing and Kollintzas (1991). The cycling occurs in their general factor demand model as a result of a specified relation between the stock of production factors in the production function and the net changes in factors in the adjustment cost function. Their interest is concentrated on the possibility of cycling in factor stocks (because of recursive interrelations), even in the absence of any stochastic disturbance, such as technology shocks. The model here is the special case of their general model where no interrelation between adjustment costs and production function is assumed, that is adjustment costs in this case are assumed to be 'strongly separable'. However, model 3 takes into account gestation lags while their model does not[25]. In model 3, endogenous cycling is possible because of the combination of adjustment costs of gross investments and a multi-period time-to-build.

---

[25] Cassing and Kollintzas claim that their model includes gestation lags. In footnote 6, page 420, they suggest that productive capital stock can always be written as a weighted sum of investments where the weights sum to 1. As can be verified from (3.6a) this suggestion is not appropriate; although investments are a weighted sum of productive capital stock (with weights summing to the depreciation rate, see (2.4)), reversing this relation with weights summing to a parameter that is constant over time is not possible.

3.4   The closed form solution of the trivariate model

The closed form solution for the model with structures, equipment and labour, as specified in section 3.2, can also be found. The derivations proceed in way similar to the derivations in section 3.3. The derivations for the model with structures adjustment costs in net capital stock, that is the trivariate model with as a first equation the structures equation, are given in appendix 3.A.

The closed form, in general form, is given in terms of productive capital stock by

$$X_t^d = C + \sum_{j=1}^{J+1} R_j X_{t-j}^d - M_1^* P_t + (R^* M_1^* - M_2^*) P_{t-1} + R^* M_2^* P_{t-2} + e_t \tag{3.22a}$$

$$P_t = M_1 P_{t-1} + M_2 P_{t-2} + e_t^p \tag{3.22b}$$

where

$X_t^d \equiv [K_{t,J-1}^s \ K_t^e \ N_t]'$,

C is a 3x1-vector of constants,

$R_1 \equiv R^* + F_1$, $R_j \equiv F_j - R^* F_{j-1}$, $j=2,3..J$, $R_{J+1} \equiv -R^* F_J$,

R^* is a 3x3-matrix used in the Koyck transformation,

$F_1 \equiv \text{diag}\{f_{1,1}, f_{1,2}, f_{1,3}\}$,

F_j is a 3x3-zero matrix with only (1,1)-element $f_{j,1}$ $(j=2,3..J)$,

M_1^*, M_2^* are 3x3-matrices that depend on M_1, M_2,

$e_t \sim N_3(0, \Sigma)$, $e_t^p \sim N_3(0, \Sigma^p)$,,

$\text{Cov}\{e_{it}, e_{js}\} = 0$, $\text{Cov}\{e_{it}^p, e_{js}^p\} = 0$, $t \neq s$, $i,j=1,2,3,$, $\text{Cov}\{e_{it}, e_{js}^p\} = 0$, $\forall t,s$ $i,j=1,2,3$,

and other symbols are defined in (3.5). Being ahead of the estimation results in the next section, it is assumed here that the process of prices is VAR(2).

The model (3.22a) is a trivariate ARX(J+1,2) model. Using the derivations in the previous section (in order to estimate), this model is to be rewritten in terms of gross investments. The result is a trivariate system with a structures equation that is ARMAX(J+1,J,J+p), a similar equation for equipment where J=1, so an ARMAX(2,1,1+p), and a labour equation that is ARX(2,p). It is assumed here that p=2 (see (3.22b)).

The structures equation equals the model with adjustment costs of net capital stock (model 2, see (3.17)) if $f_{j,1}=0$ (j=2,3..J) and the model without adjustment costs (model 1, see (3.14)) if also $f_{1,1}=0$.

In the model in section 3.3, and until so far, it was assumed that *no interrelation* in the system existed. The inclusion of *interrelation* can be accomplished in different ways. Full interrelatedness in the production or adjustment cost function (A or Γ in (3.5) are full matrices) can be taken into account. Otherwise, the assumption of technology shocks that influence one another in the persistent part (R has non-zero elements) can be assumed. Because of reasons concerning the difficulty to derive a closed form solution[26] and identification of the structural parameters, only the last solution is chosen here.

The rewriting of (3.22a) in terms of gross investments results, in the case of interrelatedness, in a system where estimation becomes difficult. Each equation contains productive structures and productive equipment, and can only be rewritten in gross investments by the transformation of (3.6) (see for example (3.13)) that causes disturbances that are time dependent. Each equation therefore contains moving average parts of order J+1. The final form is

$$\Phi(L)X_t^d = \Phi(L)[C + \sum_{j=1}^{J+1} R_j X_{t-j}^d - M_1^* P_t + (R^* M_1^* - M_2^*)P_{t-1} - M_2^* P_{t-2} + \epsilon_t] \quad (3.23)$$

where
$$\Phi(L) \equiv \sum_{i=0}^{J+1} \Phi_{J+1-i} L^i I_3$$

$$\Phi_0 \equiv (\kappa^e - 1)\, \varphi_0\, I_3$$

$$\Phi_i \equiv \varphi_{i-1} I_3 + (\kappa^e - 1)\, \varphi_i\, I_3 \quad \text{for} \quad i=1,2..J$$

$$\Phi_{J+1} \equiv \varphi_J\, I_3,$$

and L denotes the lag operator. In light of the many, non-linear restrictions across equations and above this, along with the high moving average part in each equation, estimation of this system is hardly possible or sensible.

Therefore, a conditional method is chosen. As the moving section part only depends on the time-to-build parameters $\delta_1, \delta_2..\delta_J$ and the depreciation or retirement rates of structures and equipment, κ^s and κ^e, the model becomes estimable if these parameters are fixed. This procedure is followed in the empirical section. Residual tests are carried out to verify if the fixed values are in the right direction.

---

[26]   This is the case, in particularily when adjustment costs of gross investments are assumed, see appendix 3.A.

3.5   Summary of the theoretical part and estimation aims

In part 3.2 a theoretical framework was presented with the following main assumptions:
- a rational entrepreneur invests in structures and equipment and recruits labour such that the future profit stream is maximized;
- markets clear and investments and labour demand do not influence investment prices and wages;
- structures and equipment need a multi-period time-to-build and a one period to be built, respectively;
- labour and equipment adjustment costs are incurred;
- production prices, as well as technology shocks, follow autoregressive processes;
- innovations in technology shocks and production prices do not influence one another.

The question whether structures investments incur adjustment costs is addressed.

Table 3.1   Structures investments models with time-to-build

Model 1	Time-to-build and no adjustment costs (3.14)	ARMAX(r,J+r−1,J+p−1+r)
Model 2	Time-to-build and adjustment costs of net capital stock (3.17)	ARMAX(1+r,J+r−1,J+p−1+r)
Model 3	Time-to-build and adjustment costs of gross investments (3.21)	ARMAX(J+r,J+r−1,J+p−1+r)

J = time-to-build or construction time
p = autoregressive order of vector-process of prices
r = autoregressive order of technology process

Three possibilities for adjustment costs of structures were investigated in section 3.3. Table 3.1 summarizes the three derived ARMAX-models for structures, where both variables r and p were assumed to be equal to one in section 3.2. If a one period time-to-build exists, i.e. J=1, model 2 and 3 are the same, and are even equal in their structural form if there is no depreciation (κ^s=0).

As also follows from table 3.1, an identification problem concerning technology and time-to-build seems to exist[27]. Dynamics resulting from time-to-build can in the reduced form, the ARMAX-models, also be induced by higher order technology shocks; in particularly in model 3 a low J can be offset by a high r and vice versa.

The findings in chapter 2 however empasize clearly the existence of a long time-to-build for structures. For this reason, in the following section the estimation results of the ARMAX models are given where time-to-build is imposed. All parameter restrictions are taken into account by which the identification of time-to-build and technology parameters is possible.

The equations for equipment and labour are an ARMAX(2,1,1+p) and an ARX(2,p) respectively. The three equations: structures, equipment and labour, are interrelated in their closed form by the autoregressive part, along with the prices part (the X-part) and the contemporaneous correlation of disturbances.

The following section seeks to answer two questions concerning the models in table 3.1. The first question takes as a point of departure a multi-period (more than one quarter) time-to-build for structures, and considers the relevance of adjustment costs. If adjustment costs are relevant, which adjustment cost (net or gross) is of more importance? The three models are used to answer these questions.

The second question posed here is whether the implication of time-to-build is really found to be important. The no-adjustment costs model with a multi-period construction period (J>1) in comparison with the adjustment costs models without time-to-build (J=1) seems to have a richer specification. Comparing the properties of both models is a difficult problem because a model with only adjustment costs would have to be compared with a multi-period time-to-build model. The question is whether or not the two models are capable of capturing the same investment dynamics.

Answers to these two questions are found in the next section by estimating the univariate models 1-3 of section 3.3 and the multivariate model (3.23).

---

[27]   This remark was first made by G. Laroque.

68

3.6   The estimation results

For estimation, quarterly data from the United States (1960.I-1988.IV) and the Dutch manufacturing industry (1971.I-1990.IV) are used. Investments in capital stock are disaggregated as structures (I_t^s) and equipment (I_t^e), where the structures data from the Netherlands only contain investments in structures. For both countries time series are seasonally unadjusted and indexed at 1985.II. Quarterly (uncentered) dummies are included in all analyses to account for seasonal fluctuations. A description of the data can be found in the data appendix.

Before the estimation of the closed form of model (3.5), the time series are submitted to unit root and cointegration tests. All individual series are non-stationary during the sample period, except for the real price of equipment investments (C^e) in the Netherlands[28].

The three production factors cointegrate with the three prices as might be expected from an economic point of view. This implies that the technology shock is stationary. So standard econometric estimation methods can be applied to estimate the closed form of model (3.5) with these data. The unit root and cointegration test statistics, leading to these conclusions, are given in appendix 3.B.

The outline of this section is as follows.
In subsection 3.6.1, Granger causality between production factors and prices is investigated. In subsection 3.6.2 the closed form of model (3.5) is estimated by Maximum Likelihood for both countries. The time-to-build or construction time (J) of structures is thereby varied from three to five quarters according the findings in chapter 2[29]. The different specifications for adjustment costs of structures, resulting in model

----

[28]   This price is relatively stable during the first part of the sample period, whereas all other (real) factor prices in the Netherlands as well as in the United States rise. The production factor series in the two countries, during the sample period 1970-1988, are comparable. Declines in factor demand after the two oil crises in the seventies are noticeable and the impact of the recession in the beginning of the eighties (reaching rock bottom in 1984) is very prominent. During the sixties, factor demand in the United States heavily increased.

[29]   Data used in chapter 2 give information about the gestation of plants from the Dutch industry whereas the data here are from the manufacturing industry. The industry consists of four sectors: mining and quarrying, the manufacturing industry, the public utilities industry, and the construction industry. The number of plants in the manufacturing industry obviously dominates; the annual average value of permits issued in the manufacturing industry during 1982-1990 is 82%. Beside this, the United States data that are referred to as structures possibly include other large investment projects besides plant investment.

1-3, are tested within the trivariate factor demand model. In subsection 3.6.3, impulse response functions are given, obtained with the Maximum Likelihood estimates presented in subsection 3.6.2. In subsection 3.6.4 a non-nested test is carried out between a pure adjustment costs model and a pure time-to-build model. Subsection 3.6.5 summarizes the empirical part.

3.6.1 The process of prices

Model (3.5) relies on the non-existence of Granger causality from production factors to factor prices and assumes a marginal process of prices of order p. These assumptions will now be tested.

In the analyses, the prices of structures and equipment investments (C_t^s and C_t^e) and wages (W_t) are distinguished. Using the analyses in appendix 3.B, for the United States these prices all have a unit root and do not cointegrate. C_t^e of the Netherlands is stationary and as a consequence cointegration among the three prices exists.

According to the Schwarz criterium (Schwarz (1978)) that minimizes the determinant of the covariance matrix and heavily penalizes the inclusion of additional lags, the autoregressive order of the process of prices can be determined. This is done for the vector of prices ΔP_t and P_t (where $P_t \equiv [C_t^s \ C_t^e \ W_t]'$ and $\Delta P_t \equiv P_t - P_{t-1}$) for the United States and the Netherlands, respectively.

The Schwarz criterium for the United States prices are -21.43, -21.31, -21.00, -20.74 and -20.44 for a VARI(1) up to and including a VARI(5). With the Dutch data, the Schwarz criteria are -21.38, -21.23, -20.93, -20.67 and -20.40 for a VAR(1) up to and including a VAR(5).

Thus for the United States the marginal process of prices that can be assumed is

$$\Delta P_t = M\Delta P_{t-1} + e_t^p \quad \Leftrightarrow \quad P_t = (I_3+M)P_{t-1} - MP_{t-2} + e_t^p \qquad (3.24U)$$

and for the Netherlands the process can be assumed to be

$$P_t = MP_{t-1} + e_t^p. \qquad (3.24N)$$

The disturbance vectors are assumed to be independent and normally distributed (see (3.8)).

To test for Granger causality from production factors (Y_{t-1}) to production prices (P_t) the equation

$$P_t = C_0 D_t + C_1 P_{t-1} + C_2 P_{t-2} + C_3 Y_{t-1} + e_t^p. \qquad (3.25)$$

is first estimated with the United States data. C_0 is a 3x4 matrix and C_i (i=1,2,3) are 3x3 matrices to be estimated. D_t includes quarterly (uncentered) dummies and a linear trend. A second order for the process of prices is taken, in line with (3.24U). The hypothesis $H_0 : C_3=0_3$ is tested, and according to a Likelihood Ratio statistic of 20.39, rejected at a 5%-level (χ^2 with 9 degrees of freedom). However, the χ^2-distribution according to Toda and Phillips (1993a,1993b) is not valid when there is not 'sufficient' cointegration in the vector of variables, of which the causal effect is tested. If less than three cointegration relationships exist, a distribution mix of a χ^2 and a non-standard distribution applies. In light of this and the fact that producer prices for the United States do not cointegrate, the hypothesis of Granger non-causality from factors to prices cannot be rejected.

For the Netherlands, equation (3.25) is estimated with $C_2 = 0_3$ according (3.24N), and a Likelihood Ratio test statistic of 14.89 is found. So also for the Netherlands, according to this test statistic, the hypothesis of Granger non-causality from production factors to prices cannot be rejected.

As a consequence of these results, in the closed form solution of model (3.5) (see (3.23)) the assumption is made that

$$P_t = M_1 P_{t-1} + M_2 P_{t-2} + e_t^P \qquad (3.26)/(3.22b)$$

where

$$M_1 = I_3 + M, \quad M_2 = -M, \quad \text{for the United States}$$

and

$$M_1 = M, \quad M_2 = M_2^* = 0_3 \quad \text{for the Netherlands.}$$

Notice that consequently M_1^*, M_2^* and M_1^* in (3.22a) are full 3x3-matrices for the United States and the Netherlands respectively.

3.6.2   Maximum Likelihood estimates[30]

First model (3.23) is estimated by Maximum Likelihood with $J = 3,4,5$, $f_{j,1} = 0$ ($j=2,3..J$), and no interrelation in the persistent part (R^* diagonal). For the United States, only a slight autocorrelation according to autocorrelation tests (with 2, 10 or 20 degrees of freedom, significant at a 1%-level) in the residuals of the equipment equation is found. For the Netherlands, on the contrary, a high autocorrelation in the residuals of both the labour and equipment equation exists.

As these results indicate that *interrelation* in the autoregressive part of (3.22a) seems to be important, estimation of the system without interrelation in the autoregressive part is

---

[30]   All Maximum Likelihood estimates are obtained by maximizing the 'conditional' likelihood until all elements of the relative gradient reach a value less than 0.0001 (GAUSS). The likelihood is 'conditional' in the sense that the values for the J first residuals are obtained by only taking into account the autoregressive part (where here J indicates the moving average order).

Table 3.2 Maximum Likelihood estimates structures investment models

	United States manufacturing industry 1961.IV-1988.IV								
	Model 1: ARMAX(1,J,J+2)			Model 2: ARMAX(2,J,J+2)			Model 3: ARMAX(J+1,J,J+2)		
J	3	4	5	3	4	5	3	4	5
ρ_1	0.96^{**}	0.96^{**}	0.97^{**}	0.94^{**}	0.92^{**}	0.90^{**}	[0.94]	[0.92]	[0.90]
m_1'	0.36	-1.78	-3.93	-1.10^*	-2.15^{**}	0.89^{**}	-1.39^{**}	-0.59	-3.89^*
	0.75	-0.79	0.87	1.30^{**}	1.28^{**}	-3.53^{**}	0.70	0.69	1.49
	-0.20	3.64^{**}	4.01^{**}	0.82	1.02^*	1.38	0.60	0.31	2.84^{**}
m_2'	0.45	2.82	1.41	1.08	1.73^*	2.31^*	0.97^*	0.04	0.35
	-1.25	-1.25	-2.88	-1.02^*	-1.56^*	-2.18^{**}	-1.12^{**}	-1.57^*	-2.71^*
	1.69	-0.68	0.51	-0.79	-0.32	-0.13	0.43	-0.28	-0.53
$f_{1,1}$				0.94^{**}	0.92^{**}	0.89^{**}	1.38^{**}	0.70^{**}	0.15
$f_{2,1}$							-0.27	0.13^*	0.37^{**}
$f_{3,1}$							-0.19	0.72^{**}	0.35^{**}
$f_{4,1}$								-0.74^{**}	0.07
$f_{5,1}$									-0.20^*
δ_1	0.24^{**}	0.13^{**}	0.10^{**}	0.21^{**}	0.10^{**}	0.07^{**}	0.15^{**}	[0.10]	[0.07]
δ_2	0.49^{**}	0.34^{**}	0.23^{**}	0.45^{**}	0.26^{**}	0.19^{**}	0.43^{**}	[0.26]	[0.19]
δ_3	0.27^{**}	0.36^{**}	0.30^{**}	0.35^{**}	0.37^{**}	0.27^{**}	0.42^{**}	[0.37]	[0.27]
δ_4		0.17^{**}	0.25^{**}		0.26^{**}	0.29^{**}		[0.26]	[0.29]
δ_5			0.12^{**}			0.18^{**}			[0.18]
τ	-2.57^{**}	-2.43^{**}	-2.33^{**}	-0.31	-0.36	-0.53^*	-0.29^{**}	-0.28	-0.83^{**}
LOGL	169.43	210.52	239.47	263.03	271.17	278.08	273.50	269.98	267.95
SKEW	0.56^*	0.36	0.49^*	0.02	0.06	0.29	0.12	0.10	0.30
EXKURT	-0.19	0.17	0.37	-0.05	0.04	0.20	0.10	-0.57	-0.33
Q(2)	131.47^{**}	83.40^{**}	41.45^{**}	13.69^{**}	4.93	1.85	1.02	7.85^*	0.19
Q(20)	293.33^{**}	196.86^{**}	121.72^{**}	28.91	20.64	15.22	24.42	30.26^{**}	24.25
ARCH(4)	50.60^{**}	21.76^{**}	6.91	6.17	1.67	2.04	0.54	2.65	1.77
$\sigma^2(\times 10^{-4})$	63.71	50.07	40.67	4.69	4.04	3.56	3.87	4.13	4.29

* Significant at the 5%-level

** Significant at the 1%-level

$\delta_J = 1 - \Sigma_{j=1}^{J-1}\delta_j$ and its standard error is estimated with Asymptotic Least Squares.

The depreciation of structures and equipment (r^s and r^e) are 0.0125 and 0.025 respectively.

The values between square brackets are the values at which the parameters are fixed.

τ is the coefficient of the linear trend. Coefficients of quarterly dummies are not reported.

econometrically not consistent. As a consequence of these findings, Maximum Likelihood results are presented in the following order.

First, results from *univariate* analyses for the structures equation with the United States data are presented in table 3.2. These results are (econometrically) consistent as no significant autocorrelation was found in the equipment and labour equation by estimating the *trivariate* system. The three different models (model 1-3) for structures are compared.

Second, results from trivariate analyses for the complete system with *interrelation* (**R** non-diagonal) for the Netherlands are presented in table 3.3. The time-to-build is equal to one year (J=5) here, and the moving average parameters are fixed by determining the time-to-build and retirement rate (κ). Table 3.5 gives the similar results for the United States. Some further tests are applied.

3.6.2.1 Univariate - United States

Table 3.2 contains the estimation results of model 1-3 of section 3.3 for the cases where J=3,4,5. The depreciation rates of structures and equipment are fixed at 0.0125 and 0.025 according the depreciation rates 'Flows and Stocks of fixed capital' (OECD, see the data appendix). All other structural parameters are estimated by taking into account all restrictions, except for the parameters contained in m_1^* and m_2^* that are the first rows of M_1^* and M_2^* in the process of prices (see (3.24U).

Model 1 shows for J=3,4,5 that the technology shock coefficient, ρ_1, is highly significant, as well as all time-to-build parameters δ_j (j=1,2..J) contained in the moving average part, and the linear time trend, τ. This linear trend is included according to the cointegration results (see the appendix 3.B).

The Loglikelihood values (LOGL) increase enormously when the time-to-build (J) increases. According to the tests for skewness (SKEW) and excess-kurtosis (EXKURT) in model 1 (see Jarque and Bera (1980)), the residuals when J=3 and J=5 are found to be non-normal. Furthermore, the Box-Pierce statistics with 2 and 20 degrees of freedom show that the residuals are autocorrelated. ARCH-effects (with 4 degrees of freedom, Engle (1982)) are also found.

In contrast to this, *model 2* gives reasonable results concerning autocorrelation and normality tests (SKEW and EXKURT). Only autocorrelation of a second order is found when J=3. The price variables (m_1^* and m_2^*) and in particular the price of equipment (the second element of m_1^* and m_2^*), influence the structures investments in this model. Most importantly, the eigenvalue $f_{1,1}$ that represents the adjustment costs in the model, is highly significant, and in agreement with the theory is less than one. Although the estimates of model 2 for J=3,4,5 change little, the model with J=5 seems preferable according the Loglikelihood values (LOGL).

In all three cases, no convergence was reached when *model 3* was estimated. Expecting, at first, an identification problem with respect to the technology shock parameter ρ_1, this parameter was fixed at the point estimates of model 2. This supplies in the case of $J = 3$, a reasonable result, and seems according the Loglikelihood increase of 10.47 (273.50-263.03) a preferable model to model 2. The cases where $J = 4$ and $J = 5$ did however not reach an optimum value of the Loglikelihood. This may indicate that the model is overidentified.

The results that are presented in the last two columns are estimates obtained by fixing the time-to-build parameters at the values of model 2. Although some of the eigenvalues $f_{i,1}$ ($i=1,2,3,4,5$) are highly significant, the Loglikelihood values do not increase in comparison with model 2.

To summarize this section, where the structures equation was estimated univariately, the results indicate that model 2 is preferred and the adjustment costs of net capital stock ($f_{1,1}$) are found to be highly significant.

3.6.2.2 Trivariate - The Netherlands and the United States

Table 3.3 contains the results of estimation of model (3.23) with interrelation, obtained with the Dutch manufacturing industry data. The time-to-build (J) is assumed to be five quarters. The retirement rate of structures and equipment (κ^s and κ^e) are fixed at 0.007 and 0.014, respectively, according to retirement rates in 'Statistics on stocks of capital goods' (Netherlands Central Bureau of Statistics).

In order to fix the moving average part as explained in the introduction, to obtain an estimable system, the distribution of investments during the construction, $\delta_1, \delta_2...\delta_J$, has to be chosen. Using univariate analyses[31], such as in table 3.2 for the United States data, the time-to-build parameters are assumed to be uniformly declining ($\delta_j=2j/(J.(J+1))$ for $j=1,2..J$). This declining distribution is not in accordance with the hump-shaped distribution that is found with the United States data (see table 3.2). On the other hand, it corresponds with findings of Altug (1989) where the most investments during construction are also found in the first part of the construction period. This distribution choice gives most weight to the error terms that are recent. The main reason for this distribution choice here is that the residual test statistics in table 3.3 do not indicate that the choice of weights is a wrong choice.

---

[31] The results of these univariate analyses are used to fix the distribution of investments during construction, but are further not presented here since they are not in consistence with the factor demand model (3.23). After all, with these Dutch data multivariate analyses are necessary to obtain consistent results (see section 3.4). Remarkably however, the same convergence problems as in table 3.2 were encountered with model 3.

Table 3.3 Maximum Likelihood estimates factor demand model (3.23) with J=5

	Model 1			Model 2			Model 3		
R	0.88**	0.59**	2.98	0.89**	0.63**	2.99	0.80**	0.62**	1.90
	-0.01**	0.81**	2.73**	-0.01	0.81**	2.75**	-0.02	0.83**	2.58**
	-0.00	0.06**	0.13	-0.00	0.06**	0.13	-0.00	0.07**	0.09
M₁	-5.12**	3.33**	2.63*	-5.42**	3.24**	2.69*	-5.44**	3.37**	1.87**
	-0.70**	0.86**	0.04	-0.69**	0.86**	0.04	-0.72**	0.87**	-0.01
	-0.04	0.02	0.08**	-0.04	0.02	0.08**	-0.04	0.03**	0.08*
F₁	0	0	0	-0.05	0	0	0.00	0	0
	0	0.79**	0	0	0.79**	0	0	0.80**	0
	0	0	0.70**	0	0	0.70**	0	0	0.71**
f₂,₁							0.04		
f₃,₁							0.15		
f₄,₁							0.11		
f₅,₁							0.08		
Σ x10⁻⁴	5.20			5.16			4.96		
	-1.21	1.37		-1.15	1.37		-1.07	1.37	
	-0.53	0.12	0.08	-0.52	0.12	0.08	-0.52	0.11	0.07
SKEW	-0.33	0.01	-0.10	-0.28	-0.46	-0.01	-0.39	-0.47	0.05
EXKURT	0.89	0.62	0.18	0.70	-0.25	0.68	1.15	-0.26	0.72
Q(2)	0.70	0.91	0.38	0.39	0.91	0.40	0.32	0.90	0.32
Q(10)	8.27	10.76	12.99	8.08	10.78	13.00	6.63	10.25	13.24
Q(20)	25.42	15.01	20.20	25.87	14.99	20.30	18.71	14.22	20.57
ARCH(4)	1.56	11.45*	3.00	1.74	11.33*	3.03	0.93	10.78*	3.04
LOGL	600.14			600.32			601.81		

Dutch manufacturing industry 1974.I-1990.IV

* Significant at 5%-level
** Significant at 1%-level

The time-to-build parameters δ_j (j=1,2..J) are uniformly declining: $\delta_j = 2j/(J.(J+1))$.
The retirement of plants and equipment (κ^a and κ^e) are 0.007 and 0.014 respectively.
Coefficients of quarterly dummies are not reported.

Table 3.3 shows that interrelation, that is the technology matrix R with non-zero elements, is highly significant. This in particular holds for interrelations with equipment. Diagonal elements of R are less than one by Student-tests. The matrix of the first order process of prices, M^*, predominantly contains significant elements, but has a wrong-signed element for the own-price effect of equipment (see the positive element (2,2)). The residuals only show univariate autocorrelation for the equipment series and a 20-th order autocorrelation for structures series in model 2. The significant ARCH-effect for equipment seems to be due to the first oil-crisis in the seventies.

The most important conclusion according to these results is that models 2 and 3 do not give rise to a significant increase in the Loglikelihood function in comparison with model 1.

Table 3.4 Maximum Likelihood values factor demand model (3.23)

Dutch manufacturing industry 1974.I-1990.IV			
J	Model 1: No adjustment costs	Model 2: Adjustment costs of net capital stock	Model 3: Adjustment costs of gross investments
3	527.72 (32)	527.73 (33)	532.52 (35)
4	563.50 (32)	563.83 (33)	565.12 (36)
5	600.14 (32)	600.32 (33)	601.81 (37)
The numbers of the parameters (including quarterly dummies) are given in brackets. The time-to-build parameters δ_j (j=1,2..J) are uniformly declining: $\delta_j=2j/(J.(J+1))$. The retirement of plants and equipment (κ^s and κ^e) are 0.007 and 0.014 respectively.			

In table 3.4 the Loglikelihood values are given for the same model when J=3,4,5. These results indicate that model 3 and model 2 are not preferable to model 1. Only the case J=3 seems to give a slight preference of model 3 to model 2 and model 1. And although comparison across rows in table 3.4 is econometrically not correct because the moving average part in each row is fixed in a different way, the increase in the Loglikelihood value is very large when J is increased[32].

---

[32] Also univariate analyses with the Dutch plant series (like the analyses in table 3.2 for the United States) indicate that the case with J=5 is highly significant.

Table 3.5 Maximum Likelihood estimates factor demand model (3.23) with J=5

<table>
<tr><td colspan="10" align="center">United States manufacturing industry 1963.I-1988.IV</td></tr>
<tr><td></td><td colspan="3" align="center">Model 1</td><td colspan="3" align="center">Model 2</td><td colspan="3" align="center">Model 3</td></tr>
<tr>
<td>R</td>
<td>0.96**
-0.01**
-0.01**</td><td>0.41*
0.96**
-0.00</td><td>4.64**
0.35**
0.89**</td>
<td>0.96**
-0.01**
-0.00*</td><td>0.52**
0.97**
-0.00</td><td>4.96**
0.35**
0.88**</td>
<td>0.95**
-0.01**
-0.01**</td><td>0.17
0.95**
-0.00</td><td>4.63**
0.36**
0.91**</td>
</tr>
<tr>
<td>M_1^*</td>
<td>-3.69**
0.05
0.12</td><td>3.40**
0.11
0.02</td><td>-1.83*
0.68**
-0.23**</td>
<td>-3.44*
0.04
0.12</td><td>3.75**
0.11
0.01</td><td>-2.05*
0.68**
-0.23**</td>
<td>-2.86*
0.07
0.12</td><td>3.96**
0.12
0.02</td><td>-2.29*
0.68**
-0.22**</td>
</tr>
<tr>
<td>M_2^*</td>
<td>6.39**
-0.23
0.09</td><td>-5.11**
0.07
-0.02</td><td>-2.66*
-0.18
-0.28**</td>
<td>5.68**
-0.24
0.10</td><td>-5.08**
0.06
-0.02</td><td>-2.57*
-0.18
-0.28*</td>
<td>5.29**
-0.22
0.08</td><td>-4.96**
0.05
-0.01</td><td>-2.81*
-0.19
-0.28**</td>
</tr>
<tr>
<td>F_1</td>
<td>0
0
0</td><td>0
0.84**
0</td><td>0
0
0.36**</td>
<td>-0.10
0
0</td><td>0
0.82**
0</td><td>0
0
0.37**</td>
<td>-0.12
0
0</td><td>0
0.86**
0</td><td>0
0
0.36**</td>
</tr>
<tr><td>$f_{2,1}$</td><td></td><td></td><td></td><td></td><td></td><td></td><td>0.08</td><td></td><td></td></tr>
<tr><td>$f_{3,1}$</td><td></td><td></td><td></td><td></td><td></td><td></td><td>0.17*</td><td></td><td></td></tr>
<tr><td>$f_{4,1}$</td><td></td><td></td><td></td><td></td><td></td><td></td><td>0.08</td><td></td><td></td></tr>
<tr><td>$f_{5,1}$</td><td></td><td></td><td></td><td></td><td></td><td></td><td>-0.03</td><td></td><td></td></tr>
<tr>
<td>τ</td>
<td>0.09</td><td>-0.004</td><td>-0.001</td>
<td>0.10</td><td>-0.005</td><td>-0.002</td>
<td>0.06</td><td>-0.003</td><td>-0.001</td>
</tr>
<tr>
<td>$\Sigma \times 10^{-4}$</td>
<td>4.6
0.10
0.09</td><td>0.06
0.01</td><td>0.03</td>
<td>4.6
0.10
0.09</td><td>0.06
0.01</td><td>0.03</td>
<td>4.4
0.11
0.09</td><td>0.06
0.08</td><td>0.03</td>
</tr>
<tr>
<td>SKEW</td>
<td>-0.04</td><td>0.10</td><td>-0.74**</td>
<td>0.04</td><td>0.11</td><td>-0.74**</td>
<td>0.16</td><td>0.11</td><td>-0.70**</td>
</tr>
<tr>
<td>EXKURT</td>
<td>0.20</td><td>0.36</td><td>2.94**</td>
<td>-0.10</td><td>0.36</td><td>2.88**</td>
<td>-0.22</td><td>0.34</td><td>2.85**</td>
</tr>
<tr>
<td>Q(2)</td>
<td>1.15</td><td>9.40**</td><td>0.12</td>
<td>0.85</td><td>9.50**</td><td>0.11</td>
<td>0.74</td><td>8.53*</td><td>0.11</td>
</tr>
<tr>
<td>Q(10)</td>
<td>20.18*</td><td>22.80*</td><td>6.32</td>
<td>17.71</td><td>22.89*</td><td>6.35</td>
<td>14.82</td><td>20.41*</td><td>5.87</td>
</tr>
<tr>
<td>Q(20)</td>
<td>27.93</td><td>31.35</td><td>15.88</td>
<td>25.50</td><td>31.36</td><td>16.09</td>
<td>21.67</td><td>29.07</td><td>15.61</td>
</tr>
<tr>
<td>ARCH(4)</td>
<td>0.35</td><td>5.41</td><td>1.59</td>
<td>0.52</td><td>5.39</td><td>1.58</td>
<td>0.76</td><td>5.61</td><td>1.53</td>
</tr>
<tr>
<td>LOGL</td>
<td colspan="3" align="center">1261.60</td>
<td colspan="3" align="center">1262.10</td>
<td colspan="3" align="center">1264.10</td>
</tr>
</table>

* Significant at 5%-level

** Significant at 1%-level

The time-to-build parameters δ_j (j=1,2..J) are (0.10,0.23,0.30,0.25,0.12).

The retirement of structures and equipment (κ^s and κ^e) are 0.0125 and 0.025 respectively.

τ is the coefficient of the linear trend.

Coefficients of quarterly dummies are not reported.

As models 1-3 of subsection 3.6.2.1 estimated with the United States data, indicate that adjustment costs are important and the results of the factor demand model with interrelation with the Dutch data contradict these findings, model (3.23) with interrelation was also estimated using the United States data. These estimation results are given in table 3.5. Therefore, table 3.5 is similar to table 3.3.

The time-to-build equals, in this case, five quarters $(J=5)$ and the distribution of investments during construction is chosen to be equal to the estimated distribution with $J=5$ of model 1 in table 3.2.

In agreement with table 3.3, the results in table 3.5 show that the interrelation effect (the R matrix) is highly important, the adjustment costs dynamics for equipment and labour $(f_{1,i} \quad i=2,3)$ are highly significant and the first matrix in the process of prices (M_1^*) has similarly signed diagonal elements. The matrix M_2^*, indicating a second autoregressive order in the process of prices is also estimated, and contains many significant elements. This is in contrast to the univariate estimates in table 3.2.

Most significantly, the estimates of the interrelated trivariate model indicate, like the results in table 3.4, that the model without adjustment costs does not deviate very much from the models with adjustment costs. In other words, model 2 or model 3 are not significantly better than model 1.

Furthermore and worse, in all three models, labour residuals are found to be non-normal because both the symmetry and the non-leptocurtisy hypotheses are rejected. In addition, the equipment residuals are at the second and tenth order significantly autocorrelated.

The cause for this non-normality of labour residuals is not clear. The autocorrelation in the equipment residuals might be solved by taking into account a multi-period time-to-build[33]. As solving autocorrelation in the equipment equation by assuming time-to-build will not change the main conclusion here that model 2 and 3 perform not better than model 1, and above this, needs a lot of additional assumptions concerning investments distribution whereas it makes the estimation procedure more difficult, this is not further investigated here.

Because the results in table 3.3, 3.4, and 3.5 are obtained by fixing the moving average part, some tests are carried out to verify that these fixed values are appropriate. Results from four alternative weighting schedules for the time-to-build parameters, δ_j, $j=1,2..5$, are given in table 3.6 where $J=5$.

---

[33] Univariate analyses for the equipment equation (see model 2 with $J=1$, i.e. equation (3.17)) show that the moving average parameter that according to the theory should be κ^e-1, is much larger and positive. On the other hand, specifying a two or three period time-to-build for equipment gives highly significant time-to-build parameters and solves autocorrelation.

Table 3.6 Different distributions of investments during gestation

Case	Distribution	Loglikelihood The Netherlands	Loglikelihood United States
1	$\delta_j = 2j/(J.(J+1))$, $j=1,2..5$	600.14	
1	$\delta_1 = 0.10$, $\delta_2 = 0.23$, $\delta_3 = 0.30$, $\delta_4 = 0.25$, $\delta_5 = 0.12$		1261.60
2	$\delta_j = 0.2$, $j=1,2..5$	521.69	889.78
3	$\delta_1 = 1/9$, $\delta_2 = 2/9$, $\delta_3 = 3/9$, $\delta_4 = 2/9$, $\delta_5 = 1/9$	448.67	1042.90
4	$\delta_j = 0$, $j=1,2,3,4$, $\delta_5 = 1$	397.56	759.06
5	$\delta_j = (6-j)/15$, $j=1,2..5$	no convergence	no convergence
6	$\delta_1 = 1$, $\delta_j = 0$, $j=2,3,4,5$	no convergence	no convergence

The first weighting schedule (case 1) is used in the tables 3.3 and 3.5.

For the Netherlands, the declining weights yield the highest Loglikelihood value of 600.14. For the uniform distribution, case 2, the Loglikelihood value is 521.69. The hump-shape distribution, case 3, yields a Loglikelihood value of 448.67 and the model without time-to-build, case 4, has a Loglikelihood value of 397.56. The estimates of the models with increasing investment distribution, case 5, did not give satisfactory results due to non-convergence of the estimation procedure. The same holds for case 6, the case with so-called delivery lags (see section 2.4).

For the United States, case 3 most resembles the schedule used in table 3.5. But case 1 gives the highest Loglikelihood value of all alternatives. As a result, the schedule used in the preceding econometric analyses yields the best results.

3.6.3   Impulse responses

To interpret and investigate the dynamics of the alternative models, impulse responses are calculated with the estimation results of table 3.3 and 3.5 for the Netherlands and the United States, respectively. The model (3.23) is rewritten in the moving average presentation, see for example Lütkepohl (1990). This is done in the proper way, by taking into account the existing moving average in the structural model (3.23).

The order of impulses that is chosen is C_t^s, C_t^e, W_t, I_t^s, I_t^e, N_t and the model that results for the Netherlands is

$$\begin{bmatrix} P_t \\ Y_t \end{bmatrix} = \begin{bmatrix} \hat{\Psi}_{11}(L) & 0_3 \\ \hat{\Psi}_{12}(L) & \hat{\Psi}_{22}(L) \end{bmatrix} \begin{bmatrix} \hat{e}_t^p \\ \hat{e}_t^\lambda \end{bmatrix}.$$

$\hat{\Psi}_{ij}(L)$ are 3x3-polynomial matrices and functions of the estimated structural parameters presented in table 3.3. $\hat{e}_t^i$ represent the residuals of the process of prices (e_t^p) and of technology process (e_t^λ). The contemporaneous covariance matrix Σ is decomposed in such a way that e_{1t}^p influences C_t^e, W_t, I_t^s, I_t^e, N_t but, for example, a direct response from C_t^s as an impulse in e_{2t}^p does not exist. The impulses from e_{1t}^p to I_t^s, I_t^e, N_t until e_{3t}^λ to I_t^s, I_t^e, N_t are calculated. The size of the impulse is equal to one standard deviation of the associated innovation shock.

Regarding the United States, the process of prices is assumed non-stationary for a VARI(1,1) is estimated, see (3.26). Therefore, the first difference is taken, that is $[\Delta P_t\ \Delta Y_t]'$ and the necessary corrections in the matrices of coefficients are made. So for this country, the impulses from e_{1t}^p to ΔI_t^s, ΔI_t^e, ΔN_t until e_{3t}^λ to ΔI_t^s, ΔI_t^e, ΔN_t are calculated. The responses for the three models, which are fourty periods ahead, are presented in the graphs 3.1.1-3.1.18 for the Netherlands and in the graphs 3.2.1-3.2.18 for the United States[34].

The results immediately show the very similar impulses of the models. Models 1 and 2 are hardly distinguishable because of the non-significance of net adjustment costs for structures. In comparison with these two models, the model with adjustment costs of gross investments (model 3) shows often a faster convergence to zero, thus a faster fainting of impulses that are given, and a less dynamic behaviour.

The results for the Netherlands show that the response of labour to all price shocks is inversely related to the response to investments in structures and equipment, see graphs (3.1.1)-(3.1.9). This may indicate a substitution effect between investments and labour. Unlike equipment (graph 3.1.5), the own price effect of structures (graph 3.1.1) becomes only after some periods negative, which may be due to the time-to-build. The three decision variables respond rather similarly to technology shocks.

Unlike the results for the Dutch data, for the United States labour responds in the same way as both investments to price impulses, see graphs (3.2.1)-(3.2.9). Another result with the United States estimates is that ΔN_t responds only positively to changes in wage impulses. The responses of both investments and labour to technology innovations (see graphs (3.2.10)-(3.2.18)) show a very similar and highly dynamic behaviour. This implies that an innovation of technology associated with structures, equipment or labour influence the other two decision variables, indicating complementary of the three variables.

Much caution in the interpretation here remains since the impulses for the variables of the United States are measured in first differences.

---

[34] No standard errors for the impulse response functions are given because the calculation is very complicated due to the complexity of model (3.23). Lütkepohl (1990) suggests that the calculation of errors is very easy but is himself endowed with a very simple (non-structural, linear) model with stationary variables.

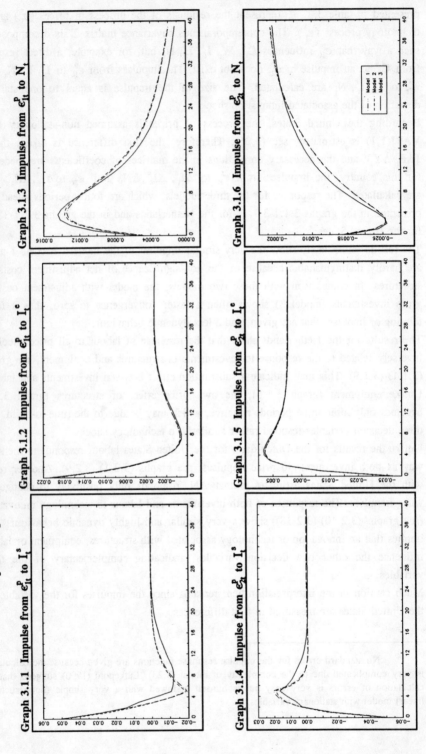

Impulse responses with the multivariate models for the Netherlands (see table 3.3)

Graph 3.1.1 Impulse from ε_{1t}^p to I_t^s

Graph 3.1.2 Impulse from ε_{1t}^p to I_t^e

Graph 3.1.3 Impulse from ε_{1t}^p to N_t

Graph 3.1.4 Impulse from ε_{2t}^p to I_t^s

Graph 3.1.5 Impulse from ε_{2t}^p to I_t^e

Graph 3.1.6 Impulse from ε_{2t}^p to N_t

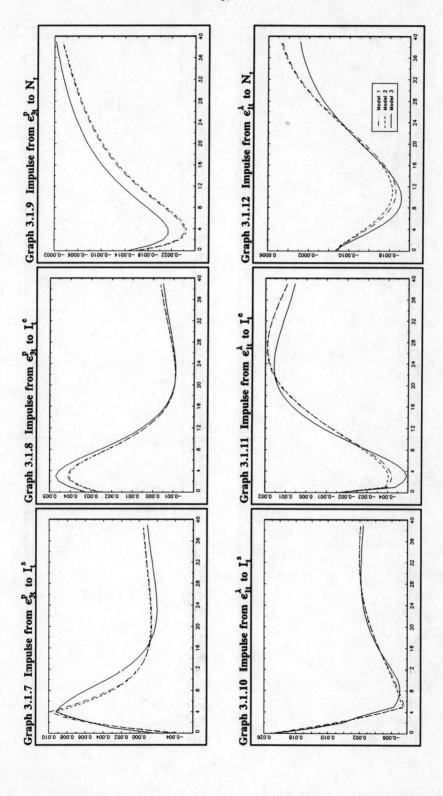

Graph 3.1.7 Impulse from ϵ_{3t}^p to I_t^s

Graph 3.1.8 Impulse from ϵ_{3t}^p to I_t^e

Graph 3.1.9 Impulse from ϵ_{3t}^p to N_t

Graph 3.1.10 Impulse from ϵ_{lt}^λ to I_t^s

Graph 3.1.11 Impulse from ϵ_{lt}^λ to I_t^e

Graph 3.1.12 Impulse from ϵ_{lt}^λ to N_t

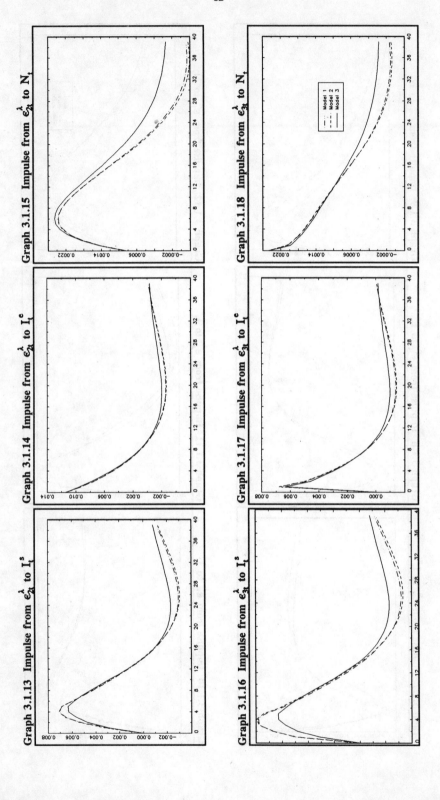

83

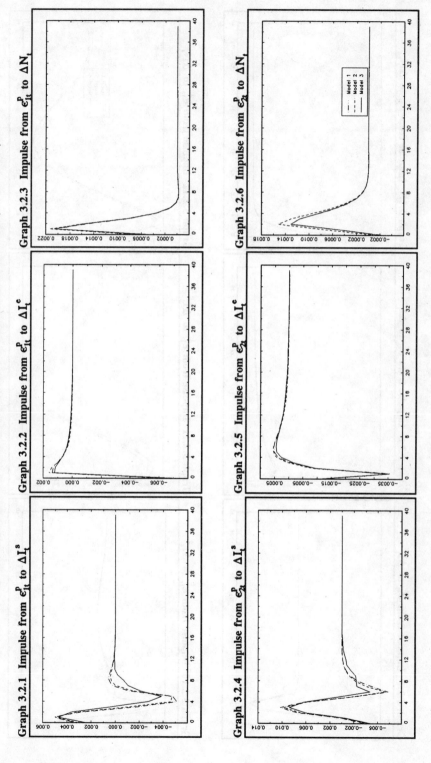

Impulse responses with the multivariate models for the United States (see table 3.5)

84

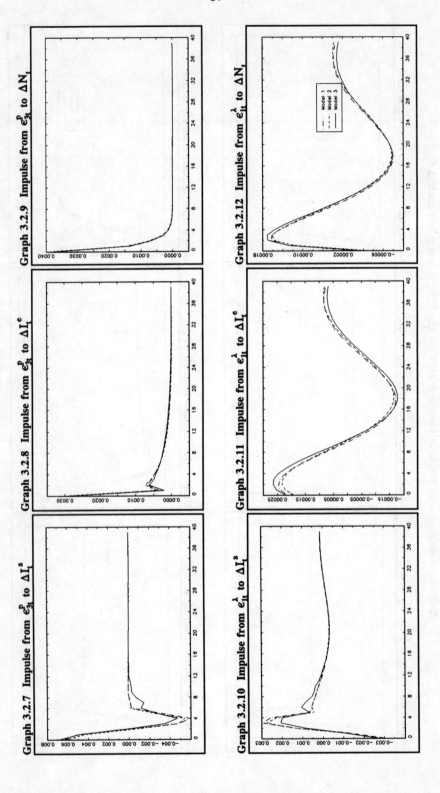

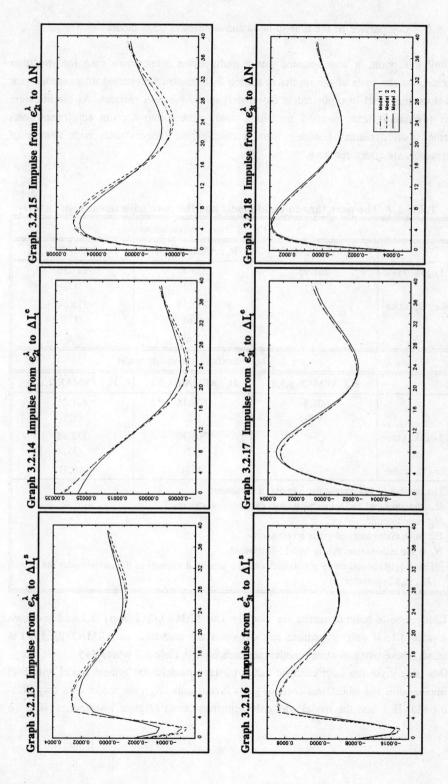

Graph 3.2.15 Impulse from e_{2t}^{λ} to ΔN_t

Graph 3.2.14 Impulse from e_{2t}^{λ} to ΔI_t^c

Graph 3.2.13 Impulse from e_{2t}^{λ} to ΔI_t^s

Graph 3.2.18 Impulse from e_{3t}^{λ} to ΔN_t

Graph 3.2.17 Impulse from e_{3t}^{λ} to ΔI_t^c

Graph 3.2.16 Impulse from e_{3t}^{λ} to ΔI_t^s

Model 1
Model 2
Model 3

3.6.4   Comparison of the time-to-build and adjustment costs model

Until this point, it was assumed that a multi-period construction time for structures exists. On the basis of the results in section 2, a construction period of about one year was assumed and incorporated in the models in the previous sections. As the literature on (dynamic) factor demand modelling usually takes into account adjustment costs rather than dynamics resulting from a multi-period time-to-build, both sources of dynamics are compared here.

Table 3.7   The pure time-to-build model and the pure adjustment costs model

United States - univariate model			
	H_0: ARMAX(6,5,7)	H_1: ARMAX(1,5,7)	H_2: ARMAX(2,1,3)
Loglik. value	267.95	239.47	187.86
	(21)	(16)	(13)
Loglik. value[*]		212.16	315.54
		(16)	(13)
N_0		-5.69	-4.61
The Netherlands - trivariate model			
	H_0: ARMAX(6,5,6)	H_1: ARMAX(1,5,6)	H_2: ARMAX(2,1,2)
	601.81	600.14	431.51
	(37)	(32)	(33)
Loglik. value		706.40	333.66
		(32)	(33)
Loglik. value[*]		-9.51	-16.91

The number in brackets is the number of parameters.
H_0: time-to-build and adjustment costs of gross investments;
H_1: time-to-build;
H_2: adjustment costs of gross investments.
N_0 is the test-statistic that is N(0,1) distributed.
[*] This Loglikelihood value is obtained with the predicted value(s) of the model under the other (H_1, H_2)-hypothesis.

If only time-to-build dynamics are modelled, an ARMAX(1,J,J+p) is found as shown in table 3.1. If only adjustment cost dynamics are modelled, an ARMAX(2,1,1+p) is found. These two non-nested models are compared in table 3.7 where J=5.
This table gives the Loglikelihood values of three models: the general model with both time-to-build and adjustment costs of gross investments (H_0), the model with only time-to-build (H_1), and the model with only adjustment costs of gross investments (H_2). To

the best of my knowledge, a test statistic to verify which of the models, that are in fact overlapping instead of non-nested as defined in Vuong (1989), does not exist. Model selection tests according to Vuong (1989) unfortunately only apply to models with serially uncorrelated series. The fall in Loglikelihood from H_0 to H_2 that is much larger than the fall from H_0 to H_1, might however indicate that the model with time-to-build is preferred to the model with only adjustment costs.

The non-nested (Cox-) test is used here according Pesaran and Deaton[35] (1978) to test the H_1-hypothesis against the H_2-hypothesis and vice versa. The test is applied assuming that cointegration between the time series used in the analysis exists, by which the obtained test statistics have stationary distributions.

For the United States the fall in Loglikelihood value is 51.61 (239.47-187.86) if a pure adjustment costs model is estimated instead of a pure time-to-build model. To test H_2 against H_1, the Cox-statistic is obtained by estimating the assumed model under H_1 by fitting the predicted values of the assumed model under H_2. This Loglikelihood value is 212.16. The test-statistic N_0 is then obtained by comparing the determinants of the covariance matrices of the three models estimated, and calculating an estimate of the variance. N_0, calculated to be -4.61, is standard normally distributed. This result therefore indicates that the H_2-hypothesis is not accepted against the H_1-hypothesis; the pure adjustment costs model is not accepted against the pure time-to-build model.

On the other hand, the reversion of the hypotheses gives the result ($N_0 = -5.69$) and indicates that the pure time-to-build model is not accepted against the pure adjustment costs model. The same exercises with the Dutch data for the multivariate system lead to the same conclusions as shown in the lower part of table 3.7.

Although these test results may seem contradictory, it is a common result of the test applied here. The conclusions that can be drawn from these results are that adjustment costs can not capture dynamics modelled by a multi-period time-to-build. Furthermore, the time-to-build model seems also to neglect some features that are modelled by the adjustment costs model. This result differs from the findings in the previous section where adjustment costs are found to be insignificant, if time-to-build is implied. Both adjustment costs and construction lags explain specific features of the dynamics of investments in structures in the Dutch and United States manufacturing industry. These findings do not contradict those obtained by Rossi (1988), using posterior odds who concludes that the time-to-build specification is favoured approximately 2:1 over a first order cost-of-adjustment model for U.S. manufacturing data.

---

[35]   A main difference between the tests of Vuong (1989) and Pesaran and Deaton (1978) is that the first tests encompas the case where models are nested. As the models here are clearly non-nested, the latter test is applicable. Tests are carried out as in Pesaran and Deaton by estimating models with moving average parts, but calculating predicted values without them.

3.6.5 Summary of the empirical part

Assuming a multi-period time-to-build for structures, models with structures, equipment and labour are estimated with United States and Dutch manufacturing industry data. The estimation results are quite reasonable in the sense that parameter estimates that are obtained fall into the admitted ranges of the theoretical model (3.5) under investigation.

Univariate analyses give highly significant values for both adjustment costs and time-to-build parameters (table 3.2). As structures investments, equipment investments and labour are interrelated (see for example appendix 1.A), an interrelated system was also estimated here.

A fixation of the multi-period time-to-build for structures made the estimation of the trivariate model possible. For both the Netherlands and the United States, no evidence was then found to take into account adjustment costs for structures (see table 3.3, 3.4, 3.5).

On the other hand, a non-nested test between a pure adjustment costs and a pure time-to-build model in section 3.6.4 gives no conclusive answers to the question which of these two models is preferred. The large difference between the Likelihood values of a pure adjustment costs model and a pure time-to-build model might however indicate the preferance of the latter.

3.7   Summary and conclusions

As shown in chapter 2, large investment projects, like the building of structures, need a considerable time to be built. The incorporation of a multi-period time-to-build in factor demand analyses that are carried out with quarterly data is thus required. The interpretation of adjustment costs regardless of a multi-period time-to-build becomes, however, less evident.

In this chapter a factor demand model for structures, equipment, and labour is specified with adjustment costs for equipment and labour and a multi-period time-to-build for structures. A closed form for the model is derived. The two different specifications for adjustment costs that prevail in the literature are analyzed together with the multi-period time-to-build assumption.

A model with *interrelation* between structures, equipment and labour is estimated with United States and Dutch manufacturing industry data. Multivariate analyses do not show evidence for the existence of adjustment costs in addition to a multi-period time-to-build.

Intuition, and descriptive and explanatory statistics, all point in the direction of preferring a multi-period time-to-build for structures to adjustment costs. On the other hand, a comparison of a pure adjustment costs and a pure time-to-build model by a non-nested test indicates that the two specifications induce mutually exclusive time series properties, which are statistically important. Hence, time-to-build dynamics might not be capable to capture fully all dynamics that are modelled by assuming only adjustment costs or, some other important features (for instance, interrelatedness in adjustment costs) might be neglected.

The econometric model adopted here could be extended by also taking into account interrelation in the production function and/or the adjustment cost function. Otherwise, the time-to-build specification can be specified in a more flexible way, as did Park (1984, see equation (2.1d*)). Although these extensions would certainly give rise to a richer and more realistic model, the conclusion that adjustment costs are not found to be significant will probably not be withdrawn. As the model would become richer in the autoregressive part, less weight would be given to the adjustment costs specification.

An improvement of the model could be made, in the sense that more simplifications are made and hence more insights are offered, if productive physical capital stock data existed. Analyses here are inevitably carried out with gross investments data because existing and available capital stock data do not fit with the multi-period time-to-build specification. Further improvements might be achieved by allowing for time-to-build gestation or delivery lags for equipment.

APPENDIX 3.A
Solving the Euler equations of the multivariate model for the rational expectations

In this appendix the Euler equations of the *trivariate* model with adjustment costs in *net capital stock* (thus $Z_t \equiv \Delta X_t$ in (3.4)) together with *time-to-build for structures* are rewritten by using the method of Blanchard and Kahn (1980). A closed form is thereafter obtained by using the marginal process assumptions of factor prices and technology shocks, see (3.7)-(3.8). This derivation method is also described in Palm et al. (1993).

The first order conditions of the optimization problem (3.5) can be obtained by differentiating with respect to $X_t^d \equiv [K_{t+J-1}^s \ K_t^e \ N_t]'$. The system of three Euler equations can then be rewritten in the expectations variables. Extending this system by adding identities yields in matrix form

$$\begin{bmatrix} X_t^d \\ E_t X_{t+1}^d \end{bmatrix} = B \begin{bmatrix} X_{t-1}^d \\ X_t^d \end{bmatrix} + \begin{bmatrix} 0 \\ D \end{bmatrix} Z_t \quad \text{where} \quad B \equiv \begin{bmatrix} 0 & I_3 \\ -\beta^{-1}I_3 & B_{22} \end{bmatrix}, \tag{3A.1}$$

and where B_{22} is a 3x3 diagonal matrix with typical diagonal element $b_i = a_i(\beta\gamma_i)^{-1} + \beta^{-1} + 1$, and

$$D \equiv (\beta\Gamma)^{-1}\begin{bmatrix} -\alpha_1 & -1 & 0 & 0 & \beta^{-J+1}\varphi_J^s & 0 & 0 & \beta^{-J+2}\varphi_{J-1}^s & 0 & \beta^{-J+3}\varphi_{J-2}^s & \cdots & \beta\varphi_0^s \\ -\alpha_2 & 0 & -1 & 0 & 0 & 1 & 0 & 0 & \beta(\kappa^e-1) & 0 & \cdots & 0 \\ -\alpha_3 & 0 & 0 & -1 & 0 & 0 & 1 & 0 & 0 & 0 & \cdots & 0 \end{bmatrix},$$

$$Z_t' \equiv \begin{bmatrix} 1 & E\{\lambda_{1,t+J-1}|\Omega_t\} & \lambda_{2,t} & \lambda_{3,t} & C_t^s & C_t^e & W_t & E\{C_{t+1}^s|\Omega_t\} & E\{C_{t+1}^e|\Omega_t\} & E\{C_{t+2}^s|\Omega_t\}..E\{C_{t+J}^s|\Omega_t\} \end{bmatrix}.$$

If matrix B in (3A.1) can be decomposed as $B = G^{-1}FG$ where F and G can be partitioned in blocks of 3x3 matrices as

$$G \equiv \begin{bmatrix} G_{11} & G_{12} \\ G_{21} & G_{22} \end{bmatrix}, \quad F \equiv \begin{bmatrix} F_1 & 0 \\ 0 & F_2 \end{bmatrix} \quad \text{where} \quad F_1 \equiv \begin{bmatrix} f_1 & 0 & 0 \\ 0 & f_2 & 0 \\ 0 & 0 & f_3 \end{bmatrix}, \quad F_2 \equiv \begin{bmatrix} f_4 & 0 & 0 \\ 0 & f_5 & 0 \\ 0 & 0 & f_6 \end{bmatrix},$$

the application of Blanchard and Kahn (1980) gives factor demand X_t^d as

$$X_t^d = -G_{22}^{-1} G_{21} X_{t-1}^d - G_{22}^{-1} \sum_{i=0}^{\infty} F_2^{-i-1} G_{22} D E\{Z_{t+i}|\Omega_t\}. \tag{3A.2}$$

The characteristic polynomial of the matrix B can be written as

$$(-f^2 + b_1 f - \beta^{-1})(-f^2 + b_2 f - \beta^{-1})(-f^2 + b_3 f - \beta^{-1}),$$

where b_1, b_2, b_3 are the eigenvalues of B_{22}. From this follows that the six eigenvalues f_i ($i=1,2..6$) of B satisfy

$$f_1 f_4 = f_2 f_5 = f_3 f_6 = \beta^{-1} \quad \text{and} \quad f_1 + f_4 = b_1, \quad f_2 + f_5 = b_2, \quad f_3 + f_6 = b_3, \tag{3A.3}$$

where it is assumed that

$$|f_i| \leq 1, \quad i=1,2,3 \quad \text{and} \quad |f_i| > 1, \quad i=4,5,6.$$

From the decomposition of B follows that

$$G B = F G, \quad \Leftrightarrow \quad \begin{bmatrix} -\beta^{-1} G_{12} & G_{11} + G_{12} B_{22} \\ -\beta^{-1} G_{22} & G_{21} + G_{22} B_{22} \end{bmatrix} = \begin{bmatrix} F_1 G_{11} & F_1 G_{12} \\ F_2 G_{21} & F_2 G_{22} \end{bmatrix},$$

such that under the condition that the submatrices are invertible, the equality of the (2,1) blocks gives

$$-\beta^{-1} G_{22} = F_2 G_{21} \quad \Leftrightarrow \quad -G_{22}^{-1} G_{21} = G_{21}^{-1} (\beta F_2)^{-1} G_{21} \tag{3A.4}$$

and with (3A.3) the equality

$$-G_{22}^{-1} G_{21} = G_{21}^{-1} (\beta F_2)^{-1} G_{21} = G_{21}^{-1} F_1 G_{21} \tag{3A.5}$$

also holds.

As B_{22} is diagonal, the decomposition of B is easy to obtain since

$$
G^{-1} = \begin{bmatrix} 1 & 0 & 0 & 1 & 0 & 0 \\ 0 & 1 & 0 & 0 & 1 & 0 \\ 0 & 0 & 1 & 0 & 0 & 1 \\ f_1 & 0 & 0 & f_4 & 0 & 0 \\ 0 & f_2 & 0 & 0 & f_5 & 0 \\ 0 & 0 & f_3 & 0 & 0 & f_6 \end{bmatrix} \qquad \text{where}
$$

$$
f_i = \frac{1}{2}b_i - \frac{1}{2}[b_i^2 - 4\beta^{-1}]^{\frac{1}{2}}, \quad i=1,2,3,
$$

$$
f_i = \frac{1}{2}b_{i-3} + \frac{1}{2}[b_{i-3}^2 - 4\beta^{-1}]^{\frac{1}{2}} \quad i=4,5,6.
$$

Thanks to (3A.5) and the diagonality of F_1, G_{21} and G_{22} formula (3A.2) reduces to

$$
X_t^d = F_1 X_{t-1}^d - \sum_{i=0}^{\infty} (\beta F_1)^{i+1} D E\{Z_{t+i}|\Omega_t\}. \tag{3A.6}
$$

The necessary conditions $|f_i| \le 1$ $(i=1,2,3)$ and $|f_i| > 1$ $(i=4,5,6)$ follow from the assumptions $0 < \beta < 1$, $\gamma_i > 0$ $(i=1,2,3)$ and $a_i > 0$ $(i=1,2,3)$. For more details about the stability of the solution, see for example Kollintzas (1985).

As should be noticed from (3A.6), the autoregressive part is diagonal. A necessary condition for this diagonality is that G_{21} is diagonal (see (3A.5)). As can be verified from the Euler equations, this follows from both the diagonality in the production function *and* the diagonality in the adjustment cost function.

Separating the components of Z_t into a constant term, a technology component and a price component, we then rewrite (3A.6) as

$$
X_t^d = C^* + F_1 X_{t-1}^d + F_1 \Gamma^{-1} E\{ [\sum_{i=0}^{\infty} (\beta F_1)^i \begin{bmatrix} \lambda_{1,t+i+J-1} \\ \lambda_{2,t+i} \\ \lambda_{3,t+i} \end{bmatrix}
$$

$$
- \sum_{k=0}^{J} D_k \sum_{i=0}^{\infty} (\beta F_1)^i P_{t+i+k}] \mid \Omega_t\},
$$

$$
\tag{3A.7}
$$

where

$$C^* = \sum_{i=0}^{\infty} (\beta F_1)^{i+1} \begin{bmatrix} \alpha_1(\beta\gamma_{11})^{-1} \\ \alpha_2(\beta\gamma_{22})^{-1} \\ \alpha_3(\beta\gamma_{33})^{-1} \end{bmatrix} = \begin{bmatrix} \alpha_1 f_1(\gamma_{11}(1-\beta f_1))^{-1} \\ \alpha_2 f_2(\gamma_{22}(1-\beta f_2))^{-1} \\ \alpha_3 f_3(\gamma_{33}(1-\beta f_3))^{-1} \end{bmatrix}$$

and

$$D_0 = \begin{bmatrix} \beta^{-J+1}\varphi_J^s & 0 & 0 \\ 0 & 1 & 0 \\ 0 & 0 & 1 \end{bmatrix}, \quad D_1 = \begin{bmatrix} \beta^{-J+2}\varphi_{J-1}^s & 0 & 0 \\ 0 & \beta(\kappa^e-1) & 0 \\ 0 & 0 & 0 \end{bmatrix}, \quad D_k = \begin{bmatrix} \beta^{-J+k+1}\varphi_{J-k}^s & 0 & 0 \\ 0 & 0 & 0 \\ 0 & 0 & 0 \end{bmatrix}, \quad k=2,3..J$$

Using the assumption that λ_t is generated by a first order VAR (3.7), the part in (3A.7) that is explained by technology shocks can be expressed as

$$F_1 \Gamma^{-1} \sum_{i=0}^{\infty} (\beta F_1)^i E\{ \begin{bmatrix} \lambda_{1,t+i+J-1} \\ \lambda_{2,t+i} \\ \lambda_{3,t+i} \end{bmatrix} |\Omega_t\} = F_1 \Gamma^{-1} \sum_{i=0}^{\infty} (\beta F_1)^i \begin{bmatrix} \rho_{11}^{i+J-1} & \rho_{12}^{i+J-1} & \rho_{13}^{i+J-1} \\ \rho_{21}^i & \rho_{22}^i & \rho_{23}^i \\ \rho_{31}^i & \rho_{32}^i & \rho_{33}^i \end{bmatrix} \lambda_t =$$

$$R^* \lambda_t \quad \text{where} \quad R^* = F_1 \Gamma^{-1} (I_3 - \beta F_1 R)^{-1} \begin{bmatrix} \rho_{11}^{J-1} & \rho_{12}^{J-1} & \rho_{13}^{J-1} \\ 1 & 1 & 1 \\ 1 & 1 & 1 \end{bmatrix}. \tag{3A.8}$$

Similarly but in a far less obvious way, if for example the assumption of a first order VAR for ΔP_t is made, it follows that

$$\sum_{i=0}^{\infty} (\beta F_1)^i E\{P_{t+i+k}|\Omega_t\} = U_k P_t - (\sum_{i=1}^{k} \overline{M}^i + \beta F_1 U_k \overline{M}) P_{t-1} \quad \text{where}$$

$$U_k - \beta F_1 U_k(I_3 + \overline{M}) + (\beta F_1)^2 U_k \overline{M} = (I_3 - \beta F_1) \sum_{i=1}^{k} \overline{M}^i + I_3, \quad k \geq 0,$$

such that

$$F_1 \Gamma^{-1} \sum_{k=0}^{J} D_k \sum_{i=0}^{\infty} (\beta F)^i E\{P_{t+i+k}|\Omega_t\} = M_1^* P_t + M_2^* P_{t-1}, \tag{3A.9}$$

where

$$M_1^* \equiv F_1 \Gamma^{-1} \sum_{k=0}^{J} D_k U_k,$$

$$M_2^* \equiv - F_1 \Gamma^{-1} \sum_{k=0}^{J} D_k (\sum_{j=1}^{k} \overline{M}^j + \beta F_1 U_k \overline{M}), \quad i=1,2..J.$$

After substituting (3A.8) and (3A.9) into (3A.7) and applying a Koyck transformation to eliminate the unobservable technology components λ_t, the model is obtained as

$$X_t^d = C + R_1 X_{t-1}^d + R_2 X_{t-2}^d - M_1^* P_t + (R^* M_1^* - M_2^*) P_{t-1} + R^* M_2^* P_{t-2} + \epsilon_t.$$

$$(3A.10)$$

C is here a 3x1-matrix of constants and

$$R_1 \equiv R^* + F_1$$
$$R_2 \equiv -R^* F_1.$$

Notice that it was assumed here that adjustment costs are in net capital stock, that is $Z_t \equiv \Delta X_t$, by which less AR-terms appear than in system (3.22). The derivation when $Z_t \equiv [I_t^s \ I_t^e \ \Delta N_t]'$ follows in a similar way as the derivation of (3A.10) (see also section 3.3.3).

APPENDIX 3.B
Stationarity tests

In this appendix some tests are applied that provide information about the stationarity of the time series used in the econometric analyses of section 3.6. All equations mentioned below are estimated with the inclusion of quarterly dummies to correct for seasonal fluctuations.

3.B.1 Unit roots

The empirical analyses contain six time series. For each time series z_t, with $z_t \in \{I_t^s, I_t^e, N_t, C_t^s, C_t^e, W_t\}$, the equation

$$\Delta z_t = c + \tau_1 t + \tau_2 t^2 + v_0 z_{t-1} + \sum_{i=1}^{k} v_i \Delta z_{t-k} + e_t^z \tag{3B.1}$$

is estimated where c, τ_1, τ_2, v_i ($i=0,1..k$) are parameters and e_t^z is a normally distributed and white noise disturbance. Table 3B.1 contains the estimation results for the time series of both the United States and the Dutch manufacturing industry.

First the equation, (3B.1) was estimated with $\tau_1 = \tau_2 = 0$. The value of k (in column (1)) is chosen such that autocorrelation is eliminated according to the Ljung-Box test (10 degrees of freedom, 5% significance level). These values of k are maintained during all unit root analyses. Column (2) contains Fuller's (see Fuller (1976)) $\hat{\tau}_\mu[z]$-statistics, belonging to the unit root hypothesis $H_0 : v_0 = 0$. In order to test for a second unit root, column (3) gives the same statistics for the time series differenced once more.

According to these (one-tailed) tests the unit root hypothesis is rejected (at the 1%-level) for the Dutch N and C^e whereas the hypothesis can not be rejected for the other series. The hypothesis of a second unit root is rejected for all of these series.

The inclusion of a linear trend (equation (3B.1) with $\tau_2 = 0$) does not alter these conclusions except for average weekly working hours in the Netherlands; the linear trend is highly significant (see column (4), where the standard t-statistics for the estimates of τ_1 are given) and the hypothesis of a unit root is now not rejected (see column (5)).

A closer look at the Dutch time series shows us that in comparison with the price variables, the course of the production factor series during 1971.I-1990.IV is completely different. Whereas the factor prices are mainly increasing (apart from slight

Table 3B.1 Unit root tests

United States manufacturing industry 1960.I-1988.IV									
(1) k	(2) $\hat{\tau}_\mu[z]$	(3) $\hat{\tau}_\mu[\Delta z]$	(4) t-stat.t	(5) $\hat{\tau}_\tau[z]$	(6) t-stat.t²	(7) LR-stat. t en t²	(8) v	(9) S_2	(10) G_2
I^a 3	-2.43	-4.11**	-1.11	-2.47	-1.23	2.98	0.97	-1.12$^@$	1.26$^@$
I^e 1	-1.85	-4.41**	2.41**	-2.97	-2.47**	12.41**	0.94	-2.07$^@$	4.30$^@$
N 1	-2.84	-5.64**	1.12	-3.02	-1.60	4.05	0.93	-4.38$^{*@}$	19.25$^{*@}$
C^s 1	-1.32	6.27**	1.23	-1.81	0.45	1.81	0.99	-2.54$^@$	6.48$^@$
C^e 2	-1.18	-5.46**	-2.32**	-2.40	-1.17	-7.12**	0.93	-3.40$^@$	11.60$^@$
W 1	-1.93	-5.76**	0.29	-1.84	0.34	0.21	0.97	-2.59$^@$	6.72$^@$
Dutch manufacturing industry 1971.I-1990.IV									
(1) k	(2) $\hat{\tau}_\mu[z]$	(3) $\hat{\tau}_\mu[\Delta z]$	(4) t-stat.t	(5) $\hat{\tau}_\tau[z]$	(6) t-stat.t²	(7) LR-stat. t en t²	(8) v	(9) S_2	(10) G_2
I^a 1	-2.60	-8.21**	1.07	-2.55	1.97	5.45*	0.65	-1.89	0.94
I^e 4	-0.33	-2.97*	2.22*	-1.92	1.63	8.54**	0.70	-1.26$^@$	-1.74$^@$
N 1	-3.83**	-3.60**	2.39**	0.27	2.13*	19.69**	0.91	1.03$^@$	1.10$^@$
C^s 1	-1.58	-6.99**	1.79	-2.37	-0.43	3.66	0.80	-0.75	0.56
C^e 1	-3.79**	-8.76**	1.09	-3.93*	1.84	4.98	0.43	-13.93**	238.98**
W 1	-1.78	4.29**	1.70	2.38	0.20	3.41	0.93	1.45$^@$	2.19$^@$

* Significant at 5%-level
** Significant at 1%-level
$^@$ Prewhitened with AR(4)-model

decreases during short periods), labour declines heavily until the last quarter of 1983 and then goes up steadily. A less prominent parabolic behaviour is found in the much more volatile structures and equipment series, where above this the equipment series has a very steep upward course from 1984 onwards.

The parabolic behaviour, especially in the Dutch labour series, suggests that a deterministic quadratic trend could be a better description for their course and probably explains the fact that the $\hat{\tau}_\mu[z]$-value is positive. Above this, the existence of higher order deterministic trends that are left out the analyses would lead to increase the likelihood of finding unit roots.

Equation (3B.1) is therefore estimated with the inclusion of a quadratic trend. In column (6) and (7) the t-statistics for τ_2 and the likelihood-ratio test(H_0 : $\tau_1 = \tau_2 = 0$) are given respectively. The quadratic trend seems significant for the Dutch labour series. In contrast to all positive (and significant) t-values of the quadratic trend for the Dutch production factor series, all United States factors have negative signs. The combination of a linear and a quadratic deterministic trend adds significantly (5%-level) to the explanation of the United States equipment series and all Dutch production factors.

As the unit root tests of Fuller are no longer applicable, the unit root tests for higher orders deterministic trends of Ouliaris, Park and Phillips (1989) are used. The equation to be estimated is

$$z_t = \sum_{i=0}^{p} \tau_i t^i + \nu z_{t-1} + e_t^z \tag{3B.2}$$

where τ_i (i=0,1..p) and ν are again parameters and e_t^z is a disturbance. To test for unit root hypothesis $H_0 : \nu = 1$ with a quadratic trend, p is taken equal to 2. The test statistics are transformations (among others) of a consistent estimate of the variance of e_t^z that is obtained by an estimate of the spectrum at frequency zero. Column (9) and (10) contain the test statistics. The spectrum window length is chosen to be 14, being relatively high (in comparison with the number of observations) in order to reduce the variance. The bias is also determined by the prewhitening of the residuals. Here an autoregressive model of fourth order (determined by Ljung-Box statistics) is used for the series marked with the symbol '@'. The statistics in column (9) are more or less comparable with t-statistics.

Table III of Ouliaris et al. (1989, page 23) contains the critical values. The unit root hypothesis ($\nu = 1$) is only rejected for the United States labour (N) series and the Dutch price of equipment investments (C^e). The test-statistics in column (10) belong to the hypothesis $H_0 : \nu = 1$ and $\tau_p = 0$. These statistics lead to similar conclusions. The estimates of ν (column (8)) also indicate that the Dutch C^e seems most distant, but the United States labour series is not far from a unit root[36].

The inclusion of higher order deterministic trends (not shown here) does not alter the conclusions that all series contain a unit root except the price of equipment investments in the Netherlands. Similar tests for a second unit root all reject the presence of a second unit root (5%-level).

It can therefore be concluded that all United States and Dutch series, except for the Dutch price of equipment investments which seems stationary, have a unit root. A deterministic quadratic trend is important in the United States equipment and Dutch production factor series.

---

[36] If a bandwidth of 10 is taken with the United States labour series, the statistics S_2 and G_2 are respectively -3.66 and 14.44 (not significant), which emplies that the hypothesis of a unit root is accepted.

3.B.2 Cointegration

The unit root findings alone do not directly have implications for the structural model specified in section 3.2. After all, the structural model contains combinations of the series that are possibly stationary. Thus although macro-economic time series are not stationary, they can be suitably modelled by a structural model, in which the disturbance terms are stationary. Consequently, standard econometric estimation methods that assume stationary distributions can be used with the data provided that cointegration exists. To estimate the system of three equations (3.23) of section 3.6, it is assumed that at least three stationary relations between the three production factors and the three factor prices exist. Cointegration tests are carried out here.

Table 3B.2 contains the cointegration test statistics along the lines of Johansen and Juselius (1990). A VAR(k)-model is rewritten as

$$\Delta Z_t = \Gamma_0 \, D_t + \sum_{i=1}^{k-1} \Gamma_i \, \Delta Z_{t-i} + \Pi \, Z_{t-k} + e_t^Z \quad \text{with} \quad \Pi = \alpha \beta', \tag{3B.3}$$

where D_t includes a constant and three quarterly (uncentered) dummies, Γ_i (i=0,1..k-1) and Π are the (constant) parameter-matrices to be estimated and e_t^Z represents the disturbance vector that is assumed to be normally distributed. Z_t contains the variables set under investigation.

Firstly, in the error correction model (3B.3) k (accounting for autocorrelation in Z_t) and the number of cointegrating relationships has to be determined. Matrix Π is therefore decomposed as $\Pi = \alpha \beta'$, where matrix α is the weighting matrix and the columns of β contain the coefficients of the cointegrating relationships. The application of the cointegration test of Johansen consists of determining the rank of the cointegration space, i.e. the dimension of matrix Π. On detailed issues see Johansen and Juselius (1990).

The upper part of table 3B.2 gives, for both countries, the trace and λ_{max}- statistics when all six variables are included in model (3.23).

For the Netherlands (k=1), the H_0-hypothesis of $r \leq 4$ where r equals the number of cointegration relationships, being the rank of matrix Π, is not rejected at a 5%-level See Johansen et al. (1990), table A.2 where a constant is contained in the non-stationary part in (3B.2) and therefore in a way resembles a drift. The H_0-hypothesis of $r \leq 3$ is not rejected at a 1%-level. The trace statistics contradict these findings and suggest that there are two cointegration relationships. The test statistics where $r \leq 2$, however, has a p-value of 10%.

It should be noticed here that the inclusion of a quadratic trend (significant in the unit root analyses) is not necessary to find cointegration relationships. The prominent trends in the labour series and investment series thus seem to move in line with each other. A

Table 3B.2 Cointegration tests

United States			The Netherlands		
Part one: $Z_t = \{I_t^a, I_t^o, N_t, C_t^a, C_t^o, W_t\}$			Part one: $Z_t = \{I_t^a, I_t^o, N_t, C_t^a, C_t^o, W_t\}$		
H_0	trace	λ_{max}	H_0	trace	λ_{max}
$r \leq 5$	5.93	5.93	$r \leq 5$	6.16	6.16
$r \leq 4$	13.57	7.65	$r \leq 4$	18.61[*]	12.46
$r \leq 3$	28.03	14.46	$r \leq 3$	35.04[*]	16.43
$r \leq 2$	47.05	19.02	$r \leq 2$	56.87[**]	21.83
$r \leq 1$	75.06	28.01	$r \leq 1$	103.83[**]	46.95[**]
$r = 0$	121.54[**]	46.48[**]	$r = 0$	159.83[**]	56.00[**]
Part two: $Z_t = \{C_t^a, C_t^o, W_t\}$			Part two: $Z_t = \{C_t^a, C_t^o, W_t\}$		
H_0	trace	λ_{max}	H_0	trace	λ_{max}
$r \leq 2$	5.47	5.47	$r \leq 2$	4.82	4.82
$r \leq 1$	15.06	9.59	$r \leq 1$	13.42	8.59
$r = 0$	35.79	20.73	$r = 0$	34.40[*]	20.99

[*]   Significant at the 5%-level
[**] Significant at the 1%-level

similar result holds for the United States.

For the United States, no cointegration was found when no linear trend was included in (3B.3). The inclusion of a linear trend in Z_{t-k} gives the statistics presented in the left part of table 3B.2. In this case k, in (3B.3), is taken to be four because of a very high autocorrelation in the residuals. This is according to the univariate Box-Pierce tests with 10 degrees of freedom. The critical values (inclusion of the linear trend) can be found in table V of Johansen (1991). According to the trace- and λ_{max}-statistics, one cointegration relationship is found for the United States statistics. However, if more lags are taken in (3B.3), $k > 4$, more cointegration relationships are found.

If the same statistics (not presented here) are calculated for the subsystems of the complete system for both countries, with one production factor and the three factor prices, in all three cases one cointegration relationship is found at the 5%-level. Therefore, these results indicate that there is 'sufficient' cointegration and the inclusion of linear trends in the United States system is important. The lower part of table 3B.2 analogously gives these statistics for the case where Z_t in (3B.3) equals the vector of the three factor prices[37]. Again, linear trends are included in the United States

---

[37]   Whether or not cointegration between the three prices exists, it is also important for the derivation of the closed form in section 3.6.

system.

The conclusions of the trace and λ_{max}-statistics are, in this case, close in line with each other; no cointegration between the United States factor prices and one cointegration relationship between the Dutch factor prices is found (the p-value of the λ_{max}-statistic is only 7.5%).

In all of these analyses, it is assumed that the residuals in (3B.3) are white noise and normally distributed. Univariate normality tests for the residuals in all equations do not reject the hypotheses of normality at a 5%-level. As the (univariate) Box-Pierce tests for autocorrelation do not indicate that a higher order for the VAR-model (equation (3B.3)) should be investigated, and the univariate tests results of normality do not interfere with the consistency of the test statistics, the conclusions drawn above can be maintained.

3.B.3 Conclusions

To summarize, the complete system with six non-stationary variables (except for the price of equipment, C^e in the Netherlands) seems for both countries to have linear relationships that are stationary. The inclusion of linear trends in the United States system is important.

The three factor prices in the United States all have unit roots. As for the Netherlands a mix of one stationary and non-stationary variables exists, the Dutch factor prices have one cointegration relationship. Therefore, the existence of at least one stationary relationships is not surprising. But the findings according to these analyses are in one way remarkable.

The unit roots test statistics in this appendix clearly suggest that all production factor are non-stationary ($I(1)$-) variables, and the presence of deterministic trends seems to be important. However, the inclusion of deterministic linear or quadratic trends in the six-variate system (first part of table 3B.2) for the Netherlands seems unnecessary when finding cointegration relations according to the test statistics; the deterministic and very prominent trends in the labour series and the investment series vanish when linear combinations of the variables are considered.

The structural model specified in section 3.2, that results in the closed form model (3.23) and implicitly assumes cointegration between the time series of the variables included, is thus by the cointegration results here not contradicted. A linear trend in the analyses for the United States is however to be taken into account.

CHAPTER 4
PERSISTENCE, ASYMMETRIES AND INTERRELATION
IN MANUFACTURING STRUCTURES, EQUIPMENT AND LABOUR DEMAND
An application to six OECD countries

4.1   Introduction

In this chapter investments and labour demand with rich interrelations are explained by profit maximizing behaviour under uncertainty. In contrast with chapter 3, first order conditions are estimated directly. The derivation of a closed form solution, like done in chapter 3, is hardly possible because of the rich interrelations together with long gestation lags for structures. The instrumental estimation method used here is also adopted, among others, by Burda (1991), Gordon (1992), Pfann and Palm (1993) and (using the dual, cost minimizing approach) Pindyck and Rotemberg (1983a,1983b) and Bresson, Kramarz and Sevestre (1993).

Three main differences with these studies exist.

Firstly, in line with the q studies of investments (see Hayashi (1982)) this chapter explains business investments whereas factor demand studies usually explain the physical capital stock. Investments and variations in physical capital stock differ in timing if lead times, delivery lags and/or construction lags, exist. Following Pindyck et al. (1983a), Lichtenberg (1988), Altug (1989) and the previous chapter structures and equipment are here separately included in the model. As the existence of lead times is confirmed by evidence for plants (including equipment) by Mayer (1960) and time-to-build appears to be of a great importance for structures (see chapter 2), Kydland and Prescott's specification is here incorporated[38]. The time-to-build specification is adopted in addition to adjustment costs.

Secondly, in the dynamic specification accounting for time-to-build and adjustment costs, two asymmetries are introduced. One asymmetry concerns the 'irreversibility' of investments. Capital projects require a gestation period (that is rather long for structures), but there is no possibility to withdraw plans in execution. Productive capital can become idle but no market exists to sell used capital goods, by which capital only depreciates or 'evaporates'. Another asymmetry is built in the 'internal' adjustment

---

[38]   For the comparison of time-to-build according Kydland and Prescott (1982) and adjustment costs dynamics in factor demand models, see Rossi (1988) who compares non-nested posterior odds, or chapter 3.

costs specification for labour by assuming that hiring costs and firing costs of labour are not necessarily equal. This approach is also adopted in Bentolila and Bertola (1990), Bresson et al. (1993) and Pfann and Palm (1993).

As a third difference, external investment adjustment costs are specified; they result from the (Granger) causality from investment demand to investment prices. For example Uzawa (1964)[39] and Brechling (1975) pay attention to these costs.

The aim of this chapter is to investigate the importance of various kinds of factor dynamics, in particular persistence, asymmetries and interrelation. Persistence in capital and labour that is often interpreted as resulting from adjustment costs, is here investigated together with persistence resulting from technological innovations and construction lags (or time-to-build).

Persistence in this context is defined as high serial correlation. As models can be dynamic having only lagged exogenous variables (in for example a factor demand model for capital stock without even adjustment costs, see Brechling (1975)), the term 'persistence' is here preferred to 'dynamics'. In this context persistence should not necessarily be associated with non-stationarity.

Contrary to the model in chapter 3, rich interrelations of investments and labour is assumed in both the production and in the adjustment costs function. As interrelations in capital and labour exist, already emphasized by Nadiri and Rosen (1969), Pindyck and Rotemberg (1983b) and appendix 1.A, the marginal productivity of capital (labour) is assumed to depend on the average weekly numbers of hours worked (capital). Interrelated costs ensued from simultaneously investing in capital and recruiting or dismissing labour, is far less frequently found in the literature. The two asymmetries in relation with these dynamics, the irreversibility of investments and asymmetric labour adjustment costs mentioned above, are also incorporated.

The outline is as follows.

Summary statistics of the manufacturing industry data of six industrial countries are presented in section 2. Section 3 specifies a model for a representative firm and presents the first order conditions. Estimation results are presented in section 4. Section 5 summarizes the main results, compares results with related studies and highlights the main shortcomings.

---

[39] Uzawa uses a model with a consumption and a capital sector. In one example the consumption sector faces external investment adjustment costs because in comparison with the capital sector, this sector is more capital intensive.

4.2 Descriptive statistics

Table 4.1 Descriptive statistics

		US	CN	UK	WG	FR	NL
SK	I^s	0.61	0.60	-0.11	-0.36	0.04	0.37
	I^e	-0.36	-0.16	-0.22	0.31	-0.26	-0.18
	ΔN	-1.19	-0.14	-0.80	-1.39	-0.55	-0.29
AR2	I^s	0.93	0.86	0.89	0.82	0.93	0.52
	I^e	0.90	0.92	0.94	0.84	0.90	0.72
	N	0.87	0.89	0.88	0.93	0.87	0.88
DW	I^s	6.24	2.09	5.56	2.29	-3.11	-0.96
	I^e	-1.58	1.35	-1.57	0.94	-2.28	-0.79
	N	-0.66	-1.16	-2.42	-2.86	2.29	-0.97
ρ_{se}		0.71	0.71	0.84	0.69	0.66	0.61
ρ_{sn}		0.53	0.31	0.67	0.64	0.64	0.56
ρ_{en}		0.68	0.68	0.80	0.72	0.63	0.34
ρ_{sdn}		-0.13	-0.18	-0.09	0.48	0.35	0.02
ρ_{edn}		-0.10	-0.11	-0.03	0.27	0.54	0.07

SK is the skewness; AR2 is the sum of the autoregressive coefficients of a (univariate) AR(2) regression; DW is the alternative Durbin's h statistic; ρ_{ij} is the contemporaneous correlations between i and j where i,j=$s(I^s)$, $e(I^e)$, $n(N)$, $dn(\Delta N)$.

Countries: Sample periods:
US = United States 1960.I-1988.IV
CN = Canada   1960.I-1988.IV
UK = United Kingdom 1960.I-1988.IV
WG = West-Germany   1960.I-1988.IV
FR = France   1970.I-1992.II
NL = The Netherlands 1971.I-1990.IV

The data used to test the model are quarterly investment and labour series from manufacturing industries. Structures and equipment investments are referred to as I_t^s and I_t^e respectively. Employment (N_t) is measured as the average number of hours worked. In table 4.1, summary statistics are given for six countries listed in the bottom part of the table together with the sample periods (see also appendix I.A where dynamics and interrelations of the annual series are investigated). Detailed data descriptions are found in the data appendix.

The investments and labour series are trending. Stationary investment series are obtained by taking the residuals from a regression of each series on a constant and a third order polynomial deterministic trend[40]. For labour, the first difference $\Delta N_t \equiv N_t - N_{t-1}$ of the employment series is used in table 4.1.

Net flows in physical capital stock and employment are respectively $\Delta K_t \equiv K_t - K_{t-1}$ and ΔN_t. Suppose that $\Delta N_t = H_t - F_t$ and $\Delta K_t = I_t - D_t$, where H_t, F_t, I_t and D_t are the number of recruitments (employment 'hired'), lay offs ('firing' or employment leaving the firm), the gross investments and depreciation (or obsolescence) at time t respectively. Then, in table 4.1 the gross flows in capital (I_t^s and I_t^e) are compared with the net flows in labour (ΔN_t).

Excess kurtosis statistics indicate the fat-tailness of a variable and thus the volatility. This statistic calculated for the series here (that are not given) indicates that for labour in the United Kingdom and West-Germany volatility is very high. The skewness (given in table 4.1 as SK) gives an indication of the importance of asymmetry.

For ΔN_t a negative skewness indicates that employment increases are relatively more frequent by which a higher persistence during recovery periods become apparent. Above this, increases in the number of employment are less high (volatile) than decreases.

The overall negative skewness for ΔN_t, confirms findings in Hussey (1992) for numbers of employed persons in the durable and non-durable goods sectors in the United States. Neftçi (1984) showed for United States unemployment rates also that asymmetries between increasing and decreasing states of the economy exist. Recessions in economic activity (increases in unemployment) tend to be steeper and more shortly lived than recoveries (decreases in unemployment).

Since the main determinants of production (physical capital and labour) are closely related, their statistical properties are expected to be similar. Table 4.1 shows a negative skewness for equipment investments, except for West-Germany. Structures investments do however not show a clear negative skewness and are even remarkably large for the United States and Canada. As significance levels for the skewness-statistics are difficult to calculate due to non-normality (see Hussey (1992) who applies a non-parametric method), nothing is here said about the significance of these values.

The sum of the autoregressive coefficients in univariate regressions (AR2) in table 4.1 indicates also the persistence of the variable under investigation. Among the three factors across countries no overall similarities are found. The relatively high persistence in net employment of about 0.88 on average is also found in Burda (1991) for annual numbers of persons employed in eight countries. A major difference is however the

---

[40] In the following section with the structural analyses, not the detrended but original series are used.

figure 0.87 for the US which is much higher than Burda's result. Burda ascribes this much lower persistence of employment in the United States in comparison with European (except Scandinavian) countries to the flexibility of the American labour market. The difference between the result of Burda (being 0.57) and the result here must be due to the detrend method used and/or the fact that Burda uses employees whereas here average working hours are used.

The AR2 statistics do not highlight the presence of autocorrelation. The alternative Durbin h statistics (see Durbin (1970)) that correct the common Durbin Watson's statistic (for static models) for several lagged dependent variables, are therefore also given. The statistic is standard normally distributed. These statistics exhibit significant autocorrelation in the structures series with the exception of the Netherlands. Often negative autocorrelation is found in the equipment for France and in some employment series.

Finally, in table 4.1 simple contemporaneous correlations are presented. Structures and equipment show considerable positive correlation of at least 60%. Similarly, considerable positive correlation occurs between structures investments and the stock of employment. These findings are plausible since structures or buildings are useless without the necessary equipment and labour and vice versa. Structures and equipment investments are also found highly positively correlated with the net flows in employment for West-Germany and France.

To summarize, equipment shows about the same skewed distribution as labour, whereas structures obviously do not. The three production factors are highly persistent, highly positively correlated among each other, except for the net flows in labour. Structures investments exhibit the largest time dependence.

4.3   A neoclassical factor demand model

In this section a model for the dynamics in structures, equipment and labour demand is specified and the associated first order conditions for profit maximization are derived.

4.3.1   Model specification

An entrepreneur is assumed to determine the demand for the physical structures stock (K_t^s), the physical equipment stock (K_t^e) and labour (N_t) by maximizing the discounted profit stream over an infinite horizon. The entrepreneur is rational, that is uses all information available when making decisions, and operates on price clearing output and factor markets. The entrepreneur's objective function is given by

$$E\{\sum_{h=0}^{\infty} \beta_{t+h}[R_{t+h}-VC_{t+h}-IAC_{t+h}] \mid \Omega_t\}, \qquad (4.1)$$

where Ω_t denotes the information set available at time t. R_t, VC_t and IAC_t denote the revenue, the variable costs and the internal adjustment costs respectively. Variable β_t is the discount factor,

$$\beta_{t+h} \equiv \prod_{i=0}^{h} \frac{1}{1+r_{t+i}}, \qquad (4.2)$$

where r_t is the going nominal interest rate during period t.

R_t is the function of revenues, thus

$$R_t \equiv P_t^q Q_t, \qquad (4.3)$$

where P_t^q is the price of the product and Q_t is the total production at t. The output price is assumed to be parametric to the firm, that is $\partial P_t/\partial Q_{t-i}=0$ for $i=0,1,2....$. A linear-quadratic approximation[41] of the underlying production function,

$$Q_t = (\alpha+\lambda_t)' X_t - \frac{1}{2}X_t' A X_t, \qquad (4.4)$$

is used where $X_t \equiv [K_t^s \ K_t^e \ N_t]'$ is the vector of production factors, $\alpha:=[\alpha_1 \ \alpha_2 \ \alpha_3]'$ and $A:=\{\alpha_{ij}\}$ for $i,j=1,2,3$ and A is symmetric. This function is concave if and only if matrix A is semi-positive definite. The term $\lambda \equiv [\lambda_{1t} \ \lambda_{2t} \ \lambda_{3t}]'$ represents a stochastic technology shock to the level of production.

If Y_t denotes the vector of structures and equipment investments and employment and P_t^q is the vector of the accompanying nominal factor prices, that are $Y_t \equiv [I_t^s \ I_t^e \ N_t]'$ and $P_t^n \equiv [C_t^{sn} \ C_t^{en} \ W_t^n]'$, then

$$VC_t \equiv P_t^{n'} Y_t. \qquad (4.5)$$

Additional costs within the firm for changing production factors, so called 'internal adjustment costs', are defined as

$$IAC_t \equiv \frac{1}{2}[I_t^s \ I_t^e \ \Delta N_t] \begin{bmatrix} \gamma_{11} & \gamma_{12} & \gamma_{13} \\ \gamma_{12} & \gamma_{22} & \gamma_{23} \\ \gamma_{13} & \gamma_{23} & \gamma_{33} \end{bmatrix} \begin{bmatrix} I_t^s \\ I_t^e \\ \Delta N_t \end{bmatrix} + \exp(\zeta\Delta N_t) - \zeta\Delta N_t - 1. \qquad (4.6)$$

If $\gamma_{ij}=0$ for $i \neq j$, the adjustment costs function is not interrelated. The adjustment costs for structures and equipment are then given by $\gamma_{11}(I_t^s)^2$ and $\gamma_{22}(I_t^e)^2$ respectively. Moreover, if $\zeta=0$ the adjustment costs of employment equal $\gamma_{33}(\Delta N_t)^2$, and are thus

---

[41]   Like in chapter 3, this assumption is made to avoid non-linearities in physical capital stock in the Euler equations (see the transition from (4.12) to (4.13)).

Graph 4.1   Example adjustment costs function

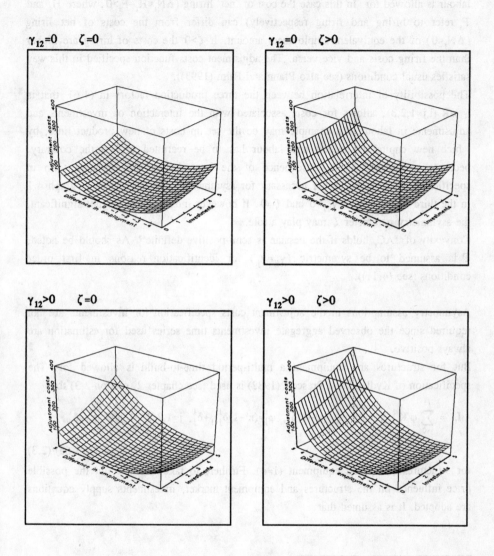

Function : $AC_t = \dfrac{1}{2}\begin{bmatrix} I_t & \Delta N_t \end{bmatrix}\begin{bmatrix} \gamma_{11} & \gamma_{12} \\ \gamma_{12} & \gamma_{22} \end{bmatrix}\begin{bmatrix} I_t \\ \Delta N_t \end{bmatrix} + \exp(\zeta\Delta N_t) - \zeta\Delta N_t - 1$

symmetric. If ζ is not equal to zero, that is $\zeta \in \mathbb{R}$, an asymmetry in adjustment cost of labour is allowed for. In this case the cost of 'net' hiring ($\Delta N_t \equiv H_t - F_t > 0$, where H_t and F_t refer to hiring and firing respectively) can differ from the costs of net firing ($\Delta N_t < 0$) of the equivalent employment amount. If $\zeta > 0$ the costs of hiring are higher than the firing costs and vice versa. The adjustment costs function specified in this way satisfies usual conditions (see also Pfann and Palm (1993)).

The possibility of interrelation between the three production factors in (4.6), that is $\gamma_{ij} \in \mathbb{R}$ ($i,j=1,2,3$), allows for costs associated with the interaction of investments and adjustments in labour. An example may be the set up costs of new product lines, by which new capital is needed and labour has to be recruited or, on the contrary, becomes redundant. As a consequence of the interrelation, the exponent term in specification (4.6) is no longer necessary for asymmetry[42]. This is shown in graph 4.1 in the third figure where $\gamma_{12} > 0$ and $\zeta = 0$. If however interrelations are not significant, the asymmetry parameter ζ may play a role.

Convexity of IAC_t holds if the hessian is semi-positive definite[43]. As should be noted, Γ is assumed to be symmetric ($\gamma_{ij} = \gamma_{ji}$) for identification reasons in first order conditions (see (4.11)).

Asymmetry assumptions in the adjustment costs specification for investments are not required since the observed aggregate investments time series used for estimation are always positive.

But for structures and equipment a multi-period time-to-build is allowed for. The specification of Kydland and Prescott (1982) is used (see chapter 2, section 2.3) thus

$$I_t^i = \sum_{j=0}^{J^i} \varphi_j^i K_{t+j-1}^i \text{ with } \varphi_0^i = (\kappa^i - 1)\delta_1^i, \quad \varphi_j^i = (\kappa^i - 1)\delta_{j+1}^i + \delta_j^i, \quad j=1,2..J^i-1 \text{ and } \varphi_{Ji}^i = \delta_{Ji}^i,$$

$$(4.7)/(3.6a)/(2.3)$$

for structures ($i=s$) and equipment ($i=e$). Further, to take into account the possible price influence on the structures and equipment market, investments supply equations are adopted. It is assumed that

---

[42]   This remark was made by Francis Kramarz. In the original paper of Bresson et al. (1993) where three types of labour are distinguished, this remark concerning specification (4.6) was also made.

[43]   Positive definiteness of the quadratic part (so positive definiteness of the matrix $\Gamma := \{\gamma_{ij}\}$ for $i,j=1,2,3$) is not a sufficient condition for convexity. If Γ is positive definite, IAC_t (see (4.6)) can be non-convex if negative elements in Γ exist. If Γ is not positive definite, IAC_t can be convex provided that $\exp(\zeta \Delta N_t) - \zeta(\Delta N_t) - 1$ is sufficiently large.

$$C_t^{in} = \eta_0^i + \sum_{j=1}^{p^i} \eta_j^i C_{t-j}^{in} + \sum_{j=0}^{q^i} \psi_j^i I_{t-j}^i + e_t^i \quad \text{for } i=s,e. \tag{4.8}$$

e_t^λ represents an independently and normally distributed disturbance. Granger causality from investments demand to investment prices was tested for and found to be present in the data for the manufacturing industry analyzed in the empirical part. The main explanation for this type of Granger causality is that the manufacturing industry can be a major demander of the domestic goods, thus its influence on investments prices might be important. Details about Granger causality tests that are applied to test for this price setting on the investments market, are given in appendix 4.A.

When supply is explained by the equations (4.8), the variable costs for investments (see (4.5)) become

$$C_t^{in} I_t^i = \eta_0^i I_t^i + \sum_{j=1}^{p^i} \eta_j^i C_{t-j}^{in} I_t^i + e_t^i I_t^i + EAC_t^i \quad \text{where} \quad EAC_t^i = \sum_{j=0}^{q^i} \psi_j^i I_{t-j}^i I_t^i \tag{4.9}$$

for $i=s,e$. The term EAC_t is known as 'external adjustment costs', being costs due to the absence of perfect competition on a factor market. For example Brechling (1975, page 40) pays attention to this 'dynamically monopsonistic' modelling of the production factors labour and capital.

In comparison with the model specified in section 3.2, the model here assumes the matrix A in the production function and the matrix Γ in the adjustment costs function to be non-diagonal and an (additional) asymmetry is allowed for in the labour adjustment costs. Furthermore, causal relationships can exist from investments demand to investments prices and the discount factor is observed (in stead of assumed constant). The technology shock, λ_t, will be assumed here to be integrated of first order. This is in contrast with the assumption of a VAR(p) in section 3.2., but is a process that follows from the estimation results. This will be discussed in section 4.4.1.

4.3.2 First order conditions

As a consequence of the fixed investments plan specification, at time t the entrepreneur chooses K_{t+Js-1}, K_{t+Je-1} and employment N_t such that profits are maximized. The entrepreneur maximizes (4.1) with respect to K_{t+Js-1}, K_{t+Je-1} and N_t under the time-to-build (4.7) and the price equations (4.8). The three first order conditions are given by

$$E\left\{\begin{bmatrix} \beta_{t+Js-1}P^q_{t+Js-1}(\alpha_1+\lambda_{1,t+Js-1}-a_{11}K^s_{t+Js-1}-a_{12}K^e_{t+Js-1}-a_{13}N_{t+Js-1}) \\ \beta_{t+Je-1}P^q_{t+Je-1}(\alpha_2+\lambda_{2,t+Je-1}-a_{12}K^s_{t+Je-1}-a_{22}K^e_{t+Je-1}-a_{23}N_{t+Je-1}) \\ \beta_t P^q_t(\alpha_3+\lambda_{3,t}-a_{13}K^s_t-a_{23}K^e_t-a_{33}N_t) \end{bmatrix}\right.$$

$$-\begin{bmatrix} \displaystyle\sum_{k=0}^{J^s}\beta_{t+k}\varphi^s_{Js-k}(C^{sn}_{t+k}+\gamma_{11}I^s_{t+k}+\gamma_{12}I^e_{t+k}+\gamma_{13}\Delta N_{t+k}) \\ \displaystyle\sum_{k=0}^{J^e}\beta_{t+k}\varphi^e_{Je-k}(C^{en}_{t+k}+\gamma_{12}I^s_{t+k}+\gamma_{22}I^e_{t+k}+\gamma_{23}\Delta N_{t+k}) \\ \beta_t W^n_t-\gamma_{13}(\beta_{t+1}I^s_{t+1}-\beta_t I^s_t)-\gamma_{23}(\beta_{t+1}I^e_{t+1}-\beta_t I^e_t)-\gamma_{33}(\beta_{t+1}\Delta N_{t+1}-\beta_t \Delta N_t) \end{bmatrix}$$

$$-\begin{bmatrix} \displaystyle\sum_{k=0}^{J^s+q^s}\beta_{t+k}I^s_{t+k}\sum_{l=max(0,k-J^s)}^{min(q^s,k)}\varphi^s_{Js-k+l}\psi^s_l \\ \displaystyle\sum_{k=0}^{J^e+q^e}\beta_{t+k}I^e_{t+k}\sum_{l=max(0,k-J^e)}^{min(q^e,k)}\varphi^e_{Je-k+l}\psi^e_l \\ \zeta(\beta_t exp(\zeta\Delta N_t)-\beta_{t+1}exp(\zeta\Delta N_{t+1})+\beta_{t+1}-\beta_t) \end{bmatrix}\left|\ \Omega_t\right\}=0. \qquad (4.10)$$

The last terms concerning the investment costs (4.5) thereby follow among others from (4.7) and (4.8) since

$$\frac{\partial C^{in}_{t+k}I^i_{t+k}}{\partial K^i_{t+Ji-1}} = C^{in}_{t+k}\frac{\partial I^i_{t+k}}{\partial K^i_{t+Ji-1}}+I^i_{t+k}\sum_{l=max(0,k-q^i)}^{min(J^i,k)}\frac{\partial C^{in}_{t+k}}{\partial I^i_{t+l}}\frac{\partial I^i_{t+l}}{\partial K^i_{t+Ji-1}} = \varphi^i_{Ji-k}C^{in}_{t+k}+I^i_{t+k}\sum_{l=max(0,k-J^i)}^{min(q^i,k)}\psi^i_l\varphi^i_{Ji-k+l}$$

for i=s,e and k=0,1..J^i+q^i where φ^i_{Ji-k}=0 if k>J^i.

Beside the necessary conditions (4.10), beginpoint and endpoint conditions have to be satisfied (see Sargent (1987), page 200-201). In most applications only the conditions (4.10) are verified by estimating the equations as done in the following section. Above this the concavity of the objective function is checked by testing the concavity of the production function and the convexity of the adjustment cost function.

To use the time-to-build specification (4.7), physical capital stocks (K^s_t and K^e_t) in the equations (4.10) have to be expressed in terms of gross investments. Rewriting the first order conditions (4.10) in terms of gross investments after dividing by the output price occurs by applying the filter (4.7), yields

$$E\left\{
\begin{bmatrix}
\alpha_1^* - a_{11}\sum_{i=0}^{J^s}\varphi_{Je-i}^e I_{t-i}^s - a_{12}\sum_{j=0}^{J^s}\varphi_{Js-j}^s I_{t-j}^e + \sum_{i=0}^{J^s}\varphi_{Je-i}^e\sum_{j=0}^{J^s}\varphi_{Js-j}^s[\lambda_{1,t+Js-1-j-i} - a_{13}N_{t+Js-1-j-i}] \\
\alpha_2^* - a_{12}\sum_{i=0}^{J^s}\varphi_{Je-i}^e I_{t-i}^s - a_{22}\sum_{j=0}^{J^s}\varphi_{Js-j}^s I_{t-j}^e + \sum_{i=0}^{J^s}\varphi_{Je-i}^e\sum_{j=0}^{J^s}\varphi_{Js-j}^s[\lambda_{2,t+Je-1-j-i} - a_{23}N_{t+Je-1-j-i}] \\
\alpha_3^* - a_{13}\sum_{i=0}^{J^s}\varphi_{Je-i}^e I_{t-i}^s - a_{23}\sum_{j=0}^{J^s}\varphi_{Js-j}^s I_{t-j}^e + \sum_{i=0}^{J^s}\varphi_{Je-i}^e\sum_{j=0}^{J^s}\varphi_{Js-j}^s[\lambda_{3,t-j-i} - a_{33}N_{t-j-i}]
\end{bmatrix}\right.
$$

$$
-\begin{bmatrix}
\sum_{i=0}^{J^s}\varphi_{Je-i}^e\sum_{j=0}^{J^s}\varphi_{Js-j}^s\sum_{k=0}^{J^s}\dfrac{\beta_{t+k-j-i}}{P_{t+Js-1-j-i}^q\beta_{t+Js-1-j-i}}\varphi_{Js-k}^s(C_{t+k-j-i}^{sn}+\gamma_{11}I_{t+k-j-i}^s+\gamma_{12}I_{t+k-j-i}^e+\gamma_{13}\Delta N_{t+k-j-i}) \\
\sum_{i=0}^{J^s}\varphi_{Je-i}^e\sum_{j=0}^{J^s}\varphi_{Js-j}^s\sum_{k=0}^{J^s}\dfrac{\beta_{t+k-j-i}}{P_{t+Je-1-j-i}^q\beta_{t+Je-1-j-i}}\varphi_{Je-k}^e(C_{t+k-j-i}^{en}+\gamma_{12}I_{t+k-j-i}^s+\gamma_{22}I_{t+k-j-i}^e+\gamma_{23}\Delta N_{t+k-j-i}) \\
\sum_{i=0}^{J^s}\varphi_{Je-i}^e\sum_{j=0}^{J^s}\dfrac{\varphi_{Js-j}^s}{P_{t-j-i}^q}[W_{t-j-i}^n-\gamma_{13}(\dfrac{\beta_{t+1-j-i}}{\beta_{t-j-i}}I_{t+1-j-i}^s-I_{t-j-i}^s)-\gamma_{23}(\dfrac{\beta_{t+1-j-i}}{\beta_{t-j-i}}I_{t+1-j-i}^e-I_{t-j-i}^e)-\gamma_{33}(\dfrac{\beta_{t+1-j-i}}{\beta_{t-j-i}}\Delta N_{t+1-j-i}-\Delta N_{t-j-i})]
\end{bmatrix}
$$

$$
-\begin{bmatrix}
\sum_{i=0}^{J^s}\varphi_{Je-i}^e\sum_{j=0}^{J^s}\dfrac{\varphi_{Js-j}^s}{P_{t+Js-1-j-i}^q}\sum_{k=0}^{J^s+q^*}\beta_{t+k}I_{t+k-j-i}^s\sum_{1-\max(0,k-J^s)}^{\min(q^*,k)}\varphi_{Js-l}^s\Psi_l^s \\
\sum_{i=0}^{J^s}\varphi_{Je-i}^e\sum_{j=0}^{J^s}\dfrac{\varphi_{Js-j}^s}{P_{t+Je-1-j-i}^q}\sum_{k=0}^{J^s+q^*}\beta_{t+k}I_{t+k-j-i}^e\sum_{1-\max(0,k-J^s)}^{\min(q^*,k)}\varphi_{Je-l}^e\Psi_l^s \\
\sum_{i=0}^{J^s}\varphi_{Je-i}^e\sum_{j=0}^{J^s}\dfrac{\varphi_{Js-j}^s}{P_{t-j-i}^q}[\zeta(\exp(\zeta\Delta N_{t-j-i})-\dfrac{\beta_{t+1-j-i}}{\beta_{t-j-i}}\exp(\zeta\Delta N_{t+1-j-i})+\dfrac{\beta_{t+1-j-i}}{\beta_{t-j-i}}-1)]
\end{bmatrix}\mid \Omega_t\right\} = 0, \qquad (4.11)
$$

where $\alpha_i^* = \kappa^s\kappa^e\alpha_i$ $(i=1,2,3)$ because (see (4.7) and (2.4))

$$\sum_{j=0}^{J^i}\varphi_j^i = \kappa^i \quad \text{for} \quad i=s,e .$$

As productive capital stock is included in each Euler equation in (4.10) as a result of the interrelation in the production function (see (4.4)), a long construction period for structures or equipment (J^s or J^e large) induces rich dynamics in all Euler equations (4.11).

4.4 Empirical analyses

In this section estimation results for the specified model are given for the six countries. The first part gives more details about assumptions made and the estimation method used. In the second part the estimation results and related tests are presented and discussed.

4.4.1 Assumptions and estimation strategy

As a consequence of the asymmetry in the labour adjustment costs specification, the Euler equations (4.10) in the previous section are (besides being non-linear in the parameters) highly non-linear in the variables. Hence no closed form solution for the production factors can be derived[44]. For this reason the Generalized Method of Moments (GMM) of Hansen (1982) is used to estimate the implicit model solution (4.11).

Before implementing GMM, the set of instruments has to be chosen. At period t in (4.10), K_{t+Js-1}^s and K_{t+Jc-1}^c are determined and can not be changed due to the fixed investments plan. At time t , in the first equation of (4.10) expectations of variables of at most J^s+q^s periods in the future are included. At time t , in the second and third equation these expectations concern variables at most J^c+q^c and one period(s) in the future respectively[45].

Hence replacing the expectations by the realized variables in (4.10) gives rise to a disturbance error that is a (J^s+q^s)-th, a (J^c+q^c)-th and a first order MA forecast error respectively. The application of the filter in (4.11) then leads to a MA of $(2J^s+J^c+q^s)$-th, $(J^s+2J^c+q^c)$-th and (J^s+J^c+1)-th order. These MA orders are taken into account when calculating the weighting matrix and choosing the instruments of GMM.

In order to estimate (4.11), assumptions are to be made concerning the technology shock, λ_t (see (4.4)). It will be assumed that the technology shock is persistent and first order integrated. Therefore,

$$\Delta \lambda_t = e_t^\lambda, \tag{4.12}$$

where e_t^λ represents an innovation. This assumption diverges from the technology assumption of an autoregressive process (not a random walk) in for example Kydland

---

[44] It should be noted that if $\zeta=0$ in (4.6), which is plausible if the interrelation coefficients γ_{ij} $(i \neq j)$ catch the asymmetry in labour, the Euler equations are linear in the variables. Because of the lead times in capital, a closed form solution is however still not within easy reach. After all, the Euler equation of structures is a stochastic difference equation of J^s+q^s-th order.

[45] If $J^s>1$, the unknown variables at t in the first Euler equation of (4.11) are P_{t+Js-1}^q, $\lambda_{1,t+Js-1}$, K_{t+Js-1}^c, N_{t+Js-1}, C_{t+k}^s, I_{t+k}^c, ΔN_{t+k} and β_{t+k} for $k=1,2..J^s$ and I_{t+k}^s for $k=1,2..J^s+q^s$. Analogously for the second equation. However, if $J^s>J^c$, K_{t+Jc-1}^c in the second equation is known at t . The only unknown variables at t in the employment equation are I_{t+1}^s, I_{t+1}^c, ΔN_{t+1} and β_{t+1}.

and Prescott (1982, page 1352) and King, Plosser and Rebelo (1988, page 212)[46]. The main difference between the study here and these studies is however that the non-stationarity of the time series used here is not eliminated by a deterministic detrending method.

The differencing of (4.11) necessary to eliminate the unit root of the (unobservable) λ_t gives then rise to a disturbance vector that has a $(2J^s+J^e+q^s+1)$-th, $(J^s+2J^e+q^e+1)$-th and a (J^s+J^e+2)-th order MA in (4.11).

In the price equations (4.8), it will be assumed that $p^s=p^e=4$ and $q^s=q^e=1$. Investments prices can thus correlate contemporaneously and with a lag of one period by investment demand (see (4.8)). The price equations are jointly estimated with (4.11), among others for reasons of identification concerning ψ_j^i.

Finally the time-to-build lags for structures (J^s) and equipment (J^e) have to be determined. In a first model, structures are assumed to be built during a period of three quarters ($J^s=3$) while the gestation lag for equipment is assumed to be one quarter ($J^e=1$). This is according to Altug (1989) and chapter 3 where different construction periods for structures and equipment are also distinguished[47]. In a second model, these gestation lags are maintained but no interrelations are imposed. Off-diagonal elements in the production as well as in the adjustment costs function are assumed zero.

Instruments are chosen from a set of the own country's variables (among which the production factors and prices themselves) by using the method of principal components to find a small set of instruments. In order to guarantee the convergence of sample moments to population moments of each instrument orthogonal to each residual (being the sum of forecast errors and a technology innovation), conditions of ergodicity need to be satisfied. Since residuals are stationary provided that (4.12) is true, non-stationary (I(1)-) instrument variables are differenced once to obtain stationary instruments. For

---

[46] The I(1)-assumption is made here since estimating the model (4.11) (after quasi-differencing) with a first order autoregressive (diagonal) process for λ_t, gives technology parameters estimates that differ not significantly from one. It should be noticed that this is in contrast with the technology assumption in chapter 3. A main difference with the closed form model in chapter 3 is that here the information from the disturbance term is not fully taken into account, hence this (instrumental) estimation method is far less efficient than the method used in chapter 3. In addition, here many interrelations are already taken into account in the production function and adjustment costs function.

[47] Kydland and Prescott (1982) and Park (1984) assume a one year and a three quarters time-to-build for US total physical capital respectively. Altug (1989) estimates a one year and one quarter time-to-build for US structures and equipment respectively. They all base their time-to-build length on Mayer (1960) who show evidence on lead times of plants including equipment by questionnaires. In chapter 3 a three, four and five quarters time-to-build for structures in the Dutch and United States manufacturing industry is estimated, a time-to-build length based on on plant construction evidence from the Dutch construction industry (see chapter 2).

each country from a large set of instruments by the method of principal components a set of ten instruments is chosen that is strongly correlated with the endogenous factor variables. In the data appendix the used instruments sets are described.

As the order of the MA in model 1 is nine in the structures equation, seven in the equipment equation and six in the labour equation, the instruments are lagged ten, eight and seven quarters. By this choice the instruments and the error (including the technology shock innovation) are uncorrelated, provided that the technology shock is indeed according (4.12) with e_t^λ white noise.

To guarantee the positive definiteness of the covariance matrix of residuals, that can be obstructed as a consequence of the presence of the MA, the Parzen kernel is used (see for example Gallant (1987), page 445). Corrections for possible conditional heteroskedascity are made.

The estimates of model 2 are obtained in a similar way.

One remark remains to be made concerning the estimations. Although there are differences in MA orders across equations, the longest MA is taken into account in all equations when calculating the optimal weighting matrix. One reason for doing this is the difficulty to adjust the estimation program used[48]. A second reason is that even if program adjustments were possible, no guarantee exists for a positive definite weighting matrix; the use of a kernel is no longer sufficient to obtain positive definiteness when lag orders differ across equations. A third reason is that (cross) correlations equal to zero should be found (where they theoretically have to be zero) if the model under investigation is correct.

4.4.2 Estimation results

Tables 4.2a and 4.2b contain the GMM-results for the two models (M1 and M2) for each country. The first panel in these tables contains the coefficients of the production function. The coefficients of α (see (4.4)) are not given since they are not identified from the Euler equations. The second panel of the table contains the parameters of the internal adjustment costs function. In the column with model 2, being the model without interrelation, panel one and panel two do not contain the off-diagonal elements of matrix A and Γ (see (4.4) and (4.6)).

The third panel contains the time-to-build parameters. As a time-to-build of three

---

[48]   All GMM estimates are obtained with the TSP version 4.2b. This version starts with the non-linear three stage least squares method (NL3SLS), calculates the optimal weighting matrix with the (NL3SLS-)residuals, by which thereafter the GMM-estimates are obtained. Different MA orders among equations are not allowed.

quarters is imposed for structures, the depreciation of structures κ^s (see the bottom part of tables 4.2) is fixed for each country according to a value from FS and the CBS (see the data appendix). This is necessary to estimate the time-to-build parameters δ_j (j=1,2,3). The restriction $\delta_3 = 1 - \delta_1 - \delta_2$ (see (4.7)) is imposed, and the standard error of δ_3 is calculated from the estimated parameters δ_1 and δ_2 with Asymptotic Least Squares.

The fourth panel gives the investments coefficients in the price equations (4.8).

The last part of tables 4.2 contains the Sargan statistic (the J statistic) for overidentifying restrictions. The statistic is calculated by a multiplication of the number of observations by the (optimal) GMM-criterium value and is χ^2 distributed. Its number of degrees of freedom equals the number of equations (5) times the number of instruments (10) minus the number of parameters.

To account for seasonality, the model was first estimated equation by equation including (uncentered) season dummy variables (except for France). In a second step the model was jointly estimated restricting the coefficients of the dummy variables to the estimates from the first step to reduce the total number of parameters to estimate.

For the United Kingdom, a convergence problem was encountered concerning the asymmetry parameter ζ in the adjustment costs specification (see (4.6)). If these parameters ζ and γ_{33} are small, an identification problem exists[49]. For this reason, in these models ζ is set equal to zero (see also footnote 42 where it is explained that the interrelation coefficients are able to account for asymmetries).

The results can be interpreted as follows.

None of the estimated models is rejected according the Sargan statistic (even if the parameters for seasonal adjustments are accounted for), which supports among others the choice of instruments. The statistic is lowest for model 1, the model where a three quarter time-to-build is imposed and is most general. A direct comparison between the two models can however not be made using the Sargan statistics since weighting matrices differ among the models.

However, it is remarkable that the Sargan statistic does not increase with the number of degrees of freedom; model 2 with 23 degrees of freedom might be expected to have a

---

[49]   For the labour adjustment costs (see (4.6)) it holds that

$$\frac{1}{2}\gamma_{33}(\Delta N_t)^2 + \exp(\zeta \Delta N_t) - \zeta \Delta N_t - 1 = \frac{1}{2}(\gamma_{33} + \zeta^2)(\Delta N_t)^2 + \frac{1}{6}\zeta^3(\Delta N_t)^3 + \frac{1}{24}\zeta^4(\Delta N_t)^4 + ...$$

Thus if ζ is small, the last terms vanish. This causes problems since γ_{33} as well as ζ are to be identified from $\gamma_{33} + \zeta$.

Table 4.2a GMM estimates (4.11) in first differences and equations (4.8)

		United States		Canada		United Kingdom	
		M 1	M 2	M 1	M 2	M 1	M 2
P r o d u c t i o n	a_{11}	-0.25*	-0.22*	-0.13	-0.04**	-0.24*	-0.19*
	a_{12}	0.28		-0.21		-0.51**	
	a_{13}	-0.10		0.03		0.00	
	a_{22}	-0.44	0.68**	0.93	0.03	-0.28	-0.83***
	a_{23}	0.03		-0.31		-0.05	
	a_{33}	0.20	0.49***	0.42*	-0.39	0.54**	0.43***
I n t A d j u s t m	γ_{11}	0.21	0.21	-0.13	-0.10	0.19	0.38**
	γ_{12}	0.01		0.60*		0.09	
	γ_{13}	0.10**		-0.22*		-0.07*	
	γ_{22}	0.10	0.11	-0.71*	0.20*	-0.13	0.07
	γ_{23}	0.16**		0.04		0.03	
	γ_{33}	-1.31***	-0.82**	-1.59***	-2.99**	-0.09*	-0.06***
	ζ	-1.14***	-0.88***	1.22***	1.76***	.	.
T i m e T B	δ_1	0.47***	0.61**	0.22***	0.48***	0.02*	0.02**
	δ_2	0.14**	0.01	0.33***	0.40***	0.25***	0.24***
	δ_3	0.39**	0.38**	0.45**	0.12**	0.73**	0.74**
	φ_0^c	-0.90***	-0.99***	-1.03***	-0.21***	-0.42***	-0.36***
C a u s a l	ψ_0^s	-0.14**	-0.10*	0.10	0.07*	0.01	0.01
	ψ_1^s	0.14**	0.12*	-0.05	-0.04*	0.01	-0.01
	ψ_0^c	0.15	0.04	0.06	0.19**	0.16*	0.08**
	ψ_1^c	-0.11	0.00	-0.08	-0.18***	-0.18**	-0.12**
	κ^s	(0.0125)	(0.0125)	(0.0092)	(0.0092)	(0.007)	(0.007)
	Sargan	12.92 [17]	13.16 [23]	11.96 [17]	11.99 [23]	13.44 [18]	13.38 [24]

Table 4.2b GMM estimates (4.11) in first differences and equations (4.8)

		West-Germany		France		The Netherlands	
		M 1	M 2	M 1	M 2	M 1	M 2
P r o d u c t i o n	a_{11}	0.77***	1.23***	0.08***	0.04***	-0.47***	-0.47***
	a_{12}	-0.05***		0.11**		-0.09*	
	a_{13}	0.06***		0.03		-0.23***	
	a_{22}	-0.13	0.23***	0.01	-0.08**	0.05	0.55***
	a_{23}	0.37***		0.16**		1.61***	
	a_{33}	-1.47	-5.21***	0.72**	0.26*	-6.93***	-9.68***
I n t A d j u s t m	γ_{11}	-0.59***	-0.66***	-0.09***	-0.09***	0.00	0.10*
	γ_{12}	0.02		-0.11**		0.34***	
	γ_{13}	-0.01		-0.14**		0.14	
	γ_{22}	-0.61**	-0.83***	-0.37***	-0.10***	0.21*	-0.46***
	γ_{23}	-0.12**		0.14**		-0.81**	
	γ_{33}	-2.85*	-5.21***	-6.48***	-4.25**	-5.86	-59.71***
	ζ	-1.79***	-2.25***	-2.16***	-1.89***	-2.95*	8.39***
T i m e T B	δ_1	0.23***	0.14***	0.29***	0.27***	0.25***	0.17***
	δ_2	0.38***	0.35***	0.34***	0.36***	0.44***	0.44***
	δ_3	0.39***	0.51**	0.37***	0.37**	0.31***	0.39***
	φ_0^e	-0.71***	-0.57***	-0.59***	-0.53***	-0.51***	-0.36***
C a u s a l	ψ_0^s	0.05	0.02	0.01	0.02**	0.37***	0.28***
	ψ_1^s	0.06***	0.06***	-0.01	-0.02**	-0.35***	-0.26***
	ψ_0^e	0.21*	0.26***	0.27***	0.07***	-0.13**	0.14***
	ψ_1^e	-0.22*	-0.27***	-0.25***	-0.07***	0.03	-0.37***
	κ^s	(0.0108)	(0.0108)	(0.0135)	(0.0135)	(0.007)	(0.007)
	Sargan	12.92 [17]	14.01 [23]	9.44 [17]	10.46 [23]	8.85 [17]	9.48 [23]

Table 4.2c Remarks

*	Absolute t-value between 2 and 3
**	Absolute t-value between 3 and 5
***	Absolute t-value larger than 5

A missing value (.) for ζ indicates that the value could not be estimated.

δ_3 follows from $\delta_3 = 1 - \delta_1 - \delta_2$ and its standard error is calculated with Asymptotic Least Squares. The autoregressive coefficients of the price equations and quarterly dummies are not mentioned. The numbers between brackets are the values at which the depreciation of structures, κ^s, are fixed.

The numbers between square brackets are the degrees of freedom.

larger Sargan statistic than model 1 with 17 degrees of freedom. One reason for this can be that relatively too many instruments are taken into account in model 2. The Sargan statistic is in this case biased towards acceptance of the H_0-hypothesis (see also Tauchen (1986)). Another reason may be that instruments are lagged too many times. As interrelation is excluded in model 2, structures stocks do not appear in the equipment and labour equations by which theoretically a much lower MA results. Instruments for equation one, two and three could theoretically be nine, five and three quarters lagged instead of ten, eight and seven (see section 4.4.1). Tauchen (1986) investigates the small sample properties of GMM-estimators and finds among others that more biased but more efficient estimators result when using instruments that are lagged more often than the theoretical model presumes.

A comparison across countries shows that the production part (the first panel) of the countries in table 4.2b have many more significant estimates than the countries in table 4.2a. In the adjustment costs part (the second panel), the asymmetry parameter (when estimated) is overall clearly significant. For the United States, West-Germany and France an overall negative asymmetry is found, indicating higher firing than hiring costs. Only Canada shows the opposite result.

Overall the empirical evidence supports the time-to-build parameters δ_j ($j=1,2,3$)[50]; they have the right sign and are highly significant. In model 1 the investments during the

---

[50]   For all countries the models were also estimated without time-to-build in which $\varphi_1^i = 1$ and parameter φ_0^i is estimated (for $i = s,e$). Theoretically, both φ_0^s and φ_0^e should be between -1 and 0 (precisely $\kappa^i - 1$, see (4.8)-(4.9)) provided that a one period time-to-build exists. The estimates for this model show differences between φ_0^s and φ_0^e, supporting the disaggregation of investments. For the United Kingdom, West-Germany and the Netherlands φ_0^s clearly is too large whereas all φ_0^e parameters are close to the right value (that is -1), but are except for Canada better in model 1 (see tables 4.1a and 4.1b). So this one period time-to-build model is not preferred above model 1.

construction period in the United Stares decline after one period ($\delta_2 < \delta_3$) and increase in the last period ($\delta_1 > \delta_2$). For the Netherlands the distribution of investments is hump-shaped, whereas all other countries show a declining investments distribution for model 1.

In the fourth panel of table 4.2 the estimates of the price equations (4.8) are highly significant, especially for West-Germany, France and the Netherlands.

Table 4.3 Tests with model 1

	d.f.	US	CN	UK	WG	FR	NL
A diagonal	3	3.82	6.26	18.13**	158.46**	28.65**	78.80**
Γ diagonal	3	33.36**	28.01**	14.39**	27.70**	64.20**	316.35**
$\psi_0^s = \psi_1^s = 0$	2	2.32	3.87	8.94**	84.56**	12.73**	142.78**
$\psi_0^e = \psi_1^e = 0$	2	5.34*	4.86*	23.50**	12.77**	30.70**	84.22**
$\delta_2 = \delta_3 = 0$	2	231.19**	87.94**	2,520.04**	35,761.66**	2,721.21**	1,687.48**
det(A)		0.009	-0.054	-0.104	0.044	-0.009	1.501
		[0.68]	[-1.27]	[-1.11]	[0.31]	[-0.64]	[5.09]
det(HAC)		-0.006	0.05	0.003	0.139	-0.024	-0.427
		[-0.84]	[1.59]	[0.92]	[1.77]	[-0.18]	[-3.49]

* Significant at the 10% level
** Significant at the 5% level

The first rows are Wald tests of the hypotheses in the first column. D.f. are the degrees of freedom. The last two rows give the determinant of matrix A in (4.4) and the hessian of the adjustment costs function in (4.6). The value in square brackets is the t-value (calculated with Asymptotic Least Squares).

To test the importance of interrelation in the production function and in the adjustment costs function, Wald statistics are calculated for model 1. For each country the off-diagonal elements of A and Γ are imposed zero, giving a test statistic that is χ^2 distributed with three degrees of freedom. The calculated statistics are given in table 4.3. The interrelation in production function is not supported by the information in the data for the United States and Canada, whereas for all countries interrelations are found in the internal adjustment costs specification.

Similar statistics for the Granger causality of investments demand to nominal prices in equation (4.8) for structures and equipment separately are given. They show that for the United States and Canada no Granger causality from structures investments to their nominal prices exists. The causality for the equipment investments is found only marginally significant. These results are in contrast with those for the European countries. A somewhat surprising result is that equipment investments in the United Kingdom and France are not found significant in table 4.2 whereas the joint test for price impact on investments demand in table 4.3 turns out to be significant.

The Wald-statistics given in table 4.3 for the non-existence of a three period time-to-build ($\delta_1=1$ and $\delta_2=\delta_3=0$) shows the significance of time-to-build. Their extremely high significance is probably an artifact of the model; the time-to-build parameters appear in the three factor Euler equations (see (4.11)) and are forced to add up to the depreciation rate. These strong restrictions boost the t-values.

Table 4.3 contains further the determinants of matrix $\mathbf{A}$ and the hessian of the adjustment costs function. A t-value is calculated by Asymptotic Least Squares.

Strict concavity of the production function (4.4) and strict convexity of the internal adjustment costs function (4.6) require that $\mathbf{A}$ and the hessian of (4.6) are positive definite[51]. As table 4.3 shows, both these conditions are not satisfied for France. The rather remarkable result is that except for the Netherlands, no significantly positive determinant is found. So for model 1 for five countries decreasing returns to scale in the production function and strict convexity (so increasingness at the margin) of internal adjustment costs at the sample mean are not confirmed.

For the function (4.1) to have a maximimum it needs to be strictly concave. The function is of the form

$$\text{PROF}_t = \sum_{h=0}^{\infty} R_{t+h} - \text{IAC}_{t+h} - \text{EAC}_{t+h} - \text{VC}_{t+h}^- \tag{4.13}$$

where $\text{VC}_t^- \equiv \text{VC}_t - \text{EAC}_t$ (see (4.1) and (4.9)), and a filter is applied before estimating the necessary conditions ($\partial \text{PROF}_t / \partial X_t^d = 0$ where $X_t^d \equiv [K_{t+Js-1}^s \ K_t^e \ N_t]'$). Hence, even if R_t is not strictly concave and IAC_t is not strictly convex, the criterium function (4.1) or (4.13) can still be strictly concave. After all, two caveats with the model in this chapter apply, being the external adjustment costs and the time-to-build. Because of the intertemporality in the EAC_t and the time-to-build, the dominance of these features above the concavity of R_t or convexity of IAC_t (see (4.13)), is not easy to verify.

The graphs 4.2 to 4.7 highlight more clearly the shifts in production and adjustment costs (Γ and ζ) parameters among models. The left figures concern model 1, the right

---

[51] As the hessian of (4.6) depends on ΔN_t, the hessian is here calculated at the sample mean of ΔN_t.

Graph 4.2 United States

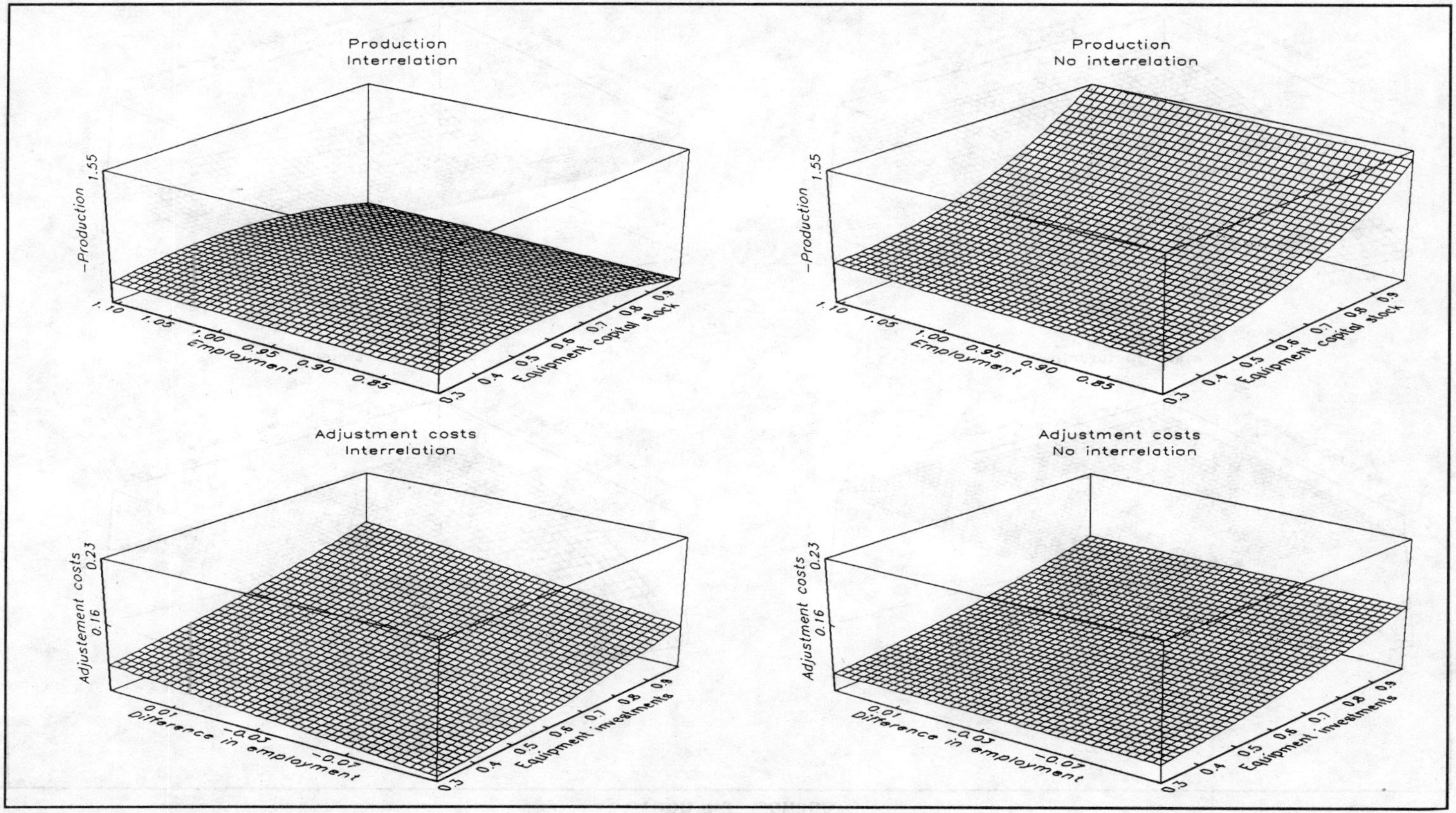

Graph 4.3 Canada

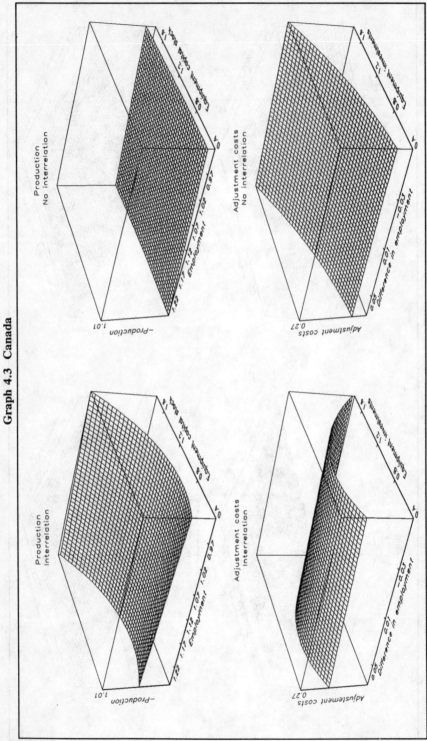

Graph 4.4 United Kingdom

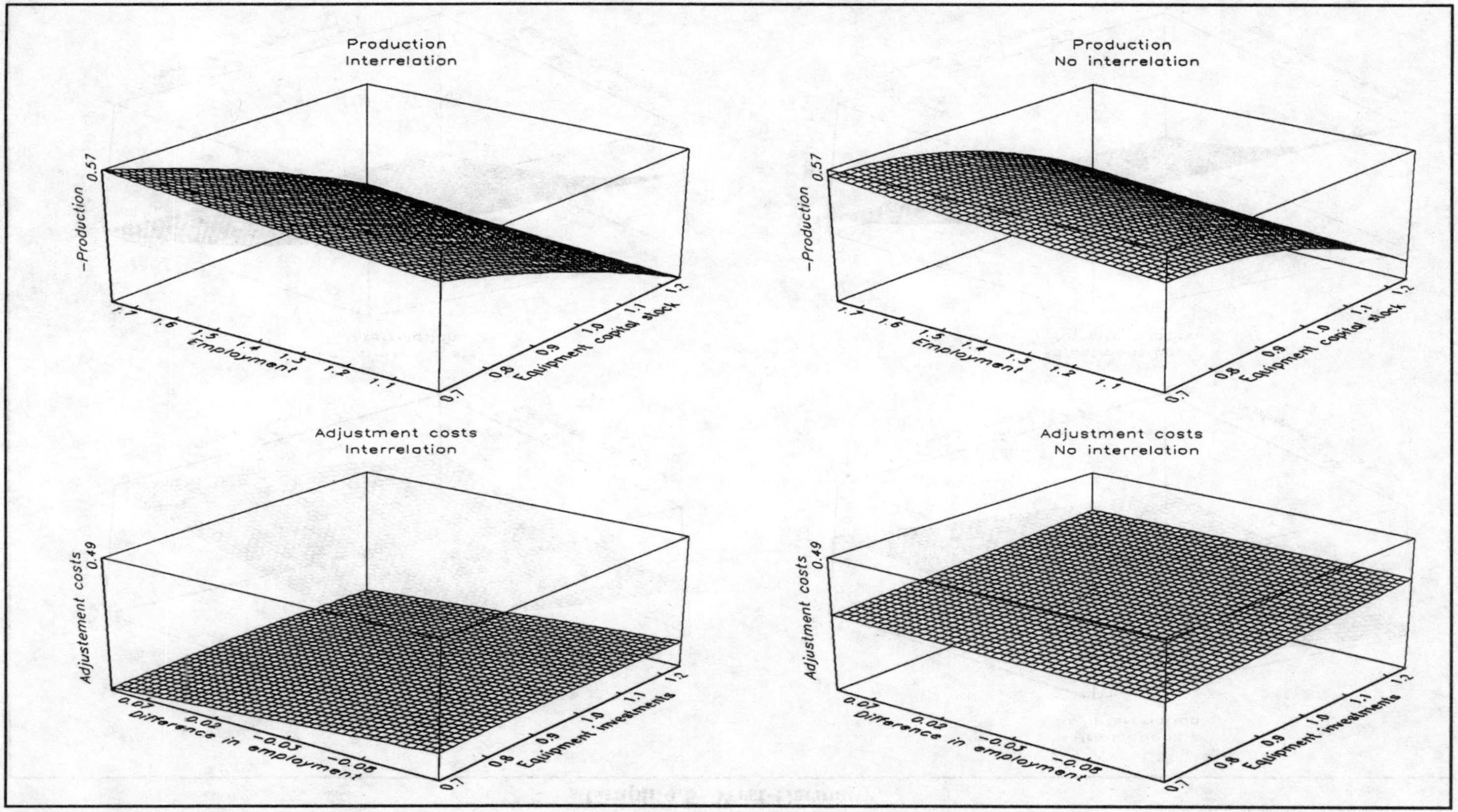

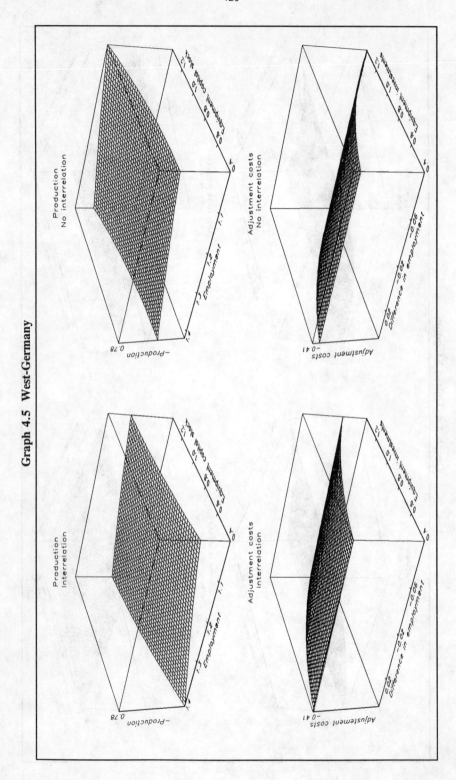

Graph 4.5 West-Germany

Graph 4.6 France

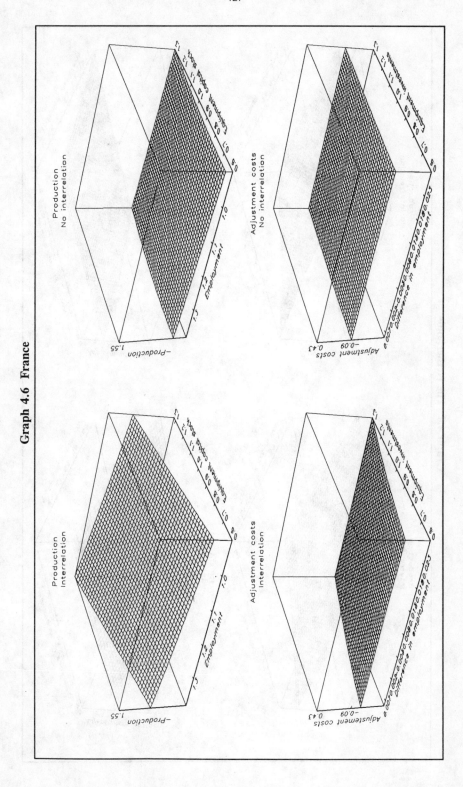

Graph 4.7 The Netherlands

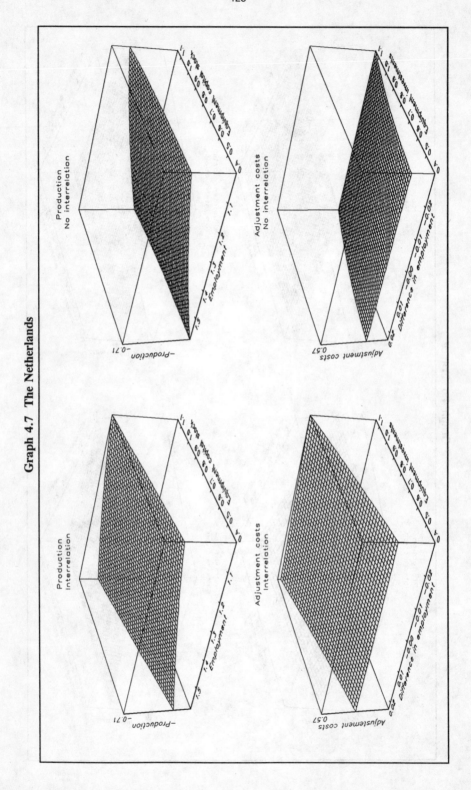

figures concern model 2. The upper part concerns the quadratic part of the production function for combinations of employment and equipment capital. The bottom part concerns the adjustment cost function (4.6) for combinations of differences in employment (ΔN_t) and equipment (I_t^e). Only the ranges of the sample values are taken into account (but ranges for capital stock are arbitrary). Structures, that have to be fixed to graph the functions, are here set at an average value. The function ranges (vertical axes) are the same across graphs horizontally to be able to compare parameter changes across models.

In order to be convex, the production figures have to be declining towards the intersection of both axis in the foreground. For example the second production figure in the United States graph (in the upper right part of graph 4.2) indicates that the marginal productivity of labour increases much if equipment capital increases.

A comparison of both models (the left figures with the right ones) shows the often considerable differences as a consequence of accounting for interrelation. Another feature that is striking in these graphs is the unobservable asymmetry in adjustment costs. This is a consequence of the much more dominating interrelations between ΔN_t and investments outlays. In addition, a negative estimate for γ_{33} plays a role.

Some reasons to worry become apparent here. Negative internal adjustment costs are found for France in the first model and for West-Germany in both models. They imply that additional investments and changes in employment incur revenues instead of costs for the entrepreneur. An explanation for these results is difficult to find.

To obtain more insights in the costs of the different production factors, measurements of the average and marginal costs are given. Table 4.4 gives the results for model 1. For each production factor the average variable costs (AVC_t) are calculated as the sample averages of the variable costs (without external adjustment costs) divided by the total costs. Average adjustment costs (AAC_t) are calculated analogously. Total costs are the sum of the variable costs (see (4.5)) and the internal adjustment costs (see (4.6)). Marginal adjustment costs (MAC_t) are calculated as the sample average of the marginal (internal and external) adjustment costs divided by the factor price. For example, for structures the sample average is calculated by

$$AVC_t \equiv [C_t^s I_t^s - \psi_0^s (I_t^s)^2 - \psi_1^s I_t^s I_{t-1}^s]/TC_t, \quad IAAC_t \equiv [\frac{1}{2}\gamma_{11}(I_t^s)^2 + \gamma_{12}I_t^s I_t^e + \gamma_{13}I_t^s \Delta N_t]/TC_t,$$

$$EAAC_t \equiv [\psi_0^s (I_t^s)^2 + \psi_1^s I_t^s I_{t-1}^s]/TC_t, \quad IMAC_t \equiv [\gamma_{11}I_t^s + \gamma_{12}I_t^e + \gamma_{13}\Delta N_t]/C_t^s$$

and

$$EMAC_t \equiv [2\psi_0^s I_t^s + \psi_1^s (I_{t-1}^s + \frac{\beta_{t+1}}{\beta_t} I_{t+1}^s)]/C_t^s$$

where

$TC_t \equiv IAC_t + VC_t$ (see (4.5) and (4.6))[52].

If no interrelations in the adjustment costs function exist, that is if Γ in (4.6) is diagonal, the sum of the AVC_t and AAC_t together should equal one. In this case also the MAC_t should be positive for labour in an expansionary, $\Delta N_t > 0$, (contraction, $\Delta N_t < 0$) regime. Because of the interrelations and the much larger investments outlays it makes however no sense to distinguish between these different regimes.

The average variable costs (AVC_t) show that between the three production factors no large divergencies exist. The average internal adjustment costs (AAC_t) show theoretically implausible negative values for Canada and, very prominently, for West-Germany and France as was already detected in graphs 4.5 and 4.6. External adjustment costs and marginal investment adjustment costs sometimes also turn out to be negative but relatively small for the other four countries. As here no significance values are given, nothing is said about the significance.

For countries where 'right' signs are found, that is the United States, Canada, the United Kingdom and the Netherlands obviously average labour adjustments are much lower than average investments costs. Average marginal labour adjustment costs are not found to be less than investments for all countries, a result that is in contradiction with the findings of Pindyck and Rotemberg (1983a) who use a model without interrelations (and thus find overall positive signs) for the United States. For the United Kingdom and the Netherlands a decrease by one unit of labour turns out to be more costly than an increase by one unit of equipment. The same result for the hiring of labour holds for the United States.

External average adjustment costs do not seem very important, but external marginal costs for structures have relatively high values for Canada, the United Kingdom and the Netherlands. However, the non-stationarity of the calculated series plays a role in these calculations (which follows from graphs that are not given here).

The main findings may therefore be that the estimation results for West-Germany and France are not interpretable and other costs, except for the average variable, differ considerably across countries. The results of Pindyck and Rotemberg of much larger marginal than average costs and much less marginal labour than marginal investment cost are only in some cases confirmed.

The calculation of marginal costs would become economically more interesting if a relation could be established with the marginal productivity. After all, if profitable

---

[52]   A feature of the calculation of the adjustment costs is that the average costs are always an overestimation of the actual AAC_t if the adjustment costs function is strictly convex. This calculation (that is averaging adjustment costs of a production factor instead of adjustment costs of the average factor flow, see for example Pindyck and Rotemberg (1983a, p. 235), is here chosen to account for non-stationarity of the series.

Table 4.4 Average and marginal costs with model 1

			US	CN	UK	WG	FR	NL
AVC		Structures	0.31	0.28	0.27	0.59	0.48	0.31
		Equipment	0.25	0.28	0.27	0.52	0.36	0.25
		Labour	0.32	0.28	0.24	0.53	0.40	0.36
AAC	I	Structures	0.08	0.31	0.24	**-0.67**	**-0.14**	0.08
		Equipment	0.02	0.17	0.05	**-0.19**	**-0.20**	0.09
		Labour	0.0003	**-0.0004**	0.0002	**-0.0004**	0.0001	0.0007
	E	Structures	**-0.0004**	0.03	0.03	0.25	0.00	0.008
		Equipment	0.01	**-0.01**	**-0.01**	**-0.002**	0.01	**-0.02**
MAC	I	Structures	0.51	0.94	1.70	**-1.49**	**-0.36**	0.25
		Equipment	0.14	**-0.01**	0.06	**-0.75**	**-0.87**	0.45
		Labour	0.45	-0.53	-0.46	-0.25	-0.10	-0.47
	E	Structures	**-0.02**	0.26	0.28	0.55	0.003	0.09
		Equipment	0.11	**-0.06**	**-0.07**	**-0.01**	0.11	**-0.13**

AVC are average variable costs. AAC are average adjustment costs. MAC are marginal
adjustment costs. I and E refer to internal and external costs respectively.
Figures printed bold should theoretically be positive.

production possibilities exist, high marginal costs can still make entrepreneurs willing to
pay high adjustment costs. Establishing this relation is here however not possible since
only the curvature of the production function (matrix A in (4.4)) is identified in the
analyses.

Finally, some statistics are given concerning the residuals of the models. In model 1 a
ninth, seventh and sixth order MA are expected. In order to draw inferences concerning
these orders, simple autocorrelations are calculated here.
The results, given in the last columns of table 4.5, indicate that for structures no
autocorrelation of tenth order is found. So, there is no reason to extend the time-to-
build to four quarters (instead of $J=3$ in model 1). Remarkable however is the high
autocorrelation left in the equipment series in the United States, France and the
Netherlands and even more prominently in the labour series of Canada, the United
Kingdom and West-Germany. The cross correlations (not given here) are also
significant. As the three production factors are interrelated, a negligence of for example
gestation lags in equipment can leave serial correlation in labour. Thus although its
existence can not be denied, the cause for the remaining serial correlations is not easy
to detect.

Table 4.5 Residuals tests for model 1

		AU7	AU8	AU9	AU10
US	S	0.02	0.07	-0.04	-0.13
	E	0.40*	**-0.32***	**0.26***	**-0.24***
	N	**0.38***	**-0.25***	0.20	-0.17
CN	S	-0.21*	-0.04	-0.11	0.12
	E	0.10	-0.12	-0.11	0.15
	N	**-0.36***	**0.29***	**-0.30***	**0.27***
UK	S	-0.14	0.25*	-0.17	0.06
	E	0.02	0.01	0.04	-0.15
	N	**-0.32***	**0.36***	**-0.38***	**0.26***
WG	S	-0.02	0.01	-0.08	-0.05
	E	-0.23*	0.18	-0.03	-0.06
	N	**0.30***	**-0.32***	0.14	-0.08
FR	S	-0.03	-0.05	-0.08	0.05
	E	-0.16	0.06	-0.01	**0.27***
	N	0.08	0.02	0.02	-0.02
NL	S	0.02	0.09	0.02	-0.16
	E	0.14	**0.45***	-0.18	**-0.32***
	N	0.10	0.04	0.02	-0.21

* Significant at 5% level
AU7-AU10 are the autocorrelations of 7,8,9 and 10 orders of the residuals of model 1. They are normally distributed with zero mean and variance $1/\sqrt{T}$, where T is the sample size. Significant autocorrelations printed bold should theoretically be insignificant.

4.5   Summary and conclusions

In this chapter a dynamic model with rich interrelations for investments and labour demand is specified. Construction lags are estimated for structures investments and asymmetric adjustment costs for labour are included in the model. Persistence, interrelation and asymmetries found in the individual series are in this way assumed to have an economic interpretation. The first order conditions are estimated using GMM, a method that accounts for serially correlated, symmetrically distributed error terms. Manufacturing industry time series of six countries are used in the empirical part.

The main results can be summarized as follows.

For all countries interrelations between investments and labour are highly significant, in particularly in the dynamic part of the specification. For the European countries also highly significant relations in the production function exist. These results imply that it is not unimportant to include investments also when labour is the main focus in empirical studies and vice versa. For example, Burda (1991) and Sensenbrenner (1991) include only labour and investments respectively in their international studies, but interrelations with the neighbour production factor (investments and labour respectively) are not mentioned to be of importance.

The implied time-to-build for structures is not rejected. Similar conclusions were found previously by Altug (1989) for structures in the United States using a general equilibrium model, Park (1984) in a multi sector model with both adjustment costs and flexible time-to-build plans for United States capital, and in chapter 3 for structures in a factor demand model for the United States and the Netherlands.

In comparison with this chapter, in chapter 3 a far less general model was specified and estimated by a different estimation method. A comparison of the results obtained in chapter 3 and 4, for the United States and the Netherlands, show that time-to-build is highly significant but, for example, a rather different investment schedule during the construction period is found. Besides the estimation method used, this is of course also due to the rather different assumptions concerning the interrelations in the technology process, the production function, the adjustment cost function and the price influencing equations. The main result of chapter 3, being the insignificance of structures adjustment costs in addition to time-to-build, seems however for the United States, Canada, the United Kingdom and the Netherlands also to be insignificant in a model with interrelations (see the parameter estimates of γ_{11} of model 1, table 4.2). The results of West-Germany and France do however not corroborate these findings, but as should be reminded, some peculiar results for these countries were obtained here.

In this chapter the concavity of the production function and convexity of the internal adjustment costs function, that are not inherent in their adopted functional forms, were checked. It turns out that except for the Netherlands, the strict concavity of the production function and strict convexity of the adjustment costs function are not significant. Decreasing returns to scale are hence rejected. Adjustment costs that are increasing at the margin are more often criticized or differently modelled (in for example Bentolila and Bertola (1990) who adopt piecewise linear labour adjustment costs), is thus also not confirmed in this chapter.

The economically more convincing existence of asymmetry in internal adjustment costs, is here corroborated. With zero investments, employment costs are higher in the expansionary than in the contractionary regime for Canada. The results for the United States, West-Germany, France and the Netherlands turn out oppositely. Asymmetries in labour adjustment for the United Kingdom could unfortunately not be estimated here. Evidence for the existence of larger firing than hiring costs in France, West-Germany, the United Kingdom and Italy was presented by Bentolila and Bertola (1990).

The importance of labour adjustment costs in the model is however overshadowed here by the investments. Unlike the studies of Pfann and Palm (1993) and Bresson et al. (1993) where labour demand is analyzed and capital demand costs do not count, the investment outlays dominate the average adjustment costs. Marginally labour costs play a considerable role but on average far less. The interrelations in the adjustment cost function seem even to be able to catch the asymmetry in labour adjustments, by which a much simpler adjustment cost function to estimate becomes possible (see footnote 42).

External investment adjustment costs are found to be much less important, except for West-Germany where they even seem to dominate the internal adjustment costs.

Like the model in chapter 3, a general problem with the time-to-build model is the observational equivalence of time-to-build and technology assumptions (see the remarks below table 3.1). Assuming longer lasting persistence of technology shocks can generate the same reduced form dynamics as a multi-period time-to-build. Therefore also in this chapter, the proposed model is estimated imposing all parameter restrictions implied by the theoretical model to verify immediately values of structural parameters.

Another problem is that as a consequence of assuming different gestation lengths for structures and equipment (and labour) together with interrelations in the production function, different orders of the moving average error terms in all Euler equations occur. With GMM this information is not fully taken into account which probably leads to a loss of efficiency. This is in contrast with the FIML estimation method used in chapter 3 that assumes a distribution and takes into account all restriction across (moving average) terms. In the model with high interrelations in this chapter, the assumption of a technology process that is integrated of first order was to be made according the estimation results.

Along with all this, to obtain reliable results with the rather long moving averages, large sample sizes would be needed whereas time series are (unfortunately) relatively short. Further improvements and extensions of models with investments gestation lags as in this chapter, like using a more general production or output market structures specifications, unfortunately are probably not feasible because of the lack of reliable capital stock series.

APPENDIX 4.A
Factor prices exogeneity, monopolistic competition or price influencing

In this appendix the possible endogeneity of prices in the model of section 4.3.1 is considered. Endogeneity of output prices may indicate monopolistic competition whereas endogeneity of nominal wages and nominal investments prices may indicate price influencing.

In chapter 3, where only simple Likelihood Ratio tests within VAR-systems were carried out, the exogeneity of real factor prices is assumed. Test statistics associated with the Error Correction Model are carried out here to verify the weak exogeneity, and causality of the variables.

4.A.1 An example

As the model in this appendix has only an illustrative purpose, no unnecessary assumptions are made.

Two production factors, K_t and N_t, referred to as capital and labour, and their nominal prices C_t^n (investments price) and W_t^n (wage) are taken into account. An entrepreneur is assumed to maximize profits,

$$\max_{K_t, N_t} \quad P_t^q Q_t - C_t^n I_t - W_t^n N_t \quad \text{where} \quad Q_t = f(K_t, N_t) \quad \text{and} \quad P_t^q = g(Q_t). \tag{4A.1}$$

The function f is a production function, giving the relation between (value added) production (Q_t) and the vector of capital and labour ($X_t \equiv [K_t \ N_t]'$), and is assumed to be marginally increasing ($\partial f/\partial X_t > 0$) at a decreasing rate ($\partial^2 f/\partial X_t^2 \leq 0$). The function g is the demand function, giving the relation between the output price P_t^q and demand for the product. The output market is assumed to clear, i.e. production and product demand coincide, by which the demand equation is a function in Q_t.

In the literature about factor demand modelling it is often assumed that $\partial g/\partial Q_{t-i} = 0$ ($i = 0,1,2..$), in which case the entrepreneur cannot affect the market price level by Q_t. As a price taker in the output market, the entrepreneur chooses X_t such that profits are maximized, i.e.

$$\max_{X_t} \quad P_t^q Q_t - C_t^n I_t - W_t^n N_t = \max_{X_t} \quad Q_t - C_t I_t - W_t N_t \tag{4A.2}$$

where $C_t \equiv C_t^n/P_t^q$ and $W_t \equiv W_t^n/P_t^q$ are the real investments price and the real wage. Modelling the entrepreneur's objective function along this line and without further assumptions, implies that real prices are assumed to be weakly exogenous and not Granger caused by labour[53].

One way to circumvent the assumption that X_t does not cause $P_t \equiv [C_t \ W_t]'$ in a model like (4A.2), is to assume that $\partial g/\partial Q_t \leq 0$ (see for example Burda (1991)). If $\partial g/\partial Q_t < 0$, the entrepreneur faces a negatively sloping demand curve, and influences his revenues $(P_t^q Q_t)$ by his labour demand not only by increasing the production but also by decreasing the product price. The entrepreneur is thus a monopolist in the output market. In this case not only production factors and output, but also real factor prices are endogenous.

For example Sargent (1978) investigates the Granger causal relationships between United States total civilian employment (in persons) and real wages. He concludes that real wages cause employment but the reverse relationship does not hold[54]. In contrast with these findings of Sargent, the insider/outsider theory supposes that the number of insiders, i.e. the number of persons employed, has a determining influence on (nominal) wages. This conclusion that N_t influences W_t^n, is in contradiction with the (for example Sargent's) conclusion that N_t does not Granger cause W_t^n.

As in the section 4.3.1 a dynamic model is specified for structures and equipment investments (I_t^s and I_t^e) and labour (N_t), the purpose here is to test for the exogeneity of the vector of real production factor prices $[C_t^s \ C_t^e \ W_t^n]' \equiv [C_t^{sn}/P_t^q \ C_t^{en}/P_t^q \ W_t^n/P_t^q]'$.

4.A.2 Weak exogeneity and Granger causality tests

As time series are used, non-stationarity properties can not be neglected. Therefore the error correction model of Johansen (see Johansen and Juselius (1990)) is used, being

---

[53] $P_t \equiv [C_t \ W_t]'$ is called weakly exogenous for the parameters in the model if these parameters can correctly be estimated and correct inference conditional on P_t is possible, whereas Granger causality implies that P_t does not depend on X_t, X_{t-1}.. (see Engle et al. (1983) for formal definitions).

[54] Although real wages are measured by him in an inappropriate way because a consumer price index is taken as the deflator (P_t^q) instead of the value added price (see Nickell and Symons (1990), who compare the differences in the potential deflators consumer, producer and value added prices), a negative influence is found from wages to employment. This Keynesian, inverse relationship between wages and labour is also confirmed in an international study by Bruno and Sachs (1985).

Table 4A.1 Weak exogeneity and Granger causality tests

	k	D_t	$H_{01} : P_t$ w.exog.	$H_{02} : I_t^a \not\to C_t^a$	$H_{03} : I_t^e \not\to C_t^e$	$H_{04} : N_t \not\to W_t$
US	4	c,q1-q3,t	43,47**	20,16**	39,87**	11,07*
CN	5	c,q1-q3,t	36,32**	15,10*	12,27	10,93
UK	6	c,q1-q3,t	58,99**	14,38*	17,05**	9,76
WG	4	c,q1-q3	18,45*	3,52	7,15	1,81
FR	4	c	73,58**	6,28	8,83	9,12
NL	2	c,q1-q3	31,60**	2,69	22,96**	1,82
D.f.			9	k	k	k

* Significant at the 5%-level
** Significant at the 1%-level

c,q1-q3 represent a constant and three quarterly dummies respectively. t represents a deterministic linear trend that is included in the cointegration (or level) space.
D.f. are the degrees of freedom.

$$\Delta Z_t = \Gamma_0 D_t + \sum_{i=1}^{k-1} \Gamma_i \Delta Z_{t-i} + \Pi Z_{t-k} + e_t^Z \quad \text{where} \quad \Pi \equiv \alpha \beta', \qquad (4A.3)/(3B.3)$$

where D_t includes the deterministic variables and Γ_i (i=0,1..k-1) and Π are the constant parameter matrices to be estimated. See also appendix 3.B on these issues. Tests for weak exogeneity can be applied by imposing zero-rows in the α matrix. Tests for Granger causality consist of imposing zero restrictions on α, β and Γ_i (i=0,1..k-1).

Firstly, in the error correction model (4A.3) k, accounting for autocorrelation in Z_t, and the number of cointegrating relationships has to be determined. For all the time series under investigation, unit root tests are applied (whose statistics are not presented here) according to Fuller (1976). The unit root hypothesis is in all cases not evidently rejected and a second unit root is not found. For each country the number of lags k in (4A.3) are then chosen as the number where no univariate autocorrelation tests in the residuals is found (according to Box-Pierce tests, 5%-level). For all countries here under investigation about three cointegration relations were found, sometimes by choosing a deterministic trend t in D_t. The dimension of α and β is thus determined to be 6x3.

First the weak exogeneity of the block of real production prices is tested. The null-hypothesis is

H_{01} : $\{\alpha_{ij}\} = 0$, i=4,5,6, j=1,2,3 ($P_t \equiv [C_t^s \ C_t^e \ W_t]'$ is weakly exogenous)

where $\alpha := \{\alpha_{ij}\}$. The test statistic is χ^2 with nine degrees of freedom.

The results are given in table 4A.1. H_{01} is in all cases rejected by which the vector of prices can not be assumed weakly exogenous in a model like (4A.3). This rejection of P_t is also a rejection of strong exogeneity[55] of P_t. The existence of monopolistic competition, that is $\partial g/\partial X_t < 0$ in (4A.3), is therefore not rejected.

The non-rejection in many cases of individual price weak exogeneity assumptions (whose statistics are not given here) does not give information about the existence of Granger causality. Price influencing behaviour may take place at the structures (I_t^s), equipment (I_t^e) and/or labour (N_t) market instead of at the output (Q_t) market. For example, if I_t^e causes C_t^{en} (in notation $I_t^e \rightarrow C_t^{en}$) and monopolistic competition does not exist ($Q_t \nrightarrow P_t^q$, so $I_t^s \nrightarrow P_t^q$ and $I_t^e \nrightarrow P_t^q$ and $N_t \nrightarrow P_t^q$), the Granger causal relationship $I_t^e \rightarrow C_t^e$ has to be found[56] but possibly $I_t^s \nrightarrow C_t^s$ and $N_t \nrightarrow W_t$. After all, monopolistic competition only exist if $I_t^s \rightarrow C_t^s$ and $I_t^e \rightarrow C_t^e$ and $N_t \rightarrow W_t$. Granger causality tests are here further applied in order to test whether such a causal relationship may exist on a factor market.

Granger causality tests in error correction models like (4A.3) are far less trivial than weak exogeneity tests. A sequential method to test for Granger causality within a system of non-stationary variables is given by Toda and Phillips (1991 and 1993b). However, difficulties arise when k in (4A.3) becomes too large, which often occurs in investments studies (see Toda et al. (1991), page 22 and section 4.3.2 here). Moreover, as they summarize in their findings according to simulation studies (Toda et al. (1991), page 24) these tests are not supported if more than three variables are used and sample sizes become smaller than 100.

Therefore, still in order to gain insights in the causality of the series, only bivariate Granger causality tests are applied here according to Mosconi and Giannini (1992) (with their RATS-program). In contrast with the Granger causality Wald tests of Toda et al. (1991,1993b) these tests are generalisations of the Likelihood Ratio tests of Johansen et al. (1990) where $\Pi = \alpha \beta'$ is maintained under both the null and alternative hypothesis. Only *bivariate* tests are easily applicable here since the only possibility to test for causality from a (set of) variable(s) to *all* other variable(s) within the system.

---

[55] P_t is strongly exogenous if and only if P_t is weakly exogenous for the parameters in the model and not Granger caused by $[I_t^s \ I_t^e \ N_t]'$. The rejection of Granger non-causality is neither a sufficient nor a necessary condition for weak exogeneity (see Engle et al. (1983)).

[56]   Here is assumed that if $I_t^s \rightarrow C_t^{en}$ and/or $I_t^s \rightarrow P_t^q$ then $I_t^s \rightarrow C_t^s \equiv C_t^{en}/P_t^q$.

the calculation of the likelihood value under the H_0 is an iterative procedure that becomes more complicated if the number of causal variables exceeds the number of cointegration relationships.

For these reasons, the hypotheses for the statistics presented are

$$H_0 : \{\Gamma_i\}_{21} = 0 \quad \text{for } i=1,2..k-1, \qquad \{\Pi\}_{21} = 0, \quad \Pi = \alpha\beta' \qquad (VF_t \nrightarrow VP_t)$$

where $(VF_t, VP_t) \in \{(I_t^s, C_t^s),(I_t^e, C_t^e),(N_t, W_t)\}$ is taken as the vector under investigation in H_{02}–H_{04} and the dimension of Π is imposed to be 1 (thus $\alpha, \beta \in \mathbb{R}^{2x1}$). The order k is maintained as under H_{01}.

The results in table 4A.1 show that for the United States $I_t^s \nrightarrow C_t^s$, $I_t^e \nrightarrow C_t^e$ and (marginally) $N_t \nrightarrow W_t$ are rejected. Thus either the hypothesis of price influencing at the output market or the hypothesis of price influencing by investments demand at the individual factor input markets cannot be rejected. In contrast with these United States results, the assumptions of price influencing in the other countries is often rejected. Real wages seem clearly not influenced by employment. Hence the assumption of monopolistic competition in the manufacturing industry output market is rejected.

4.A.3   Conclusions

The results can be summarized as follows.

Weak exogeneity test rejections indicate that parameter estimation and inference might be improved by explicitly taking into account the process of each factor price (that may depend on the other prices). For elaborations on the issue of weak exogeneity, see for example Urbain (1993). The tests that are carried out here, reject the hypothesis of weak exogeneity of the three (real) product prices within a system of six variables.

Granger causality tests are applied to test whether a causality from a production factor to a real price exists. Non-stationarity properties of the time series are taken into account. As these tests are not applicable within large systems of variables and in small samples (see Toda et al. (1991), page 24), only bivariate tests among one production factor and its real price are carried out.

The results show that employment (measured in hours) does not evidently influence real wages. On the equipment market a price influencing behaviour $(I_t^e \rightarrow C_t^{en})$ is accepted for the United Kingdom and the Netherlands. Results for the United States can be interpreted as monopolistic competition in the output market and/or a price influencing behaviour on the structures, equipment and/or labour market. As however labour influencing real wages is only marginally accepted, the second interpretation seems most appropriate.

Monopolistic competition can be expected in closed economies; the manufacturing industry is the only supplier of manufacturing goods, so output prices influencing can be expected to exist. The existence of price influencing by investments demand can be expected if the manufacturing industry is a large demander on the domestic capital goods market in open economies; as the manufacturing industry is a supplier of capital goods, price influencing of these input investments goods will most naturally occur if no monopolistic competition occurs. The test results here do not contradict these reasonings.

In order to take account of the possible Granger causal relation between investments and their prices, in section 4.3.1 for each country a price equation for both structures and equipment separately (see (4.8)) is estimated.

As should be noticed, the results obtained here concerning the United States and the Netherlands differ from the assumption made in chapter 3 that no Granger causality from production factors to real prices exist. The model in chapter 4 is hence on this point more general.

CHAPTER 5
INTERRELATIONS IN PHYSICAL CAPITAL STOCK, LABOUR AND INVENTORY INVESTMENTS
An application to French industrial sectors

5.1   Introduction

In the previous two chapters, a factor demand model was specified with structures, equipment and labour that incur adjustment costs and structures that need time to be built. In this chapter the role of inventories in a factor demand model is investigated.

Most factor demand studies do not include inventories by which it is assumed that, either inventories may exist but do not incur costs, or inventories do not exist and consequently each good that is produced is sold instantaneously. As inventories generally entail costs and certainly exist in industries that do not always produce to order, both assumptions seem to be inaccurate, in particular on aggregate levels.

To investigate the role of inventories, a factor demand model is specified that includes inventories. The specified model differs from the models used in the previous chapters in some respects to simplify the econometric analyses.

A first difference is that a cost minimizing approach (see for example Diewert and Wales (1987), instead of a profit maximizing approach is adopted. Thus in this chapter no attention is paid to the market structure on the goods market and input prices are assumed exogenous. The reason for adopting this cost minimizing approach is the difficulty to suitably endogenize production and/or input prices and to focus on the production cost structure at the same time.

A second difference is that structures and equipment investments are not distinguished, but comprised as total investments. Evidence for long time-to-build periods that was found in previous chapters, is accounted for by the calculation of productive capital stock according to a time-to-build scheme. Hence, a multi-period time-to-build is incorporated in the capital stock series that will be used in a flexible cost function.

One objective of this chapter is to investigate the importance of inventories in relation with physical capital stock and labour. Accumulating inventory stocks, for example, requires investments to keep these stocks. A relation between inventories and labour seems even more clear. The possibility to hold inventories may let entrepreneurs hoard labour or delay recruitments when it is costly to change the incumbent labour force.

A second objective of this chapter is to compare the factor demand model including inventories with the production smoothing model. This last model is used very often in the inventory literature, but seems far less specific concerning costs modelling than the factor demand model.

In literature inventories, indicating a disequilibrium on the product market and thus differences between production and sales, have received much attention.

For example Blinder (1986) induced a critical review of production smoothing models. If costs of adjusting production are high relative to inventory costs, inventories may be held to smooth production. In this case the variability of production must be less than the variability of sales. However, empirically opposite results are found. Blinder (1982 and 1986) emphasises among other things the importance of the demand side, the persistence in demand shocks. He thus implicitly casts doubt on factor demand studies that only take into account the supply side of the goods markets.

On the other hand, several studies rationalize the higher volatility (measured by the variance) of production above sales. For example West (1987) indicates that the backlog of unfilled orders acts as a buffer between production and sales, whereas most studies take into account net inventories, that is inventories minus backlogs. Ramey (1991) finds producers bunching production as a consequence of concave instead of (the often assumed) convex production costs. Gregoir and Laroque (1992) pay attention to the non-stationarity of time series used. They emphasize the fact that a higher variance of production in comparison with sales is not necessarily in contradiction with sales and inventories correlating negatively. Using French industrial micro data, they do not confirm earlier findings of sales and inventories increases (decreases) accompanying each other.

Whether or not inventories smooth production, a major fact is that they exist, are only a small part of production (or GNP), but are highly volatile (see for example Blinder (1986) or Christiano (1988)). Their impact in producer's decision making concern the costs they entail, and their interrelation with the main determinants in the production process, such as capital and labour.

Quarterly balance sheet time series data from French sectors (1970.I-1992.IV) are used here as an application. The sectors are the agricultural, the intermediate goods, the professional equipment, consumers equipment, transport equipment and consumption goods sector. The following three main inventory literature fields are then consecutively crossed.

First, the non-stationarity of the individual series and multi-cointegration between production, sales and inventories are tested. As goods are produced to be sold, production and sales must cointegrate. The cointegration (or so called multi-cointegration) with inventories stocks is less evident. This is however very often modelled, following Holt, Modigliani, Muth and Simon (1960) who assume inventory stocks gearing to sales. It is also in this multi-cointegration literature field (see Granger and Lee (1989,1990)) that asymmetries concerning the entrepreneurs' objectives associated with inventories are modelled.

In a different literature field on inventories, attention is paid to inventories by specifying a production cost model with sales assumed exogenously. These models are more structural than the above mentioned Error Correction Models in the sense that they rely on economic theory. Costs associated with the levels and the changes in production are modelled, and nominal cost shocks of input prices can be incorporated. Studies in this field are West (1986a), Eichenbaum (1989), Ramey (1991) and are mainly concerned with the question whether or not inventories smooth production. In these studies time series are used, but non-stationarities are captured by traditional detrend methods instead of testing and assuming cointegration.

A third literature field is the factor demand field. A model is specified here that is even much more structural than the fields mentioned above, as each production factor with its assumed cost(s) is specified. The number of first order conditions then equals the number of factor input variables. Studies in this field are for example Eichenbaum (1984) and Dolado (1987). Many other factor demand studies exist, but do not incorporate inventories.

The organisation of this chapter is as follows. Section 2 gives some descriptive statistics for the data used and pays attention to the non-stationarity of the series. Section 3 is subdivided into three parts. The first part contains a specification with only production as decision variable, in the second part a factor demand model is specified. The third part clarifies similarities and differences between this production and factor demand model. Section 4 contains the estimation results of both models, obtained by the General Method of Moments (Hansen (1982)). Section 5 summarizes and concludes.

5.2   Volatility and multi-cointegration

Inventories are here defined as investments in finished goods that are not yet sold. The identity that holds is

$$Q_t^s = Q_t^d + \Lambda V_t \tag{5.1}$$

where Q_t^s represents the supply of goods or production, Q_t^d the demand of goods or sales, and $\Delta V_t \equiv V_t - V_{t-1}$ the changes in the inventories stock V_t. Data used in the

Table 5.1 Descriptive statistics

	Sector 1				Sector 2				Sector 3			
Z	lev.	int.	std.	cont.	lev.	int.	std.	cont.	lev.	int.	std.	cont.
Q^d	97.4	85.7	37.1	125.7	99.5	105.1	62.3	51.1	98.0	112.5	85.8	139.1
ΔV	2.6	14.3	62.9	37.1	0.5	-5.1	37.7	62.3	2.0	-12.5	14.2	85.8
*		0.46		-0.64		0.39		0.31		0.75		-0.55

	Sector 4				Sector 5				Sector 6			
Z	lev.	int.	std.	cont.	lev.	int.	std.	cont.	lev.	int.	std.	cont.
Q^d	98.7	102.4	2.9	183.0	98.7	95.9	44.5	79.7	99.3	102.8	57.7	111.0
ΔV	1.3	-2.4	97.1	2.9	1.30	4.1	55.5	44.5	0.7	-2.8	42.3	57.7
*		1.30		-0.80		0.75		-0.41		0.5		-0.52

Sector 1 = Agriculture, silviculture and fishery   Sector 4 = Consumers equipment
Sector 2 = Intermediate goods   Sector 5 = Transport equipment
Sector 3 = Professional equipment   Sector 6 = Consumption goods

$$\text{'lev.'} = \frac{\bar{x}\{Z\}}{\bar{x}\{Q^s\}}; \quad \text{'int.'} = \frac{\bar{x}\{\Delta Z\}}{\bar{x}\{\Delta Q^s\}}; \quad \text{'std.'} = r\{\Delta Z, \Delta Q^s\}\frac{s\{\Delta Z\}}{s\{\Delta Q^s\}};$$

$$\text{'cont.'} = \frac{s^2\{\Delta Q^d\}}{s^2\{\Delta Q^s\}} \quad \text{or} \quad \text{'cont.'} = r\{\Delta Q^s, \Delta Q^d\}\frac{s\{\Delta Q^d\}}{s\{\Delta Q^s\}}.$$

$\bar{x}$, s and r are the sample mean, sample standard deviation and sample correlation coefficient.

* the statistics in this rows are $\bar{x}\{\Delta Q^s\}$ and $r\{\Delta Q^d, \Delta^2 V\}s\{\Delta Q^d\}s\{\Delta^2 V\}$ respectively.

subsequent analyses are quarterly and mainly come from the National Accounts. A description is found in the data appendix.

Some descriptive statistics (all in percentages) for the sectors under investigation are given in table 5.1. The calculated statistics, as well as the sector names, are given in the bottom part of the table.

The column 'lev.' gives the average demand (or variation in inventories) divided by the average production. The column 'int.' gives similar statistics for the series in first differences. Hence, these second statistics are obtained by the once differenced (integrated) variables and are similar to the first statistics that concern the levels. As both production and sales are integrated of first order according to augmented Dickey-Fuller tests (see Fuller (1976)) that are not shown here, these last averages give more valuable information. The column 'std.' gives the standard deviation of sales (or variation of inventories) divided by the standard deviation of production, and can be taken as a measure of 'volatility'. A correction is made here for the correlation between first differences in production and integrated sales (or second differences in inventories) such that the two percentages given under 'std.' add to 100. The number (below) in column 'int.' is the growth of production, which is highest in the consumers equipment sector.

The results in the 'lev.' column show a very small proportion of about 2% for the mean first differences in inventory stock. The first differenced series ('int.') show that for the sectors 2, 3, 4 and 6, a value for sales exceeds one. This indicates that the average increase in sales is higher than the average increase in output. Overall the variation of inventories has no dominance over the variation of sales. The standard deviations column ('std.') shows, on the other hand, that volatility of variations in inventories is high, ranging from 14.2% in the professional equipment sector to 97.1% in the consumers equipment sector. It is this high volatility of the overall relatively small average inventory changes that has attracted the attention in many macroeconomic studies.

The 'cont.' column gives a measure for whether or not production is more variable than sales (the contribution of sales with respect to production). From (5.1) follows that

$$\sigma^2\{\Delta Q_t^s\} = \sigma^2\{\Delta Q_t^d\} + \sigma^2\{\Delta^2 V_t\} + 2 \operatorname{cov}\{\Delta Q_t^d, \Delta^2 V_t\}, \tag{5.2}$$

where σ^2 and cov represent the variance and the covariance respectively of the variables within curled brackets and Δ represents the first difference operator. It immediately follows that the covariance between sales and the variation in inventories must be negative if the variance of sales exceeds the variance of production. If sales is however less variable than the production, the sign of the covariance is not determined. If $\operatorname{cov}\{\Delta Q_t^d, \Delta^2 V_t\} > 0$, an overproduction and/or underproduction exists since inventories change contemporaneously in the same direction as sales changes. This clearly rejects the smoothing role of production since $\sigma^2\{\Delta Q_t^s\} > \sigma^2\{\Delta Q_t^d\}$.

The sample covariance is given at the bottom under column 'cont.'. The number in the row Q^d gives the variance from the sales as a percentage of the variance from the production series in first differences. This number shows that sales is more volatile than production in sector 1, 3, 4 and 6, where the (sample) $\operatorname{cov}\{\Delta Q_t^d, \Delta^2 V_t\}$ is by consequence negative. Sector 2 shows a positive covariance between sales and the variation of inventories. Hence for this sector the increases (decreases) in inventories accumulation took place while sales increased (decreased). For this reason for this sector the smoothing role of inventories is rejected[57].

For all sectors production and sales are non-stationary (according to unit roots tests, see Fuller (1976)), as already stated above. The cointegration of production and sales, that is the existence of a stationary linear combination of both series, is expected to exist on the basis of economic considerations and is also clearly observed in the data.

However, if the difference between production and sales (thus the variation in inventories, see (5.1)) is stationary, the possibility of multi-cointegration exists. This is the case if the inventory stock, i.e. the accumulation of the variation of inventories, cointegrate with production. In this case inventories are consequently also cointegrated with sales. The notion of multi-cointegration is hence the existence of N, instead of N-1 or less, cointegration relationships between N variables. To verify whether or not multi-cointegration for the sectors under investigation exists, the methodology of Granger and Lee (1989) is applied in the following.

Augmented Dickey-Fuller tests are first applied. The equation

$$\Delta V_t = v_0 V_t + \sum_{j=1}^{4} v_j \Delta V_{t-j} + e_t^v, \tag{5.3}$$

is estimated, where v_j (j=0,1..4) are parameters and e_t^v is a white noise disturbance. The hypothesis H_0: $v_0=0$ of a unit root is then tested. In table 5.2 the t-statistics of v_0 are given for each sector. As the critical value is -2.89 (at 5%-level, see Fuller (1976)), a unit root is accepted for all sectors at a 10%-level although the sectors 1 and 5 show strangely positive values. To test for a second unit root, (5.3) is estimated replacing V_t by ΔV_t. The results (the second column in table 5.2) show that for all sectors the presence of a second root is rejected at a 10%-level.

To test for (multi-)cointegration, V_t is regressed on Q_t^s and on Q_t^d separately, that is

$$V_t = \alpha_s + \beta_s Q_t^s + e_t^s, \tag{5.4a}$$

and

$$V_t = \alpha_d + \beta_d Q_t^d + e_t^d \tag{5.4b}$$

and estimated by ordinary least squares (OLS). The residuals, e_t^s and/or e_t^d, are then used in an Error Correction Model (ECM). Here only e_t^d is used. The ECM

$$\Delta Q_t^s = a_{s0} + \beta_{s1} \Delta V_{t-1} + \beta_{s2} e_{t-1}^d + \beta_{s3} \Delta Q_{t-1}^s + \beta_{s4} \Delta Q_{t-1}^d + u_t^s \tag{5.5a}$$

---

[57] In a similar way Gregoir and Laroque (1992) give a measure to verify whether inventories do not smooth production; from $\sigma\{\Delta Q^s\}=\rho\{\Delta Q^s, \Delta Q^d\}\sigma\{\Delta Q^d\}+\rho\{\Delta Q^s, \Delta^2 V\}\sigma\{\Delta^2 V\}$ they draw the conclusion that inventories do not smooth production if both $\sigma^2\{\Delta Q^d\}/\sigma^2\{\Delta Q^s\}<1$ and $\sigma^2\{\Delta Q^d\}/\sigma^2\{\Delta Q^s\}-\rho\{\Delta Q^s, \Delta Q^d\}\sigma\{\Delta Q^d\}/\sigma\{\Delta Q^s\}<0$. So a substraction of both percentages in column "cont." should be negative, which is the case for sector 2.

Table 5.2   Tests for (multi-)cointegration

Sector	$t_1(v_0)$	$t_2(v_0)$	β_{s1}	β_{d1}	β_{s2}	β_{d2}	β_{s1}^-	β_{s1}^+	β_{s2}^-	β_{s2}^+
1	2.10^*	-3.69^{**}	-0.16^{**}	0.20^{**}	0.01	0.02^{**}	-0.14	-0.16^{**}	-0.01	0.02^*
2	-1.99	-3.17^{**}	-0.53^{**}	-0.06	-0.14^{**}	-0.05	-0.76^{**}	-0.43^{**}	-0.18^*	-0.14^*
3	-1.94	-2.68^*	-0.06	0.23^{**}	0.00	0.05^{**}	0.36	-0.17^*	0.02	-0.03
4	-2.38	-4.02^{**}	-0.21^{**}	0.30^{**}	-0.00	0.06^{**}	-0.07	-0.34^{**}	-0.05	0.04
5	-1.82	-4.43^{**}	-0.38^{**}	0.03	-0.05^*	0.02	-0.11	-0.54^{**}	-0.11^*	0.02
6	0.46^*	-3.15^{**}	-0.12	0.25^*	0.03	0.06^*	-0.17	-0.08	0.05	0.00

$t_1(v_0)$ and $t_2(v_0)$ are the t-values of v_0 to test for a unit root in V_t and ΔV_t (see 5.3).

β_{s1}, β_{s2}, β_{d1}, β_{d2} are coefficients of the ECM-model (5.5) whereas β_{s1}^-, β_{s1}^+, β_{s2}^-, β_{s2}^+ come from a similar model (see text).

* Significant at the 5%-level
** Significant at the 10%-level

$$\Delta Q_t^d = a_{d0} + \beta_{d1}\Delta V_{t-1} + \beta_{d2}\epsilon_{t-1}^d + \beta_{d3}\Delta Q_{t-1}^s + \beta_{d4}\Delta Q_{t-1}^d + u_t^d \qquad (5.5b)$$

is estimated by OLS. To have Q_t^s and Q_t^d cointegrating, either β_{s1} or β_{d1} has to be significant. Above this, to have multi-cointegration, either β_{s2} or β_{d2} has to be significant.

In table 5.2 the coefficients β_{s1}, β_{d1}, β_{s2} and β_{d2} are given. It follows that cointegration between production and sales is confirmed, as either β_{s1} or β_{d1} is significant. This result is not surprising. For all sectors, either β_{s2} or β_{d2} is found significant, which implies that multi-cointegration exists. Inventory stocks thus seem to move in line with production and sales.

A logical reaction to an inventory increase (decrease) is a decrease (increase) in production in the subsequent period. Increases (decreases) in ΔV_{t-1}, see (5.5a), should then decrease production Q_t^s by which β_{s1} is negative. A same reasoning holds for β_{s2} if entrepreneurs want to keep inventories in line with sales; increases (decreases) in V_t in comparison with $\beta_d Q_t^d$ (see (5.4b)) should thus decrease (increase) production in the subsequent period.

As the reaction of production may be different on both sides of the two objectives, being production in line of sales *and* inventories in line with sales, Granger and Lee (1989) pay attention to the asymmetric ECM. They estimate the equations (5.5) by separating the series $\Delta V_{t\,1}$ and ϵ_{t-1}^d each into two series, one with the negative and one with the positive values. A similar model as theirs is also estimated here and the corresponding coefficients are referred to as β_{s1}^-, β_{s1}^+, β_{s2}^- and β_{s2}^+ that accompany $\Delta V_{t-1}<0$, $\Delta V_{t-1}>0$, $\epsilon_{t-1}^d<0$ and $\epsilon_{t-1}^d>0$ respectively.

These parameter estimates are also given in table 5.2.

The results show that the estimates for β_{s1}^- and β_{s1}^+ that are significant, are negative. This corroborates the theory that production increases when inventories fall and vice versa. Asymmetry between the increasing and decreasing states of inventories thereby seems to exist since both parameter estimates clearly diverge. This is especially true in the investment sectors (sector 3-5) where only the reaction to $\Delta V_{t-1} > 0$ is significant. A rather remarkable result here is that sector 2, for which a positive contemporaneous correlation between sales and inventories was found in table 5.1, has negative and significant coefficients.

The estimates of β_{s2}^- and β_{s2}^+ show that significant coefficients are negative, except for the first sector. This sector comprising agriculture, silviculture and fishery differs largely from the industrial sectors since production is much harder to control. For this reason this result is not very difficult to interpret. The sector of intermediate goods and the sector of transport equipment (on one side) show behaviour of changing production when inventories diverge from sales. For the sectors 3-6, the non significant parameter estimates indicate that the objective of gearing inventory stocks to sales to each other may not always be an objective.

To summarize, inventories are only a small part of production but are in particular highly volatile in the agricultural, consumers and transport equipment sector. These characteristics of inventories have already been confirmed, among others by Christiano (1988) and Gregoir and Laroque (1992) for inventories at the macroeconomic level. Inventory accumulation covaries negatively with sales in the agricultural, investments and consumption good sector. Strangely, the sector of intermediate goods shows the opposite result. Thus for this sector a smoothing role for inventories seems not to exist since the volatility in production is higher than the volatility in sales (see (5.2)). It is however this sector that most significantly shows that production reacts with a lag of one period in answer to inventory changes, and sales in comparison with inventories.

The existence of multi-cointegration is confirmed for all sectors, so inventories seem to tend to stay in line with production and sales. Asymmetry in production reactions on both sides of the objective attractors is not rejected, although this attractor of inventories being contemporaneously in line with sales (see Holt et al. 1960), is not significant for the professional equipment, consumers equipment and consumption good sector. This result, that contradicts the quadratic specification of Holt et al. (1960), is confirmed in Rossana (1993), who estimates a symmetric ECM with monthly data for several United States industrial sectors. Rossana tests the restriction that shipments and inventories in the long-run relationship have opposite sign in the ECM, and rejects this hypothesis.

For the agriculture, silviculture and fishery sector a result is found more in coherence with production bunching instead of inventories and sales in line with each other. This sector is in the subsequent analyses, where a cost minimizing objective is modelled, not further investigated because of this characteristic.

5.3 Two structural models with inventories

In this section three parts are distinguished. In part one a model is specified in which production and inventories are endogenous, known in the literature as the production smoothing model. In part two another model is specified in which also the production factors are jointly modelled with inventories. In part three both models are compared.

5.3.1 A production smoothing model

An entrepreneur is assumed to choose production and inventories in order to minimize the costs of production, that are

$$L_1 \equiv [\psi_{11}P_{mt}^n + \psi_{12}C_t^n + \psi_{13}W_t^n]Q_t^s +$$

$$P_t^q[\frac{1}{2}\omega_1(Q_t^s)^2 + \frac{1}{3}\omega_2(Q_t^s)^3 + \frac{1}{2}[\Delta Q_t^s \ \ \Delta^*V_t]\begin{bmatrix} \eta_{11} & \eta_{12} \\ \eta_{12} & \eta_{22} \end{bmatrix}\begin{bmatrix} \Delta Q_t^s \\ \Delta^*V_t \end{bmatrix}], \qquad (5.6)$$

where $\Delta^*V_t \equiv V_t-\theta_0-\theta_1Q_t^d$ and $Q_t^s = Q_t^d+\Delta V_t$.

P_t^q, P_{mt}^n, C_t^n and W_t^n are the nominal production price, the nominal price of materials (including energy), the nominal price of investments and the nominal wages respectively. ψ_{11}, ψ_{12}, ψ_{13}, ω_1, ω_2, η_{11}, η_{22}, η_{12} are parameters to be estimated.

The first term in (5.6) represents cost shocks by nominal factor prices to the marginal costs of production. The shocks are proportional to production, and together with the quadratic and cubic term in production are assumed to represent the total costs associated with the level of production. $\eta_{11}(\Delta Q_t^s)^2$ represent the costs for making changes in production capacities, like hiring and lay off costs of labour. $\eta_{22}(\Delta^*V_t)^2$ represents the objective of entrepreneurs to keep inventories in line with sales according to Holt et al. (1960). The optimal level of inventories is proportional to sales, $V_t=\theta_0+\theta_1Q_t^d$, and deviations of this optimum give rise to costs. If $\theta_0=\theta_1=0$, costs are only occurred with increases in the inventories level V_t. The multiplication of the latter components in (5.6) by the nominal production price, P_t^q, indicates that (5.6) is in nominal terms.

The interrelation in costs between ΔQ_t^s and Δ^*V_t is here adopted ($\eta_{12}\neq0$) to catch asymmetries on both sides of the attractors $\Delta Q_t^s=0$ and $\Delta^*V_t=0$; asymmetries of the first are confirmed in the factor sales literature, for instance asymmetric adjustment costs, whereas the second asymmetry was confirmed by Granger and Lee (1989) and in the previous section (see table 5.2 where $\beta_{s2}^- \neq \beta_{s2}^+$).

The cost function (5.6) is only slightly different from the production smoothing models adopted in the literature. For example West (1986a) assumes $\psi_{11}=\psi_{12}=\psi_{13}=\theta_0 =\omega_2=\eta_{12}=0$, Eichenbaum (1989) assumes a stochastic process for the cost shocks and $\theta_0=\omega_2=\eta_{12}=0$, Ramey (1991) assumes $\psi_{12}=\theta_0=\eta_{12}=0$. Durlauf and Maccini (1993) assume $\psi_{11}=\omega_2=0$ but include energy prices and additional inventory stock costs. Hence (5.6) is a generalisation of these production smoothing models used in the literature.

Under neoclassical assumptions, an entrepreneur is rational in the sense of using all information available at period t and aims at minimizing costs over an infinite horizon. Thus,

$$E\{\sum_{h=0}^{\infty} \beta_{t+h}[\ L_1(P_{m,t+h}^n, C_{t+h}^n, W_{t+h}^n, Q_{t+h}^d, V_{t+h})\ ]\ |\ \Omega_t\} \quad \text{where} \quad \beta_{t+h} \equiv \prod_{i=0}^{h} \frac{1}{1+r_{t+i}}, \quad (5.7)$$

is minimized where L_1 denotes the restricted cost function (5.6), Ω_t the information set and r_t the going nominal interest rate[58]. Endogenous variables are only Q_t^s and V_t. As the two equality restrictions mentioned under (5.6) can be substituted in (5.6), the restricted cost function L_1 in (5.7), is not dependent on Q_t^s.

The necessary first order condition is then given by differentiating (5.7) with respect to V_t,

$$E\{\psi_{11}[P_{mt}^n - \frac{\beta_{t+1}}{\beta_t}P_{m,t+1}^n] + \psi_{12}[C_t^n - \frac{\beta_{t+1}}{\beta_t}C_{t+1}^n] + \psi_{13}[W_t^n - \frac{\beta_{t+1}}{\beta_t}W_{t+1}^n] +$$

$$P_t^q(\omega_1[Q_t^s - \frac{\beta_{t+1}}{\beta_t}Q_{t+1}^s] + \omega_2[(Q_t^s)^2 - \frac{\beta_{t+1}}{\beta_t}(Q_{t+1}^s)^2] +$$

$$\eta_{11}[\Delta Q_t^s - 2\frac{\beta_{t+1}}{\beta_t}\Delta Q_{t+1}^s + \frac{\beta_{t+2}}{\beta_t}\Delta Q_{t+2}^s] + \eta_{22}(V_t - \theta_0 - \theta_1 Q_t^d) +$$

$$\eta_{12}[V_t - \theta_0 - \theta_1 Q_t^d + \Delta Q_t^s - 2\frac{\beta_{t+1}}{\beta_t}(V_{t+1} - \theta_0 - \theta_1 Q_{t+1}^d) + \frac{\beta_{t+2}}{\beta_t}(V_{t+2} - \theta_0 - \theta_1 Q_{t+2}^d)]\ |\ \Omega_t\} = 0.$$

$$(5.8)$$

Necessary conditions for an optimal solution to (5.7), the Legendre-Clebsch conditions that are obtained by differentiating (5.8) with respect to V_t and necessary (second order) conditions for marginally increasing costs in Q_t^s, found by twice differentiating (5.7) with respect to Q_t^s, can be verified after estimation.

5.3.2 A factor demand model with inventories

---

[58] A nominal interest rate is taken here since L_1 in (5.6) is also in nominal terms.

In a factor demand model an entrepreneur is assumed to minimize the variable costs of each production factor together with the adjustment costs. These costs can be specified as

$$P_{mt}^n M_t + C_t^n I_t + W_t^n N_t + P_t^q AC_t,$$ (5.9)

where M_t, I_t and N_t represent materials, gross investments and employment respectively. P_t^q denotes the production price. As a consequence of its multiplication with (real) adjustment costs, represented by AC_t, the last component is in nominal terms. AC_t are here specified as

$$AC_t \equiv \frac{1}{2} [I_t \ \Delta N_t \ \Delta^* V_t] \begin{bmatrix} \gamma_{11} & \gamma_{12} & \gamma_{13} \\ \gamma_{12} & \gamma_{22} & \gamma_{23} \\ \gamma_{13} & \gamma_{23} & \gamma_{33} \end{bmatrix} \begin{bmatrix} I_t \\ \Delta N_t \\ \Delta^* V_t \end{bmatrix}.$$ (5.10)

Physical capital stock and labour are thus assumed to be quasi-fixed variables and adjustment costs of capital are specified in gross investments. The cross-coefficients in the specification allow for asymmetries in the factors. For example, if $\gamma_{12}>0$, $\gamma_{22}>0$ and $\gamma_{23}=0$, the hiring costs for labour are higher than the firing costs of labour at a level where $I_t>0$. After all, $\gamma_{12} I_t \Delta N_t + \gamma_{22} (\Delta N_t)^2$ is an asymmetric function around $\Delta N_t = 0$. The function AC_t represents non-linear convex costs if and only if the matrix $\Gamma := \{\gamma_{ij}\}$ $(i,j=1,2,3)$ is positive definite.

The entrepreneur thereby faces the restrictions

$$Q_t^s = Q_t^d + \Delta V_t \quad \text{and} \quad Q_t^s = f(M_t, K_t^*, N_t),$$ (5.11)

denoting the inventory accumulation identity and the production restriction. $K_t^* \equiv K_t U_t$ is the physical capital stock used for production, K_t is the potential capital stock, U_t is the utilisation rate and f the production function. Q_t^d are exogenous sales, as in the previous model. Substitution of both restrictions in (5.9) then gives the objective function

$$E\{\sum_{h=0}^{\infty} \beta_{t+h} [\ L_2(P_{m,t+h}^n, C_{t+h}^n, W_{t+h}^n, Q_{t+h}^d, K_{t+h}^*, N_{t+h}, V_{t+h}) \ ] \ | \ \Omega_t\}$$ (5.12)

where

$$L_2(P_{mt}^n, C_t^n, W_t^n, Q_t^d, K_t^*, N_t, V_t) \equiv RC(P_{mt}^n, Q_t^d, K_t^*, N_t, V_t) + C_t^n I_t + W_t^n N_t + P_t^q AC_t.$$ (5.13)

The discount factor β_t is defined as in (5.7). RC represents the restricted cost function, here specified as

$$RC(P_{mt}^n, Q_t^d, K_t^*, N_t, V_t) = \alpha_0 + \alpha_m P_{mt}^n + \frac{1}{2}\alpha_{mm}(P_{mt}^n)^2 + P_{mt}^n[\alpha_{md}Q_t^d + \alpha_{mv}\Delta V_t + \alpha_{mk}K_t^* + \alpha_{mn}N_t]$$

$$+ P_{mt}^n[\frac{1}{2}\alpha_{dd}(Q_t^d)^2 + \alpha_{dv}Q_t^d\Delta V_t + \alpha_{dk}Q_t^d K_t^* + \alpha_{dn}Q_t^d N_t +$$

$$\frac{1}{2}\alpha_{vv}(\Delta V_t)^2 + \alpha_{vk}\Delta V_t K_t^* + \alpha_{vn}\Delta V_t N_t + \frac{1}{2}\alpha_{kk}K_t^{*2} + \alpha_{kn}K_t^* N_t + \frac{1}{2}\alpha_{nn}N_t^2].$$

$$(5.14)$$

If inventories do not exist, $\Delta V_t = 0$, and thus $Q_t^s = Q_t^d$, this restricted cost function is similar to that used by, among others, Berndt, Fuss and Waverman (1979) and Mohnen, Nadiri and Prucha (1986). It should be noticed however that in these studies, like in many others, more than one variable production factor exists. Consequently the choice of a price as numéraire becomes important. Here both capital and labour are assumed quasi-fixed and only materials are a variable production factor. The function (5.14) is non-separable in the quasi-fixed production factors (since $\alpha_{kn} \neq 0$). Unlike the study of Mohnen et al., (5.14) is however assumed to be separable from the adjustment part (5.10), but interrelations in this adjustment part exist.

Function (5.14) is more general than Ramey (1989), who investigates stage-of-processing inventory investments, specifies no adjustment costs and assumes a predetermined capital stock. Dynamics in both capital and labour, specified here as adjustment costs, are more often confirmed to be important (in for example Berndt et al. (1979), Pindyck and Rotemberg (1983a/b) and the previous two chapters).

Gross investments, I_t, are not included as a decision variable in the restricted cost function (5.14) since they are a function of K_t. It is here assumed that capital needs to be constructed according to the time-to-build specification introduced by Kydland and Prescott (1982). The construction period is set at three quarters. Since this multi-period time-to-build specification is used it holds that

$$I_t = \sum_{j=0}^{3} \varphi_j K_{t+j-1} \quad \text{where} \quad \varphi_0 \equiv \delta_1(\kappa-1), \quad \varphi_j \equiv \delta_{j+1}(\kappa-1)+\delta_j \text{ for } j=1,2, \quad \varphi_3 \equiv \delta_3,$$

$$(5.15)/(2.3)$$

where κ is the constant depreciation rate. δ_3, δ_2, δ_1 describe the distribution of investments during construction and are fixed at 3/6, 2/6 and 1/6. Hence half of the investments outlays occur during the first period of the construction. Further details are given in the data appendix.

The variable K_{t+2} instead of K_t is then the instrument variable at t and it follows that

$$\frac{\partial I_{t+i}}{\partial K_{t+2}} = \sum_{i=0}^{3} \varphi_{3-i} \quad \text{for} \quad i=0,1..3.$$

The first order conditions for capital, labour and inventories are then[59]

$$E\{\sum_{j=0}^{3} \frac{\beta_{t+j}}{\beta_{t+2}} \varphi_{3-j}[C_{t+j}^n + \gamma_{11}P_{t+j}^q I_{t+j} + \gamma_{12}P_{t+j}^q \Delta N_{t+j} + \gamma_{13}P_{t+j}^q \Delta V_{t+j}] + \frac{\partial RC_{t+2}}{\partial K_{t+2}} \mid \Omega_t\} = 0 \qquad (5.16a)$$

$$W_t^n + P_t^q[\gamma_{12}I_t + \gamma_{22}\Delta N_t + \gamma_{23}\Delta V_t] + \frac{\partial RC_t}{\partial N_t} - E\{\frac{\beta_{t+1}}{\beta_t}P_{t+1}^q[\gamma_{12}I_{t+1} + \gamma_{22}\Delta N_{t+1} + \gamma_{23}\Delta V_{t+1}] \mid \Omega_t\} = 0 \qquad (5.16b)$$

$$P_t^q[\gamma_{13}I_t + \gamma_{23}\Delta N_t + \gamma_{33}\Delta V_t] + \frac{\partial RC_t}{\partial V_t} - E\{\frac{\beta_{t+1}}{\beta_t}P_{t+1}^q[\gamma_{13}I_{t+1} + \gamma_{23}\Delta N_{t+1} + \gamma_{33}\Delta V_{t+1}] + \frac{\beta_{t+1}}{\beta_t}\frac{\partial RC_{t+1}}{\partial V_t} \mid \Omega_t\} = 0 \, (5.16c)$$

Shephard's lemma for the variable production factor materials,

$$M_t = \frac{\partial RC_t}{\partial P_{mt}}, \qquad (5.16d)$$

thereby holds.

5.3.3 Similarities and differences between the production and factor demand model

The production smoothing model (5.7) and the factor demand model (5.12) are at first glance similar since Q^s is a function of M_t, K_t and N_t. The arguments in the criterium function (5.7) and (5.12) are thus the same. From an economic point of view, the minimisation of costs of production and inventories (modelled in (5.6)) must be equivalent with the minimisation of the costs of production factors and inventories (see (5.9)). After all, costs of production concern the costs of employment, capital, materials and energy. Above this lump sum, costs (for example rents or interest costs) may exist but are not of importance in the minimisation process as they are fixed costs. Between both cost specifications (5.6) and (5.13), a strict equivalence does however not hold.

To simplify, even if one assumes that $\omega_2=0$, and that inventories do not exist by which $\Delta V_t=0$ and $Q_t^d=Q_t^s$, both specifications do not coincide. Costs associated with the level of production in (5.6), that are $[\psi_{11}P_{mt}+\psi_{12}C_t+\psi_{13}W_t]Q_t^s+1/2P_t^q\omega_1(Q_t^s)^2$, are not appropriately specified. In the literature on the production smoothing model the terms between square brackets are said to represent 'cost shocks' to the production. On the contrary, the variable costs together with interrelations for each production factor are

---

[59] U_t may seem at first sight a decision variable because an entrepreneur can choose, besides the capital stock, the utilisation rate of it. However, U_t is most probably an increasing function of Q_t^d in relation to Q_t^s, so $U_t = g(Q_t^d/Q_t^s) \equiv g(1-\Delta V_t/Q_t^s)$ with $\partial g(x)/\partial x \geq 0$. Q_t^s depends on M_t, N_t and the predetermined K_t. As K_{t+2}, N_t, V_t and M_t are decision variables, U_t is determined.

incorporated in (5.13). If the interrelations between the different production factors (including inventories) are important, the two models certainly diverge. As already said above, additional to the variable factor costs, fixed costs, may be incorporated in (5.6) but may not be important in the minimisation process.

Like these 'level' costs, adjustment costs specified in (5.6) by $1/2\eta_{11}(\Delta Q_t^s)^2$ are specified in less detail than in (5.10) and without factor interrelations. Only if a linear production function with only one production factor holds in (5.6), for example $Q_t^s = \alpha_1 N_t$, could cost specification (5.9) be obtained.

To give another example, suppose that production is linearly homogenous in the production factors capital and labour and specified by $Q_t^s = \alpha K_t + (1-\alpha)N_t$. In this case the level costs of production are investment costs $C_t^n I_t$ and labour costs $W_t^n N_t$, that do not interrelate as specified by $(\psi_1 C_t^n + \psi_2 W_t^n)Q_t^s$. After all, investment price shocks affect only investments, and wage shocks affect only labour. If the production smoothing model holds, in this example adjustment costs are specified by $\eta(\Delta Q_t^s)^2 = \eta\alpha^2(\Delta K_t)^2 + \eta(1-\alpha)^2(\Delta N_t)^2 + \eta\alpha(1-\alpha)(\Delta K_t \Delta N_t)$. This specification seldom encompasses the case where capital, labour and interrelations of capital and labour incur adjustment costs, being $\gamma_{11}(\Delta K_t)^2 + \gamma_{22}(\Delta N_t)^2 + \gamma_{12}\Delta K_t \Delta N_t$. Stated the other way around, this last specification of a production function is comparable with the adjustment costs specification in the production smoothing model only for very special cases.

To the best of my knowledge, in the literature either specification (5.6) or a similar of (5.9) is used but a comparison has not been made. By using a model similar to (5.6), Eichenbaum (1989) concentrates on the nominal cost shocks. He compares a production-level smoothing model (*without* costs shocks) with a production-cost model *with* cost shocks and concludes on the basis of monthly time series analyses of the United States sectors that the latter model is preferable. Unfortunately the cost shocks in his model are specified by a rather ad hoc stochastic process, in this case an autoregressive process of first order. Durlauf and Maccini (1993) criticize this way of modelling also, and incorporate price shocks of wages, materials and energy. Contrary to the factor demand models, they do not take production factors into account but estimate coefficients (like ψ_{11}, ψ_{12}, ψ_{13}). Furthermore, in all these studies deterministic detrending methods are applied before estimating the structural model.

Much more elaborate factor demand studies than the model (5.6) with restricted cost function (5.14) exist, but inventories are not often incorporated. An exception is Ramey (1989), who also includes inventories and sales in a restricted cost function instead of (the usual) production, but refrains completely from specifying factor dynamics. As dynamics are omnipresently found to be important, they are specified here by (5.10) and (5.15).

Econometrically the solutions to the factor demand model (5.13) may diverge from the production smoothing model (5.6) because four equations are estimated, hence more structure is imposed by which more efficient estimates can be obtained.

Three questions are raised at this moment and intended to be answered by the empirical analyses. First of all, the differences between both models should become clear when estimating first order conditions (5.8) and (5.16). If the models were equivalent, the estimates of θ_0, θ_1 would be equal in both models, provided of course that the same estimation method is applied to both models. The parameter estimates η_{22} and γ_{33} must be equal in this case also. Secondly, the influence of including inventories in the models should become apparent. This can be verified by testing the hypothesis that inventories do not exist. Thirdly, if including inventories is important, their associated costs ($\eta_{22}(\Delta^* V_t)^2$ or $\gamma_{33}(\Delta^* V_t)^2$) should be compared with the associated costs of changing production ($\eta_{11}(\Delta Q_t^s)^2$ or AC_t). The question whether holding inventories or adjusting production is most costly can then be answered and the smoothing role of inventories is verifiable for the sectors under investigation.

5.4   Empirical results

The two models specified in the previous section are estimated by the General Method of Moments[60] (see Hansen (1982)) using the GMM-routine of TSP 4.2b with a tolerance of 0.001. GMM-estimates are presented in the first part of this section. In the second part calculations of elasticities with the factor demand model are presented.

5.4.1   GMM estimation results

The model with only production as a decision variable (5.7) has only one first order condition (see (5.8)). This equation contains variables two periods in the future (Q_{t+2}^s, Q_{t+2}^d and V_{t+2}). Thus a substitution of these expected future variables by their realisations entails a residual that is a second order moving average. The factor demand model (5.12) has the four first order conditions (5.16a)-(5.16d). Because of the time-to-build, equation (5.16a) contains variables of at most three periods in the future. The

---

[60]   The production smoothing model and factor demand model can also be estimated by a Full Information Maximum Likelihood method. In this case the demand process must be specified, which is difficult because much less consensus exists on demand than on costs specifications. See also West (1993), who compares full and limited estimation methods for the production smoothing model, and tries to explain the differences in estimation results of various authors who all estimate a production smoothing model.

second and the third equation have only variables one period in the future and the fourth equation has none (and is even static if $\Delta V_t = 0$).

One additional remark needs to be made about serial correlation. The residuals may be autocorrelated because of specification errors or for example, persistent technology or persistent demand shocks that are incorporated in Q_t^s and Q_t^d but not explicitly modelled. For example Blinder (1986) emphasizes the existence of persistent demand shocks, especially in macroeconomic time series. Gregoir and Laroque (1991) also emphasize the importance of non-stationarities in production, sales and inventory series (see also section 5.2). Corrections for autocorrelation seem therefore necessary unless residuals do not have a unit root and consequently cointegration between all variables in the models exists.

The first model is consecutively estimated by corrections (by quasi-differencing (5.8)) for autocorrelation of fourth, third, second and first order. As these experiments show that the residuals turn out to be non-stationary, (5.8) is finally estimated in first differences for all sectors. The moving average is thus of the third order.

Corrections for autocorrelation in the second model are made by quasi-differencing once each equation. Their autocorrelation coefficients are referred to as ρ_1, ρ_2, ρ_3 and ρ_4. The moving average order for the four equations is then four, two, two and one (provided that the all ρ's are significant). Clearly here a trade off with the dynamic part (5.10) seems to exist. As the 'right' order of autocorrelation in the disturbance is thus difficult to disentangle from the dynamics specified by adjustment costs, the assumption $\rho_1 = \rho_2 = \rho_3 = \rho_4 = 1$ is made. Thus in line with the production smoothing model, the residuals are assumed to have a unit root. Probably this stochastic detrending method followed here in comparison with the deterministic detrending methods used elsewhere (see for instance Eichenbaum (1989) and Ramey (1991)) makes a significant difference for the estimation results.

Instrumental variables that are used in the estimations of both models are an intercept, Q_t^s, Q_t^d, ΔV_t, production in value added, I_t, N_t, M_t, C_t^n, W_t^n, P_{mt}^n and P_t^q, all of each sector under investigation, GNP and national gross investments and national value added, all in constant and current prices. Except for the intercept, they are differenced once to satisfy conditions of ergodicity. For both models (5.8) and (5.14), instruments are lagged two quarters to account for the correct moving average error structures imposed by the theoretical model. The moving average used in the factor demand model when calculating the weighting matrix is of fourth order.

Because of the moving averages, a kernel (in casu the Parzen-kernel) is used in order to guarantee the positive definiteness of the weighting matrix. Corrections are made to account for heterogeneity in the factor demand model. Unfortunately, the number of observations in the factor demand model is less than the number of observations in the first model because the utilisation rate of capital stock exists only from 1977 onwards

Table 5.3 GMM-estimates model (5.8) in first differences

Parameters	Interm. goods	Prof. equip.	Cons. equip.	Trans. equip.	Cons. goods
ω_1	-2.96*	-2.46*	-2.02	-1.92*	-3.03*
	(-1.88)	(-1.76)	(-1.09)	(-1.77)	(-1.87)
ω_2	1.22	0.49	0.69	0.69*	1.19
	(1.49)	(0.66)	(0.95)	(1.55)	(1.31)
η_{11}	0.07	0.37	0.47*	0.03	0.28
	(0.51)	(1.34)	(1.50)	(0.14)	(1.29)
η_{12}	0.01	0.001	-0.02	0.04	-0.03
	(0.34)	(0.001)	(-0.21)	(0.26)	(-0.27)
η_{22}	-0.08	-0.002	0.09	-0.001	-0.03
	(-0.92)	(-0.001)	(0.44)	(-0.23)	(-0.19)
θ_0	-5.91	-34.04	5.19	-28.47	-9.47
	(-0.78)	(-0.01)	(0.51)	(-0.23)	(-0.21)
θ_1	4.36	7.39	-0.84	-1.11	4.68
	(0.86)	(0.01)	(-0.29)	(-0.41)	(0.28)
J	10.12	11.97	3.27	10.13	6.43

* Significant at the 10%-level.

Figures in brackets are t-values. J is the test-statistic for overidentifying restrictions with 11 (=18-7) degrees of freedom. Number of observations = 84.

Table 5.4 (first part) GMM-estimates model (5.16) in first differences

Parameters	Interm. goods	Prof. equip.	Cons. equip.	Trans. equip.	Cons. goods
γ_{11}	-0.09*	0.16	2.19*	0.17*	0.01
	(-4.26)	(1.55)	(8.22)	(3.80)	(0.10)
γ_{12}	-0.004	0.33	0.08	-0.03	0.93*
	(-0.06)	(0.46)	(0.44)	(-0.30)	(2.51)
γ_{13}	-0.0003	0.04*	0.003	-0.01*	0.02*
	(-0.04)	(1.80)	(0.04)	(-1.99)	(1.99)
γ_{22}	3.31	3.12	-0.18	0.51	-4.92
	(1.48)	(0.36)	(-0.34)	(0.44)	(-0.98)
γ_{23}	0.03	-0.16	0.003	-0.05	-0.10
	(0.24)	(-0.56)	(0.18)	(-0.73)	(-0.60)
γ_{33}	0.005	0.04	0.002	-0.04*	-0.01
	(0.24)	(0.62)	(0.76)	(-2.14)	(-0.75)

Table 5.4 (second part) GMM-estimates model (5.16) in first differences

Parameters	Interm. goods	Prof. equip.	Cons. equip.	Trans. equip.	Cons. goods
α_{mm}	-0.19* (-2.56)	0.05 (0.37)	-0.68* (-2.46)	0.04 (0.35)	-0.23* (-3.04)
α_{md}	1.79 (1.00)	-1.06 (-0.47)	1.96 (1.29)	0.67 (0.55)	-3.37 (-1.29)
α_{mv}	-0.02 (-0.80)	0.05* (1.73)	0.01* (2.45)	-0.08* (-4.86)	0.01 (0.60)
α_{mk}	-0.61 (-0.51)	-0.82 (-0.50)	-0.40 (-0.51)	-1.92* (-2.52)	1.68 (1.56)
α_{mn}	0.76 (0.89)	0.50 (0.15)	-0.91 (-1.27)	0.40 (0.49)	2.00 (1.00)
α_{dd}	-2.03 (-1.25)	1.52 (0.85)	-0.85 (-0.43)	0.17 (0.19)	4.61* (1.77)
α_{dv}	0.01 (0.74)	-0.004 (-0.20)	-0.001 (-1.08)	-0.01 (-0.36)	-0.01 (-0.56)
α_{dk}	0.11 (0.19)	-0.54 (-0.66)	-0.18 (-0.26)	-0.12 (-0.27)	-0.78 (-1.01)
α_{dn}	1.09* (2.19)	1.09 (0.96)	-0.13 (-0.77)	0.19 (0.46)	0.50 (0.62)
α_{vv}	0.0003 (0.73)	-0.001* (-2.26)	-0.00001 (-1.27)	-0.0004 (-0.41)	-0.0001 (-0.41)
α_{vk}	0.0002 (0.02)	-0.03* (-2.59)	-0.00004 (-0.02)	0.03* (2.08)	0.001 (0.32)
α_{vn}	-0.005 (-0.64)	-0.04* (-2.01)	-0.0004 (-0.49)	0.03* (3.31)	-0.004 (-1.46)
α_{kk}	1.28 (1.35)	1.31 (1.41)	0.44 (1.30)	1.51* (3.20)	-0.17 (-0.37)
α_{kn}	-0.37 (-0.77)	0.11 (0.10)	0.01 (0.03)	0.77* (2.26)	-0.83 (-1.27)
α_{nn}	-1.69* (-3.39)	-1.76 (-0.73)	0.22 (0.54)	-1.38* (-2.19)	-2.29* (-1.63)
θ_0	[0]	[0]	[0]	3.62* (2.24)	[0]
θ_1	[0]	[0]	[0]	0.30 (0.57)	[0]
J	22.39	37.53	29.81	22.98	33.96

* Significant at 5%-level

Figures in brackets are t-values. Figures in square brackets are the numbers at which the parameter is fixed because of convergence problems. J is the test-statistic for overidentifying restrictions with 49 (=4*18-23) degrees of freedom for sector 5 and 47 for the other sectors. Numbers of observations = 63.

Table 5.5 GMM-estimates model (5.16) without inventories, in first differences

Parameters	Interm. goods	Prof. equip.	Cons. equip.	Trans. equip.	Cons. goods
α_{mm}	-0.34* (-2.44)	-0.01 (-0.06)	-0.33 (-0.71)	-0.30 (-0.93)	-0.22 (1.37)
α_{md}	5.05 (1.34)	0.27 (0.12)	1.41 (0.85)	-1.83 (-0.70)	1.52 (0.31)
α_{mk}	-1.21 (-0.79)	-0.58 (-0.39)	-1.60* (2.07)	-0.28 (-0.36)	-1.06 (-0.80)
α_{mn}	-0.59 (-0.60)	3.95 (1.22)	-1.37* (-3.07)	-0.57 (-0.92)	-1.69 (-0.61)
α_{dd}	-6.03* (-1.67)	-0.12 (-0.06)	-1.72 (-0.81)	1.89 (0.79)	0.29 (0.06)
α_{dk}	1.08 (0.82)	0.21 (0.25)	0.51 (0.70)	0.01 (0.01)	0.11 (0.11)
α_{dn}	1.12* (2.01)	0.17 (0.15)	-0.03 (-0.41)	0.05 (0.17)	-0.83 (-1.11)
α_{kk}	1.27 (0.91)	1.02 (1.33)	0.55* (1.55)	0.90* (1.68)	0.07 (0.14)
α_{kn}	-0.55 (-1.07)	-0.26 (-0.27)	0.36 (1.28)	-0.30 (-0.89)	0.60 (1.00)
α_{nn}	-0.65 (-0.97)	-3.85* (-1.66)	0.40* (1.65)	-0.08 (-0.12)	1.02 (0.55)
γ_{11}	-0.12* (-2.49)	0.17 (1.46)	2.14* (8.57)	0.14* (3.08)	0.02 (0.18)
γ_{12}	-0.04 (-0.62)	0.12 (0.20)	0.06 (0.54)	0.01 (0.24)	0.16 (0.58)
γ_{22}	2.87 (1.30)	1.20 (0.15)	-0.18 (-0.60)	0.36 (0.40)	0.51 (0.14)
J	24.01	37.03	48.22	20.62	31.63

* Significant at 5%-level
Numbers in brackets are t-values. J is the test-statistics of overidentifying restrictions with 41 (3*18-13) degrees of freedom. Numbers of observations = 63.

(see the data appendix).

When estimating the production smoothing model, a normalisation is necessary since the optimal solution for model (5.6) without restrictions is the solution where all parameters equal zero. Instead of fixing one parameter in the adjustment part (see for example Blanchard (1983) who fixes $\eta_{11}=1$ or Ramey (1991) who fixes $\eta_{22}=1$) the normalisation $\psi_{11}=\psi_{12}=\psi_{13}=1$, that is more in line of (5.9), is chosen.

The GMM-estimates of model (5.8) and (5.16) are given in table 5.3 and table 5.4 respectively. The J-statistic, given in the last row, is the test statistic for the overidentifying restrictions. For model (5.8) and (5.16) this statistic has eleven and forty nine degrees of freedom respectively (see the bottom of table 5.3 and 5.4). For the factor demand model some parameters were set at zero because of convergence problems. For this reason for some sectors the number of degrees of freedom is higher. The J-statistics show that for none of the sectors the model is rejected, which supports the choice of instruments.

The estimation results for the model (5.8) show very low t-values (given in square brackets in table 5.3). The costs of production in levels and changes in production, estimated by ω_1, ω_2 and η_{11}, η_{12}, η_{22} are significant for some sectors at a 10%-level. For the factor demand model (5.16) the estimation results are much more significant as follows from table 5.4. According these results model (5.16), where the same set of instruments and even less observations (63 instead of 84) are used, appears to perform much better.

As should be noted here, a major difference between the analyses here and other inventory studies is the use of quarterly instead of monthly data. The major reason for using quarterly data, is that capital stock and employment data are not easily available on a higher frequency. It turned out that even no improvement was obtained with model (5.8) by analyses (not presented here) with pooled data of all five sectors.

To investigate the importance of inventories in the factor demand model, the model (5.16) is estimated without inventories, using the same set of instruments. These estimation results are given in table 5.5. In this case one equation less is estimated and the parameters associated with inventories are set at zero. The degrees of freedom in this model is forty one and thus less than in the model (5.16) of table 5.4. The J-statistic is thus expected to be higher in table 5.4, which is clearly not the case for the consumers equipment sector.

To illustrate the differences between the estimation results of the models, with and without inventories, graphs 5.1 are given. In these graphs the adjustment costs function (5.10) is calculated, where $\Delta V_t^* = 0$ is assumed and the estimates of the adjustment costs parameters γ_{11}, γ_{12}, γ_{22} are used. The ranges of I_t and ΔN_t, given on the y-axis and x-axis in the graphs, are the sample ranges. The ranges of the adjustment costs (the z-axis in graphs 5.1) are in model 1 (estimates of table 5.4) and model 2 (estimates of table 5.5) kept equal, in order to see the shifts in the function clearly.

The graphs show that changes between the two models is most apparent in the sector of consumer goods. For the other four sectors, the incorporation of inventories in interrelation with investments and labour changes seems less significant. Another feature that becomes apparent by these graphs is that for the sector of intermediate goods and partly for the sector of consumption goods, negative adjustment costs are found. These result are in contradiction with the objective function of the theoretical models used here, since the existence of negative costs makes producers bunch production (see also Ramey (1991) on this issue).

Unfortunately, the importance of inventories in the restricted cost function, is more difficult to investigate using graphs because in addition to capital, labour and inventories, also the price of materials, materials and sales are included.

Graph 5.1   Adjustment cost functions table 5.4 (model 1)   - table 5.5 (model 2)

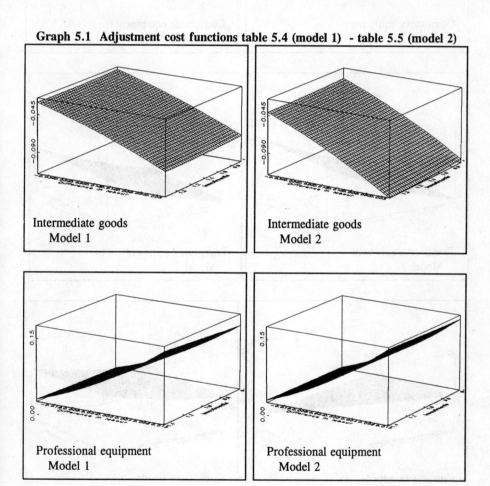

Intermediate goods
Model 1

Intermediate goods
Model 2

Professional equipment
Model 1

Professional equipment
Model 2

x-axis: ΔN_t; y-axis: I_t; z-axis: adjustment costs (5.10) where $\gamma_{13}=\gamma_{23}=\gamma_{33}=0$.

Graph 5.1 Adjustment cost functions table 5.4 (model 1) - table 5.5 (model 2)

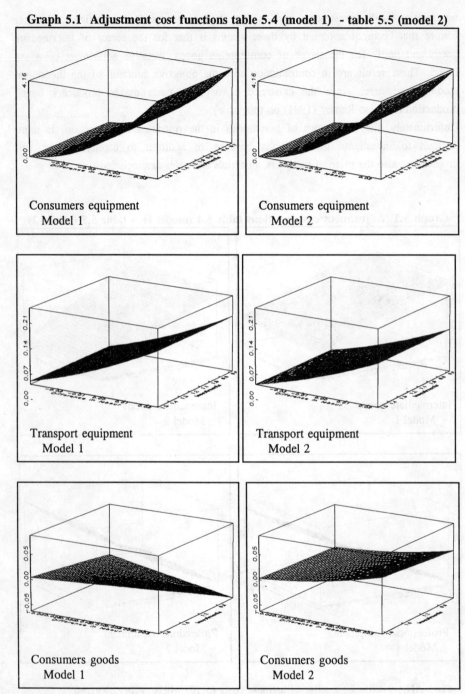

Consumers equipment
Model 1

Consumers equipment
Model 2

Transport equipment
Model 1

Transport equipment
Model 2

Consumers goods
Model 1

Consumers goods
Model 2

x-axis: ΔN_t; y-axis: I_t; z-axis: adjustment costs (5.10) where $\gamma_{13}=\gamma_{23}=\gamma_{33}=0$.

Table 5.6 Wald tests with model (5.16)

Parameters	Interm. goods	Prof. equip.	Cons.equip.	Trans. equip.	Cons. goods
H_{01}	191.21*	50.67*	37.14*	112.57*	191.52*
H_{02}	0.02	2.71	2.56	63.40*	2.26

* Significant at 5%-level
H_{01}: $\alpha_{dd}=\alpha_{vv}=\alpha_{dv}$, $\alpha_{dk}=\alpha_{vk}$, $\alpha_{dn}=\alpha_{vn}$
H_{02}: $\theta_0=\theta_1=\gamma_{13}=\gamma_{23}=\gamma_{33}=0$

In order to investigate in which part of the cost function inventories are most important, Wald tests are applied. The results of two tests are given in table 5.6.

The first hypothesis tests if inventories are important in the restricted cost function. If this hypothesis, i.e. H_{01}: $\alpha_{dd}=\alpha_{vv}=\alpha_{dv}$, $\alpha_{dk}=\alpha_{vk}$, $\alpha_{dn}=\alpha_{vn}$ were true, the restricted cost function in terms of production $(Q_t^s=Q_t^d+\Delta V_t)$ held. As the results show, this hypothesis is clearly rejected for each sector. Hence, inventories turn out to be important in the restricted cost function.

The hypothesis of inventories not interrelated with investments and labour adjustment costs and, without the objective $V_t=\theta_0+\theta_1Q_t^d$ is then tested. The hypothesis is H_{02}: $\theta_0=\theta_1=\gamma_{13}=\gamma_{23}=\gamma_{33}=0$. The results indicate that the hypothesis is only rejected for the transport sector. This is the only sector where θ_0, θ_1 did not cause convergence problems and were estimated. For this sector the adjustment costs for investments seem higher than the costs for keeping inventories (since γ_{11} is significant and positive, whereas γ_{33} is negative).

The result of inventories in line with sales for the transport sector corresponds with the results in the multi-cointegration part in section 5.2. After all, for this sector multi-cointegration was confirmed when investigating Q_t^s, Q_t^d, ΔV_t. The objective of inventories in line with sales was confirmed when $V_t<Q_t^d$, i.e. β_{s2}^- in table 5.2 is significant. The result of inventories gearing towards sales that was clearly found for the intermediate goods sector (see section 5.2, table 5.2) is however not confirmed here. For the other three sectors, both in section 5.2 and in table 5.6 an entrepreneur's objective of having inventory stock in line with sales, is not confirmed.

5.4.2   Price and sales elasticities

In this study elasticities are estimated such that the role of inventories in relation to capital stock and labour can be investigated. In order to calculate these elasticities, the Euler equations ((5.16a)-(5.16c)) are to be rewritten such that an explicit expression for the production factors in terms of prices and production results. There are two approaches to establish this.

The usual approach is to solve the Euler equations (5.16) for the rational expectation and estimate this solution with a Full Maximum Likelihood method. Several caveats then apply. First of all, an explicit solution needs to be obtained in an analytical way. Morrison and Berndt (1981) and Mohnen et al. (1986) are examples of the calculation of elasticities in dynamic factor demand models. No time-to-build is assumed and adjustment costs (thus dynamics) are specified in capital stock, research and development and/or labour under static expectations. For example Ramey (1989) also calculates elasticities from Euler equations, but does not assume adjustment costs by which the explicit form is easy to obtain. For the model under investigation here, this becomes however rather difficult because of the long lead times of capital, being the time-to-build of three periods, and the interrelations in the cost and adjustment costs function. The fact that a closed form is hard to find for a multivariate model with time-to-build follows from chapter 3. The assumptions of interrelations make finding an explicit solution difficult. A second caveat is that the interest factor needs to be constant in time for a closed form to be obtained. As a third caveat, in order to derive an explicit form, more assumptions need to be made concerning the prices when rational expectations are assumed.

As a consequence of the time-to-build together with the interrelations in the four-variate system the analytical solution is (if possible) hard to find. Therefore a different approach is adopted here. Elasticities are calculated from the estimated Euler equations. The estimated system (5.16a)-(5.16.c) is rewritten as[61]

$$\sum_{j=0}^{6} \hat{B}_j \Delta X_{t+5-j} + \Delta \hat{A}_t = e_t \quad \text{where} \quad X_t \equiv [K_t \ N_t \ V_t]', \quad (5.17)$$

where B_i (i=0,1..6) are 3x3 matrices whose parameters are functions of the structural parameters,

$$A_t \equiv \begin{bmatrix} \sum_{j=0}^{3} \beta^{j-2} \varphi_{3-j} C_{t+j}^{n*} + \alpha_{mk} P_{m,t+2}^{n*} + \alpha_{dk} P_{m,t+2}^{n*} U_{t+2} Q_{t+2}^{d} \\ W_t^{n*} + \alpha_{mm} P_{mt}^{n*} + \alpha_{dn} Q_t^{d*} \\ \alpha_{mv}^* + \alpha_{dv} Q_t^{d*} - \beta(\alpha_{mv}^* + \alpha_{dv} Q_{t+1}^{d*}) \end{bmatrix},$$

---

[61] In these derivations the rewriting of (5.17) in real prices (that is a division by P_t^q) is assumed to occur before the Euler equations are estimated. The discount factor is then assumed to be in real terms. In addition to this, the assumption is made that the restricted cost function (5.14) is in terms of the output price instead of the materials price (P_m^n) by which the form (5.17) is found.

and a variables with a star indicates that the variable is divided by the product price. The hats over B_i, (i=0,1..6) and A_t indicate that the GMM-estimates are used and e_t represents the error, i.e. the prediction and measurement error.

Two assumptions were made here. Fluctuations in the interest rate were taken into account when estimating the Euler equations. To calculate the elasticities the assumption of constancy must however be made. In the following calculations it is therefore assumed that $\beta_t \equiv \beta = 0.98$, $\forall t$. It is also assumed that all prices are real, by which the objective function (5.12) is divided by the production price P_t^q.

The system (5.17) is thus a trivariate difference equation system. The first equation contains a difference equation of sixth degree in capital stock and a fourth degree in both labour and inventories. The second and third equations are at most of fourth order. From Morrison and Berndt (1979) it follows that for the case where a one period time-to-build exists and variables are not in first differences, the solution is of the flexible accelerator form

$$\Delta X_t = M (X_t - X_{t-1}^*).$$

X_t^* is defined as the long run solution. The elements of matrix M are functions of the parameters in the structural model. From this model elasticities can then be derived[62].

As a consequence of the three period time-to-build, system (5.17) has a similar flexible accelerator solution, i.e. the representation[63]

$$\Delta X_t = \sum_{i=1}^{3} \hat{M}_i \Delta X_{t-i} + \hat{M}_4 \Delta X_t^* \quad \text{where} \quad X_t^* \equiv -(\sum_{i=0}^{6} B_i)^{-1} A_t^*. \tag{5.18}$$

According to the estimation of models (5.8) and (5.16), first differences are taken. Short run, 1, 2 and 3 medium term, and long run 'elasticities' from first differences of factor price or sales Δp_t ($p_t \in \{C_t^n, W_t^n, P_{mt}^n, Q_t^d\}$) to factor Δf_t ($f_t \in \{K_t, N_t, V_t\}$) can then be defined, respectively, as

$$e_{fp}^s \equiv \frac{\partial \Delta f_t}{\partial \Delta p_t} \frac{\Delta p_t}{\Delta f_t}; \quad e_{fp}^{mi} \equiv \frac{\partial \Delta f_{t+i}}{\partial \Delta p_t} \frac{\Delta p_t}{\Delta f_{t+i}}, \quad (i=1,2,3); \quad e_{fp}^l \equiv \frac{\partial \Delta f_t^*}{\partial \Delta p_t} \frac{\Delta p_t}{\Delta f_t^*}. \tag{5.19a}$$

f_t^* here indicates the long run solution for f_t. The elasticities concerning materials, being the variable production factor, follow from (5.16d) as

---

[62]   A third approach to calculate elasticities could be to derive from (5.17) the total derivative and calculate directly the reaction of prices and output to factors. The definition of elasticities is then different from (5.19a)-(5.19b) since no stable solution is first obtained.

[63]   The assumption $e_t = 0$ in (5.17) and stability of the solution (5.18) are made.

$$e_{Mp}^s \equiv \frac{\partial \Delta M_t}{\partial \Delta p_t} \frac{\Delta p_t}{\Delta M_t}, \qquad p_t \in \{P_{mt}^n, Q_t^d\}$$

$$e_{Mp}^{mi} \equiv [\frac{\partial \Delta M_{t+i}}{\partial \Delta p_t} + \frac{\partial \Delta M_{t+i}}{\partial \Delta K_{t+i}} \frac{\partial \Delta K_{t+i}}{\partial \Delta p_t} + \frac{\partial \Delta M_{t+i}}{\partial \Delta N_{t+i}} \frac{\partial \Delta N_{t+i}}{\partial \Delta p_t}] \frac{\Delta p_t}{\Delta M_{t+i}}, \qquad (i=1,2,3), \qquad (5.19b)$$

$$e_{Mp}^1 \equiv [\frac{\partial \Delta M_t}{\partial \Delta p_t} + \frac{\partial \Delta M_t}{\partial \Delta K_t^*} \frac{\partial \Delta K_t^*}{\partial \Delta p_t} + \frac{\partial \Delta M_t}{\partial \Delta N_t^*} \frac{\partial \Delta N_t^*}{\partial \Delta p_t}] \frac{\Delta p_t}{\Delta M_t}.$$

Notice that materials do not react to investment price and wage changes in the short run because of the quasi-fixedness of capital and labour. Thus $e_{MC}^s = e_{MW}^s = 0$ in (5.19b). The elasticities calculated can in a way be interpreted as impulse responses (see chapter 3, section 3.6.3). The only difference is the appearance in (5.19) of $\Delta p_t / \Delta f_t$.

To obtain (5.18), the matrices M_i $(i=1,2..4)$, being functions of the structural parameters, must be found. As this is far from easy, a heuristic method is used. The residuals e_t are regressed on ΔX_{t-i} $(i=0,1..3)$ and ΔX_t^*. Hereafter, the elasticities (5.19a)-(5.19b) are calculated with the estimated $\hat{M}_i$ $(i=1,2..4)$.

It should be noticed that the method used here to derive elasticities is very heuristic because several times approaches are used in order to obtain the equations (5.18). First, the assumptions of a constant interest rate and having real prices was necessary, whereas the GMM-estimation results incorporated in e_t and X_t^* were obtained without them. Second, a second estimation method was used to obtain (5.18) since its derivation analytically is far from easy. As a consequence of these rough approaches, the calculated elasticities will be biased and the results must thus be interpreted with caution.

The results seem nevertheless worthwhile, because by (5.18), insights can be obtained concerning, for instance, the reaction of inventory changes to price and sales changes. As these reactions of inventories are most interesting, their sample averages are given in table 5.7. Each reaction is given for the short, medium (1-term), and long run.

As a production factor's own price elasticity is negative, also the reaction of inventory stock changes to price changes can be expected to be non-positive. After all, if for example wages increase and consequently labour demand falls, production falls and thus inventory stocks do not accumulate. But, as should be reminded, here not the reaction to price and sales changes but the reaction's decrease or increase of these changes (second derivative) is measured.

The results in table 5.7 indicate that the reaction of inventory stock is negative with respect to price changes. Long and short run elasticities often only slightly differ. As follows from (5.19) (or see Berndt et al. 1979) this only holds if inventories and the other production factors are no strong substitutes.

Inventory changes in response to sales changes, turn out to be much larger than to price

Table 5.7 Price and sales elasticities

		Interm. goods	Prof. equip.	Cons. equip.	Trans. equip.	Cons. goods
ΔC_t^n	long	0.0004	-0.0001	-0.00003	-0.0001	-0.0011
	medium	-0.0002	-0.002	0.000008	-0.01	-0.0001
	short	-0.0008	-0.006	0.000006	-0.02	-0.0002
ΔW_t^n	long	0.0017	-0.001	0.00012	-0.002	-0.0009
	medium	0.0003	-0.02	0.00006	-0.03	0.000001
	short	0.0013	-0.05	0.00009	-0.04	0.000001
ΔP_{mt}^n	long	0.0009	-0.0007	0.00002	-0.0006	-0.0003
	medium	-0.0002	-0.0096	0.00002	-0.05	-0.0003
	short	-0.001	-0.028	0.00003	-0.06	-0.0004
ΔQ_t^d	long	0.53	-0.22	0.07	-0.65	-0.84
	medium	0.03	0.05	0.01	-0.02	-0.005
	short	0.15	0.15	-0.001	-0.01	-0.007

For each sector the sample average of $\dfrac{\partial \Delta V_t}{\partial \Delta z_t} \dfrac{\Delta z_t}{\Delta V_t}$, $\quad z_t \in \{C_t^n,\ W_t^n,\ P_{mt}^n,\ Q_t^d\}$ in the long, medium (1-term) and short term is given.

changes. From the results it clearly follows that a negative correlation that should exist between sales and inventories, at least in the short run, is not corroborated for the intermediate goods and professional equipment sector. Even in the long run increases (decreases) in sales changes, increase (decrease) inventory stock changes in the intermediate sector. This is a result that may indicate a constant production irrespective of the inventory accumulation or a possible production bunching character for this sector. This last result was also suggested earlier, see graph 5.1a where negative costs are found, along with the positive correlation between sales and inventories found in table 5.1.

5.5   Conclusions

In this chapter an ECM with production, sales and inventory stocks, a production smoothing model and a factor demand model with inventories are estimated.

The ECM is used among others to verify whether the inventory objective specification of Holt et al. (1960), that implies inventory stocks in line with sales, holds. This specification assumes cointegration between sales and inventories (and thus production).

For the French industrial sectors under investigation, this objective is accepted for the intermediate goods and the transport equipment sector. For the professional equipment, consumers equipment and consumers goods sector this objective is rejected.

Two structural models, being the production smoothing model and factor demand model with inventories, are thereafter compared. They differ theoretically because costs are differently specified.

One major advantage of the factor demand model is that a normalisation rule is unnecessary because variable factor costs are observed. For example, West and Wilcox (1993) find that estimation results highly depend on the normalisation rule that is chosen. Another advantage is that the factor demand model imposes more structure in the factor demand model. Hence more efficient results can be obtained. The factor demand model is, because of these two major differences, preferable above the production smoothing model that is often used in the literature, see for example Eichenbaum (1989), Durlauf and Maccini (1989), West (1986a, 1993) and West and Wilcox (1993).

The results obtained by the structural models show that the factor demand model is favourable since this model gives more efficient and more satisfying estimation results. For the sectors under investigations, only for the transport sector the objective of gearing inventory stocks to sales, seems to hold. This objective was also confirmed by the multi-cointegration tests, according to Granger and Lee (1990), in the ECM. For the four other sectors, including this objective in the factor demand model, incurred convergence problems. This may indicate that the objective concerning inventories is misspecified.

As a consequence, the question whether holding inventories or adjusting production is more costly can only be answered for the transport equipment sector. The estimation results seem here to point out that adjusting production (capital stock) is more costly.

For all sectors, the inclusion of inventories in the restricted costs function is however highly significant. It seems thus necessary to include inventory changes and sales, instead of production (as usually done) in restricted cost functions.

The question concerning the importance of inventories in economic modelling is not yet answered clearly. Inventories exist but, unlike physical capital stock and labour, their role in the production process and their associated costs are not easy to specify. Both the relation of inventories to total production and the associated costs are not evident and will (in general) depend on the 'inventoriablity' of the final good produced.

Theoretical results obtained here are appealing in the sense that the cointegration tests can be used to verify the cointegration between inventory stocks and other relevant variables. Above this, in any case the factor demand model turns out to be a better model than the production smoothing model to verify the importance of inventories.

From an economic point of view this conclusion holds since costs are directly associated with production factors. From an econometric point of view this also holds since more structure is imposed on the model that is confirmed by (more significant) results.

In addition to the specification issues, many improvements could be made concerning inventory analyses.

First of all the analyses could better be carried out using monthly rather than quarterly data. Inventories highly fluctuate and the balance sheet inventory data that were used here are calculated as being the residual of the balance disequilibrium. The use of quarterly data here in comparison with monthly data elsewhere (see for example Eichenbaum (1989) and Ramey (1991)) can of course be one source of their much better performance of the production smoothing model (5.6). The reason for working with quarterly data is that investments, labour, production and sales data are used that are not easily available.

Another issue concerns seasonal adjustments. Data used here are all seasonally adjusted by the X-11 procedure. In addition to the fact that this procedure may change the properties of statistical tests, also the fact that inventories can be used to smooth production in response to seasonal variations in sales can uphold.

The importance of seasonal adjustments is for example paid attention to by Kahn (1990), Nerlove, Ross and Willson (1993) and Krane (1993). Kahn investigates whether or not inventories smooth production at seasonal and/or at business cycle frequencies. He finds only little evidence of production smoothing for seasonal and no evidence of production smoothing at the business cycle fluctuations for three-digit industry levels in the United States. Along with Nerlove et al. (1993) who investigate this issue for Swiss manufacturing firms, he finds that production and sales move in line with each other. Hence, seasonality (in inventories) does not play a significant role. The role of inventories as production smoothing remains nevertheless a crucial question; if production smoothing were important, it could at least be expected at seasonal frequencies (see Krane (1993)).

The factor demand model investigated here with sales and inventory changes (instead of production), in line with Ramey (1989), might thus be improved by using seasonally unadjusted data, on a higher frequency and also on a less aggregate level. The question whether changing the production factors (and thus production) is a reason for entrepreneurs to keep inventories, thus whether 'inventories smooth production', can then be more thoroughly discussed.

CHAPTER 6
SUMMARY, CONCLUSIONS AND SHORTCOMINGS

6.1 Summary

Main theoretical results can be summarized for each chapter as follows.

In the *overview* it was shown that gestation lags are periods of time that occur between the placement of orders and the delivery of capital goods. In comparison with other economic factors that directly influence economic growth, a lagging behind or leading ahead of capital growth over the business cycle exists as a consequence of gestation lags. An illustration of the business cycle by Kalecki (1935) clearly shows this.

Several studies in the literature, mentioned in *chapter 1*, bring the occurrence of gestation lags up for discussion. Different aspects are discussed by Kalecki (1935), Jorgenson (1963), and Kydland and Prescott (1982,1988).

Chapter 2 empirically scrutinizes the process of, literally put, the 'capital construction' of houses and plants. This process consists of the designing of plans, the acquisition of building permits, the placement of orders and the start and completion of projects. Construction lags obviously apply to construction projects like houses and plants. Apart from these construction lags, delivery lags can be distinguished as being another 'lead time'. A delivery lag is defined as a lead time where investments fully occur at the beginning *or* at the end of the lead time, whereas the delivery of the capital good occurs at the end. These kinds of lags most logically exist for equipment which is customly made or affected by transportation lags.

An empirical foundation for the existence of lead times is also given by Mayer and Sonenblum (1955) and Mayer (1960). Abel and Blanchard (1988) give statistical information on delivery lags. From their results and the results presented in chapter 2, it follows that construction lags seem longer than delivery lags and are more evidently underpinned by the descriptive statistics presented.

The 'time-to-build' specification of Kydland and Prescott (1982) encompasses both kinds of gestation, being construction lags and delivery lags. In subsequent chapters, 'construction lags' and 'time-to-build' are used interchangeably. The occurrence of delivery lags is further not investigated.

The difference between an investment series subject to a multi-period construction lag and a series subject to a delivery lag is shown in chapter 2 to be a difference in serial correlation. Much more correlation is present in the former as a consequence of the stagewise investment scheme. The specification of Kydland and Prescott is used to calculate physical capital stock series with the different assumptions about gestation. Calculations of the capital growth rates obtained by assuming a multi-period construction period and a multi-period delivery lag highlight the difference of fluctuations and autocorrelation. These two growth rates also differ from a series with a one period time-to-build, being the 'Perpetual Inventory Method', that is very often used by Central Bureaus of Statistics.

Physical capital stock series that take into account the construction lags entail a stagewise investment in current projects, like the multi-period time-to-build of Kydland and Prescott (1982), are unfortunately not available. For this reason it is emphasized that in order to test the existence of dynamics resulting from time-to-build, economic models should be formulated in terms of gross investments.

Chapter 3 analyses a neoclassical intertemporal linear-quadratic model in which the inclusion of a multi-period time-to-build is investigated. Intertemporality in these kinds of models is usually explained by adjustment costs. This adjustment costs theory assumes that production factors can be changed within one period. But particularly large physical capital stock projects, called 'structures', need a relatively long period to be built, according to the findings in chapter 2. Instantaneous changes seem thus to be impossible for structures, even if high compensations would be possible.

In the model, the three production factors structures, equipment and labour are distinguished. For structures, a multi-period time-to-build is specified while adjustment costs are specified for structures, equipment and labour.

The closed form derived from this model is a trivariate VARMAX-model with non-linear cross equation restrictions. As a consequence of the time-to-build in the structures equation, a high order moving average parts results. A first principle result is that time-to-build can be identified from adjustment costs. Time-to-build is associated with the moving average (MA-) part, the prices (X-) part and, in case of adjustment costs of gross investments, also the autoregressive (AR-) part. As was already well-known from other factor demand studies, adjustment costs without time-to-build only entail an autoregressive part.

The VARMAX-model could be estimated by Full Maximum Likelihood. However, estimation unfortunately turns out to be very complicated. Interrelations between the three production factors together with the high order moving average parts, make convergence to optimum values wretchedly slow. For this reason the existence of a multi-period time-to-build model for structures is imposed, fixing the parameters of the moving average part at a priori selected values. Maximum Likelihood estimates are then obtained for the other structural parameters in the model, although convergence is still not fast.

A major difference between this model and the model investigated by Palm, Peeters and

Pfann (1993) is that the latter only takes into account interrelations in the contemporaneous disturbances of prices and technology shocks. Estimation of the time-to-build parameters is then possible, but no interrelations in the autoregressive part exist. The model of chapter 3 takes into account interrelations in the autoregressive part of the technology process that turn out to be highly significant. For this reason this model is more appealing from an economic point of view.

Unfortunately, interrelations in the production function and adjustment costs function are not taken into account. For these specifications the model solution would become very tricky because of the time-to-build in combination with the adjustment costs in the trivariate setting.

Chapter 4 focuses on interrelations between both the production function (in the factor part) and the adjustment costs function. In this way the marginal productivity of, for example, structures stocks can depend both on equipment stocks and the number of working hours of employees. Relations in the opposite direction also hold. Interrelations in the adjustment costs account for costs associated with simultaneous changes of both the capital stock and labour force. Apart from this economic interpretation of interrelated adjustment costs, it is important that allowances in dynamics are modelled.

The model here is more general than the model of chapter 3, and obviously more appealing from an economic point of view. The main drawback is that a closed form, like the model solution in chapter 3, is cumbersome to derive theoretically, let alone to manage empirically. For this reason an instrumental estimation method is used, the General Method of Moments. Transversality conditions are in this case not satisfied by estimation. Furthermore, these instrumental methods are always less efficient than estimation by Full Information Maximum Likelihood, where information concerning marginal processes is taken into account. In addition, for the model under investigation in this chapter, a lot of efficiency is lost because high order moving averages that are only implicitly estimated appear in all disturbance terms.

As in chapter 3, time-to-build specified for structures remains to be identified as a consequence of transforming the first order conditions into terms of gross investments. Gross investment data, instead of productive capital stock data, that do not exist (see chapter 2, section 2.6), can be used in this way for estimation.

Contrary to chapters 3 and 4, *chapter 5* takes into account inventory stocks. If producers do not instantaneously sell their production, inventory stocks accumulate. Vice versa, if inventory stocks exist, producers need not increase production to meet demand increases. Inventories stocks are included in chapter 5, among others, in a similar factor demand model such as the model analyzed in chapter 3 and 4.

Three main differences with models of chapter 3 and 4 exist. First, a cost minimizing approach is adopted. In this way the main focus is on costs of inventories, labour, and capital stock. Revenue specifications that are more difficult to model, need not be chosen. Secondly, aggregate instead of structures and equipment investments are modelled. Thirdly, a multi-period time-to-build is imposed instead of tested. This is justified by the fact that time-to-build already turned out to be significant in chapters 3 and 4. A three quarter time-to-build is assumed for the aggregate physical capital stock. With these capital stock data, more flexible production functions or cost functions, can easily be specified and maintained in the econometric analyses.

In this chapter, three inventory models are investigated: an Error Correction Model, a production smoothing model, and a factor demand model with inventories. The first model is estimated using Least Squares regressions, while the last two structural models are estimated by the General Method of Moments. The impact of inventories, entailing costs for entrepreneurs and their possible interrelation with capital stock and labour, is investigated.

From an economic point of view, one can conclude that the factor demand model with inventories is more appealing than the very often used production smoothing model. Costs associated with the level of production as well as costs associated with 'adjustment costs' seem more appropriately specified in the factor demand model. Also interrelations among physical capital stock, labour and inventories seem more appropriately specified.

From an econometric point of view, a similar conclusion holds. More structure concerning parameters and variables are imposed by the factor demand model with inventories. For this reason, the estimation results are more efficient.

From the factor demand model, price and sales elasticities are derived and calculated, thus making the dynamics resulting from adjustment costs and time-to-build apparent. Flexible accelerator models are often directly associated with models with adjustment costs. The inclusion of a multi-period time-to-build calls for the use of difference equations of a higher order and thus a more 'stagewise' flexible accelerator model.

In comparison to the models of chapter 3 and chapter 4, the factor demand model with inventories presented in chapter 5 is a more general model. Bearing in mind that inventories certainly exist on aggregate levels, as demand almost never coincides with supply, theoretically this model must be an improvement of the former models. A major difficulty is however the specification of inventory costs and their implications to production. Until now literature has not reached a consensus on the role of inventories such as, for example, the specifications of adjustment costs of capital stock and/or employment.

6.2   Conclusions from empirical results

Main empirical results can be summarized for each chapter as follows.

In *chapter 2* data for plants and houses from the Dutch and French building industry, 1986.I-1991.IV and 1980.I-1992.IV respectively, illustrate the existence of time-to-build, preconstruction or construction lags. With quarterly data from the Netherlands on reconstruction, expansions, and new plants for projects from Dfl. 50.000 onwards, an average time-to-build ranging from 10 to 17 quarters is found. The 'average' time-to-build for plants is about one year. This is however difficult to indicate exactly, because of a changing time-to-build over the business cycle and the lack of detailed data for all (plant) projects. Nevertheless, the existence of a multi-quarter time-to-build seems evident.

As a consequence of these findings, *chapter 3* investigates a multi-period time-to-build for structures of three, four, and five quarters. Although the main focus is on structures, interrelations between the three production factors can not be denied according to simple, non-structural, analyses presented in the appendix of chapter 1.

The empirical analyses, using manufacturing industry data from the United States and the Netherlands, show that the existence of adjustment costs for structures within the model with interrelation between equipment and labour, seems to be unpersuasive. This does not seem surprising from an economic point of view, because adjustment costs besides time-to-build for structures, are difficult to interpret.

As a result of the many (cross equation) restrictions in the model, and the very high dynamics (including high order moving averages) and the ensuing difficulty in estimation, only adjustment costs other than time-to-build for structures are tested. At first sight the results indicate that in an interrelated model adjustment costs are not significant besides time-to-build, for both structures in the United States and in the Dutch manufacturing industry.

The reverse case, which is imposing adjustment costs and testing for time-to-build, is only carried out using a non-nested hypotheses test. This test indicates that for the United States, as well as for The Netherlands, none of the pure models (adjustment costs *or* time-to-build) is accepted. This might also indicate that other features in the multivariate model are not quite well specified.

In line with the model analyzed in Palm, Peeters, and Pfann (1993), where few interrelations are taken into account, the result that both adjustment costs and time-to-build for structures are significant is thus upheld.

In *chapter 4,* a highly interrelated model is estimated. As estimation is less cumbersome here than in chapter 3 because of the instrumental estimation method used, the model is applied to data from six industrial countries. The rejection of adjustment costs for structures other than time-to-build is not confirmed. Both adjustment costs and time-to-build parameters are estimated. The time-to-build parameter estimates are within proper ranges and are highly significant. This significance is however at least partly due to the high restrictions on these parameters.

In the model under investigation a distinction is made between internal and external adjustment costs. The former are costs that are incurred within the firm, the latter are costs incurred at the capital good markets. As in chapter 3, internal adjustment costs seem important. This, in particular, holds for equipment and labour. A peculiar result is that, unlike the presumptions of the theoretical model, internal adjustment costs are not convex for two countries. France and West-Germany show negative and concave, instead of convex costs. This contradicts the objective function of profit maximising behaviour. It could indicate that production bunching may occur.

The presence of external adjustment costs seems to be confirmed for West-Germany. According to these results, the German manufacturing industry is able to influence its investment prices. West-Germany is however the country for which adjustment costs turned out negatively, both in a model with and a model without interrelations. As these latter results are peculiar, and a clear reason for these findings is not on hand, other results for this country must be interpreted with some caution.

An important result is, that for all six countries, investigated time-to-build parameters are highly significant. Interrelations are highly significant too, particularly in the adjustment costs function.

In *chapter 5,* the existence of inventories and their high volatility is confirmed, especially in French agricultural, transport equipment, and in the consumer sector. Simple analyses further show that inventories increase (decrease) when sales decrease (increase), except in the intermediate goods sector. The objective of entrepreneurs of having inventory stock in line with sales, as specified by Holt et al. (1960) and often thereafter, is not confirmed in an Error Correction Model for the French sectors. This objective supposes that sales and inventory stock cointegrate. Assuming sales as given, an entrepreneur is then supposed to gear inventory stocks to sales. This result is clearly not overall confirmed by the estimation results.

In a structural factor demand model applied to four French investment sectors and one consumption sector, the significance of this objective is only confirmed for the transport equipment sector. Interrelations between inventory changes, physical capital stock, and labour are confirmed to be important in the restricted cost function that is specified. The hypothesis that inventories do not exist, implying that sales and output always coincide, is rejected. This finding casts doubt on studies in which inventories are not mentioned and a clearing goods market is assumed.

The major difference with this factor demand inventory model in comparison with the models of chapter 3 and 4, is that far less restrictions are imposed and significance levels consequently decrease. It can be concluded, however, that the inclusion of inventories in the production function seems important from an economic point of view and is found significant in econometric modelling. The inventory objective specified by Holt et al. (1960), which is used very often in the literature, is not confirmed.

6.3   Shortcomings

The analyses summarized above can be criticised in many different ways. Some shortcomings concerning specification, econometric, and data issues are mentioned here.

In all analyses the time-to-build specification of Kydland and Prescott (1982) is used. This specification is restricted to investment projects that, once started, are completed. Evidence shows that cancellations certainly occur, see for example Lee (1992), although the percentage of cancellations in comparison with the total amount of started projects seems small.

But apart from these cancellations, changes during construction are in reality always possible. For entrepreneurs who start building large projects and foresee profitable sales opportunities, high compensations may exist that accelerate construction. The opposite is also true; slow down possibilities can exist. Allowing for these changes in projects that are under construction would result in a so called 'multi-period adjustment cost' model (see Park (1984)). In this case, entrepreneurs not only decide on capital projects to be started, but also decide on all projects that are under construction. This last statement already indicates the difficulty in solving the optimization problem of the entrepreneur. For example, a model where a three period time-to-build is assumed for structures entails three decision rules that need to take into account the fact that changes made in a certain period can be revised in subsequent periods. This issue is addressed by Park (1984), who solves his specified model with the use of Riccatti methods.

Another assumption in the time-to-build specification which could be criticized is the constancy of the depreciation rate. Depreciation is, among other things, subject to the level of capital utilization and the maintenance of capital. Maintenance outlays can lead to improvements of the productivity of capital goods, capital goods that during recession or depression periods would be depreciated. Periods of prosperity might lead to higher utilization, instead of extending the actual capital stock, and at the same time keep depreciation low. Therefore, a difference between economical and technological decay of capital goods should be made (see for example Nickell (1975)). Here again, more realistic modelling of depreciation is restrained by the difficulty of conceiving a suitable model.

The models adopted in chapter 3 and 4 can be criticized more broadly. For example, the often made assumption of price taking by entrepreneurs on the output and factor input markets seems appropriate on a microeconomic level but is difficult to defend at an aggregate level. A major problem is that choosing a more general model leads to identification problems. If, for instance, monopolistic competition is assumed on the output market, parameters in the production function are difficult to disentangle from the parameters in the price setting equation.

The efforts made in chapter 4, in order to assume causal relationships from investment demand to investment prices when the representative entrepreneur is the aggregate manufacturing industry, are steps in the right direction. After all, investment prices can be influenced by a large demander like the manufacturing industry. Again, the econometric drawback applies as this more realistic way of modelling is hampered by identification and estimation issues.

Assumptions that are made concerning stochastic technology shocks in chapter 3 and 4 seem to be very important because they also entail dynamics, as confirmed in Real Business Cycle studies. The main problem with technological developments is that the impact of innovations is observable, but the source and nature is hard to identify. Hence, modelling the process of technology remains a guess. Unfortunately, a trade off seems to exist between the modelling of dynamics, or persistence, induced by technology innovations and time-to-build. A higher persistence in technology shocks can lead to the same dynamics that are described by a multi-period time-to-build, and vice versa. But as the empirical evidence in chapter 2 showed, the time-to-build dynamics for structures are very well-founded.

Another not yet mentioned feature is the negligence by all models is the financial structure of firms. Investments depend on available equity or the possibility of acquiring financial means. In all analyses made in this thesis, it is assumed that no financial restrictions occur, an assumption that on a microeconomic level is certainly not upheld, but seems less serious on aggregate levels.

An empirical econometric issue concerning the structural models adopted in chapters 3, 4, and 5 is the non-stationarity of the time series used in the analyses. These time series are mostly non-stationary and are assumed to cointegrate in the structural models in which they appear. If cointegration did not hold, the structural models would be unusual from an economic point of view. Cointegration seems to be a necessary condition because, for example, investment and employment together with their prices can not differ widely, and be at the same time the most important variables in the linear-quadratic criterium function to be optimized (see for example Nickell (1985) and Dolado, Galbraith and Banerjee (1991)).

Long term stationary relationships obtained when Error Correction Models are estimated should coincide with the estimation results obtained when using the structural model as a vantage point. A verification of both estimation results seems important in order to test both models. It is important because two different approaches are used, one that takes theory (the structural model) and the other (the ECM) taking data to start from. The fact that these different approaches can have very different results, follows from chapter 5 where both kind of models are adopted. A very thorough comparison is however in this thesis not given.

All analyses carried out here, could be simplified and improved by the availability of data that are more in line with theory. Examples are the physical capital stock data, which do not exist, at least not using a multi-period time-to-build. If these data would exist, the estimation of the very complicated model in chapter 3 would become much easier. After all, less dynamics result if the solution in productive capital stock could be estimated directly.

A drawback when using the investment data is that some interpolations are necessary. Although these interpolations are carried out by the 'Ginsburgh' method, allowing for mimicking fluctuations of closely associated series by a method that does not cause serial correlation, some caution is necessary.

Another data improvement could be achieved in the inventory analyses of chapter 5. Inventories highly fluctuate, thus making the use of data at a high frequency important. Also, the use of rough data instead of seasonally adjusted inventory data would be much better in these inventory analyses.

6.4   Overall conclusions and some policy implications

Overall insights that are gained can be summarized as follows.
Intertemporal modelling of inventories, investments, and labour together with their interrelations is appealing both from a theoretical and an empirical point of view. Interrelations certainly exist, as already emphasized for labour and capital by Nadiri and Rosen (1969) or Brechling (1975). Dynamics are also very important, as the use of the adjustment costs specification in many factor demand studies already have emphasized.

The question whether investment gestation lags are important or not, the major question addressed here, can be answered in the affirmative. Firstly, data on the construction of houses and plants from the Netherlands and France show that a considerable construction period exists. Secondly, the dynamics induced by gestation lags turn out to be identified in factor demand models with investments. Earlier, gestation lags were mentioned in univariate studies, like Jorgenson (1963), or in general equilibrium models, like Kydland and Prescott (1982). As turns out here, gestation lags are another source of dynamics besides, the often used, capital adjustment costs dynamics. Thirdly, from an economic point of view long gestation lags for large investment projects seem to be more plausible than adjustment costs. These latter costs are in the literature unclearly referred to as 'scrappage' and 'installation' costs whereas, as said before, time-to-build investments are well-founded. Fourthly, from the econometric analyses it follows that time-to-build is statistically significant.

Drawbacks certainly remain. Analyses with time series on employment (number of hours worked), capital stock investments, and inventory investments show that these three factors are increasing in degree of volatility. Consequently, it is increasingly difficult to find a specification by which they are well explained. The average number of hours worked remains relatively stable in time, causing the theory of adjustment costs that results in a model where labour is autoregressive of first order, to be almost trivially upheld (see also appendix 1). On the contrary, series on inventory stocks are for most industries very volatile, making the formation of an economic explanation much more difficult. A consensus about the explanations of fluctuations of capital stock and inventory investments seems as yet unreached (see for example Chirinko (1993), Christiano (1982)). As interrelations among factors exist and can not be neglected, models become even more complicated.

No one can doubt the occurrence of adjustment costs (at least for labour), the existence of long time-to-build periods for large investment projects, or the existence of inventory stocks. To what extent they are of importance in econometric modelling is a question that can only be answered by making simplifying assumptions. As shown here, despite slight differences, the specified and estimated dynamically interrelated multivariate models can be said to be relatively robust across countries (chapter 3 and 4) and across industrial sectors (chapter 5).

The concept of gestation lags and the associated irreversibility of investments, is here only applied to large investment projects. They could however even be extended to small investment projects and/or labour.

Many equipment investments may gestate more rapidly than structures investments. Nevertheless, delivery lags or other lags resulting from delays in the acquisition of specific capital goods certainly exist. An enterpreneur's decision to invest or delay investments, can also for particular goods be of major importance. For example, Dixit and Pindyck (1994) pay attention to these kind of investment decisions. The impact of the irreversibility -in particular along with lead times- or delay -in the case of waiting- on aggregate investments is, however, hard to overlook.

Also labour, the human capital that is an input for production, can have gestation lags. For specific kinds of labour an entrepreneur may need time to find a person able to fulfil his requirements, see also Smolny (1993) on this point. The gestation of human capital, i.e. the gaining of required job skills, seems even more evident. Each person that is hired needs a certain period to do 'on-the-job-training' or an 'apprenticeship', during which job specific skills are acquired. This is a period where human capital gestates, but from an entrepreneur's point of view, costs (search costs, wage costs and possibly training costs) are incurred. During this period no optimal productivity is obtained. Both Schultz (1961) and Spence (1973) compare investments in human capital with investments in capital goods, although Schultz is reasoning more from an employee's point of view. Spence states that: ... *The job may take time to learn. ... The fact that it takes time to learn an individual's productive capabilities means that hiring is an investment decision. The fact that these capabilities are not known beforehand makes the decision one under uncertainty...* (page 356). From an entrepreneur's point of view, hiring costs are sunk costs and thus irreversible and spent before the on-the-job-training period.

Individual firms are usually driven by increasing profits and depend to a great extent on (uncertain) sales potentials. As the acquisition of capital and labour takes time, along with the time needed to obtain the optimal productivity from new recruitments, entrepreneurs or firm management may need long periods before optimal 'profits' are obtained. Firms should therefore not base policy decisions only on current developments, but forecast future events while accounting for the long gestation of capital and labour during firm set-ups or capacity extensions ('upturns').

When sales are low for a long time, firms' revenues may become lower than costs. In order to reduce costs, the actual capital stock may become idle, may even be scrapped and employees may be fired. In the worst case, complete firm shut downs could follow.

For individual firms, these 'downturns' will generally occur much more suddenly and more quickly than the constructive 'upturns'. After all, capital scrappage can be much faster than capital construction and installation. Hiring or better stated, the acquisition of human capital that is optimally productive, seems also to be a longer phase than the firing phase. Of course these phases depend highly on associated costs and regulations.

A government's policy concerning investments and labour subsidies should be concerned with the possibly long 'time-to-build' and relatively quick 'time-to-destruct' phenomena. Governments that want to establish high economic growth and at the same time high incomes, might take investment funds into consideration in order to stimulate quicker investments during upturns. Such investment funds were used, for example, during the late 1950s and 1960s in Sweden, see Taylor (1982) who also takes into account time-to-build considerations according Kydland and Prescott (1982). Investment fluctuations can be destabilized by the existence of such funds, although this result is not fully proven by Taylor's analyses for the Swedish system. Concerning labour, bearing in mind the enormous unemployment rates of today, governments could stimulate starting firms and subsidize hiring and wages in order to compensate for the relatively long unproductive periods of employees, which can be very costly for an entrepreneur.

The results in the previous chapters emphatically indicate that structures investment gestation periods are rather long. Unfortunately, attention was paid to neither equipment nor labour gestation during these 'constructive phases' of firms, nor to the opposite 'destructive phases'. Empirical evidence on these issues (on micro, let alone on macro levels) is probably harder to find, but might be of similar importance to the occurrence of the construction lags observed for structures.

DATA APPENDIX
Quarterly aggregate data

I.1   Data sources

CNT   'Les Comptes Nationaux Trimestriels - Séries longues 1970-1991 en base 1980' (and database), Institut National de la Statistique et des Etudes Economiques (INSEE);

FS   Flows and Stocks of Fixed Capital, Organisation for Economic Cooperation and Development (OECD, Paris), various issues;

MEI   Main Economic Indicators, OECD, various issues or databank DATASTREAM from the OECD;

QNA   Databank of Quarterly National Accounts, OECD;

SOC   'Sociale maandstatistiek/Sociaal-economische maandstatistiek', various issues, Central Bureau of Statistics (CBS).

TC   'Tendances de la Conjuncture', INSEE, various issues.

I.2   Aggregate manufacturing industry data of six OECD countries

Dutch national gross investment series, described below, are used in chapter 2, section 2.5-2.6. The data described below of the United States, Canada, the United Kingdom, West-Germany, France and the Netherlands are used in chapter 4. Data from the United States and the Netherlands are also used in chapter 3.

I.2.1   Variables used as production factors and prices in chapter 3 and 4

I^s, I^e gross fixed capital formation (GFCF) in volumes, structures and equipment respectively;

N   average weekly working hours, that is $NP*NH$ where NP and NH equal respectively the number of all employees and the average weekly hours of work;

C^{sn}, C^{en} I^{in}/I^i, i=s,e, price of gross investments, structures and equipment respectively. I^{in} and I^i equal respectively GFCF of i in values (current prices) and GFCF of i in volumes (constant prices);

W^n nominal hourly wages;

P^q producer price;

r   official nominal discount rate.

I.2.2   Data description

United States, Canada, United Kingdom and West-Germany: 1960.I-1988.IV

The time series I^s, I^e, I^{sn}, and I^{en} are taken from FS and are annual, where the constant prices have as a base year 1982, 1981, 1985 and 1980 for the four countries respectively. The other time series are taken from MEI and are quarterly. The annual (end of the year) series I^s, I^e, I^{sn}, and I^{en} are interpolated using the Ginsburgh method (Ginsburgh, 1971). National non-residential investments series from QNA for structures and equipment in both current and constant prices are used to describe quarterly fluctuations.

One remark has to be made concerning these interpolations. For the United Kingdom the national investments series in constant prices are not available during 1960.I-1964.IV and for West-Germany the national investments series are not available during 1960.I-1967.IV. For these periods the structures and equipment series have fluctuations that are generated by assuming the fluctuations of 1968 for West-Germany and the fluctuations of the current prices for the United Kingdom. As experiments showed, this seems not to harm the results in chapter 4 since many observations in the beginning of the sample period are not used in the dynamic model.

NP are all employees, W^n are hourly earnings and P^q is the producer price index of manufacturing goods. As an exception, the United States W^n are gross earnings and P^q is the producer price index of industrial goods. For the United Kingdom both NH and W^n are for Great Britain (instead of the United Kingdom) and where NH is seasonally adjusted.

France: 1970.I-1992.II

All variables in constant prices have as base year 1980. The series that is 'Formation brute de capital fixe' (FBCF) in current and constant prices of the manufacturing industry are disaggregated as structures and equipment investments (I^s, I^e, I^{sn}, and I^{en}). This disaggregation is done with help of end of the year and annual distribution codes on investments in current and constant prices from FS. All other variables are from CNT or TC.

Instead of the producer price, P^q is the gross value added ('Valeur ajoutée brute: valeur en francs 1980'). The nominal interest rate used, r , is the yield of government bonds. All series from CNT are quarterly adjusted with the X11-ARIMA method.

The Netherlands: 1971.I-1990.IV

The series NP, I^n (GFCF in values), I (GFCF in volumes), P^q, W^n and r are from MEI.

Annual data of I^{in} and I^i (i=s,e) for the manufacturing industry are provided by the department 'Bedrijfstakkencoördinatie' from the Central Planning Bureau (CPB) and include investments of small firms. Constant prices have as base year 1980. Structures investments include only plant investments and equal investments in non-residential buildings, that is CBS-code 2 for type of capital good. Equipment investments equal total gross manufacturing investments minus plant investments. The annual data are interpolated with the Ginsburgh method; to describe the quarterly fluctuations the quarterly series of national gross investments in values and volumes are used. They are disaggregated as current and constant plants and equipment investments based on unpublished national quarterly data from the CBS for plants (type of capital good code 2) and equipment (type of capital good code 3,4 and 6). As these unpublished data (unfortunately) only exist from 1977 onwards the distribution codes of 1977.I and 1971.I are assumed to be equal to 1977.I.

NH are biannual data from SOC up to 1985. Annual unpublished data from 1985 onwards were provided by the CBS. These series are interpolated with the Ginsburgh method into quarterly series.

W^n are nominal hourly wage rates of the manufacturing industry. P^q is the producer price of finished products (output of industry).

The series described above, together with the instrumental variables described in I.2.3, are in the econometric analyses all indexed at 1985.II. Series that are not mentioned as seasonally adjusted, are seasonally unadjusted. Table I.1 contains the average investments in volumes and the average employees of the six countries.

I.2.3   Variables used as instruments in chapter 4

Instruments US (the last eight variables in first differences): a constant, average weekly hours of work, GFCF of structures and equipment in constant prices, GFCF of structures in current prices, employment, persons employed, production in constant prices, retail sales, unemployment.

Instruments CN (the last seven variables in first differences): a constant, official discount rate, yield of government bonds, employment, persons employed, real wages, product price, unemployment, share prices, GFCF of structures in current prices.

Instruments UK (the last seven variables in first differences): a constant, average weekly hours of work, yield of government bonds, GFCF of structures and equipment in constant and current prices, persons employment, product price, unemployment.

Instruments WG (the last nine variables in first differences): a constant, GFCF of structures and equipment in constant and current prices, employment, real price of structures and equipment investments, retail sales, unemployment.

Instruments France (the last nine variables in first differences): a constant, GFCF of structures and equipment in constant prices, GFCF in the manufacturing industry in current and constant prices, GFCF of structures in current prices, national GFCF in constant prices, production manufacturing industry, retail sales, gross national product.

Instruments The Netherlands (the last nine variables in first differences): a constant, GFCF in structures and equipment in constant and current prices, the real price of structures and equipment investments, real wages, nominal wages, retail sales in current prices.

The series that were not mentioned until this section, are all from MEI and/or DATASTREAM.

Table I.1 Averages of production factors

	US	CN	UK	WG	FR	NL
Sample	'60-'88	'60-'88	'60-'88	'60-'88	'70-'92	'71-'90
I^s	15,048	1,885	3,629	4,087	4,261	0,826
	[3,100]	[0,423]	[1,703]	[1,064]	[1,309]	[0,244]
I^e	49,573	5,765	16,196	14,750	13,023	3,379
	[14,546]	[1,552]	[3,590]	[6,968]	[2,987]	[1,327]
NP	20,947	1,965	7,300	9,459	4,499	1,229
	[1,338]	[0,156]	[1,212]	[0,692]	[0,481]	[0,146]
Base year	1982	1981	1985	1980	1980	1980

I^s = Structures investments in volumes (thousands) in US dollars
I^e = Equipment investments in volumes (thousands) in US dollars
NP = Number of persons employed (thousands)
Numbers in square brackets are standard deviations.
The base year is the year for constant price calculations. As a consequence of differences in base years, I^s and I^e are columnwise not all comparable.

I.3   Aggregate sectorial data of France 1970.I-1992.IV

Data descriptions in this part only concern chapter 5.

I.3.1   Variables used

Q^s	Supply of goods, production in constant prices;
Q^d	Demand of goods, sales in constant prices;
V	Investments in inventory stocks, in constant prices;
I	gross fixed capital formation (GFCF), in constant prices;
N	average weekly working hours, that is $NP*NH$ where NP and NH equal respectively the number of all employees and the average weekly hours of work;
M	materials, including energy;
C^n	nominal price of gross investments, that is I^n/I. I^n and I equal respectively GFCF in values (current prices) and GFCF in volumes (constant prices);
W^n	nominal hourly wages;
P_m^n	nominal price of materials (including energy);
P^q	producer price, calculated as the sales in values divided by the sales in volumes;
U	physical capital stock utilization rate;
r	nominal official discount rate, yield of government bonds.

I.3.2   Data description

The interest rate is from TC, U is from an INSEE database. All other variables are from CNT and are seasonally adjusted with the X11-ARIMA method. Constant prices have as a base year 1980. In the econometric analyses, see chapter 5, section 5.4, variables are indexed at 1985.II.

The following sectors are included in the analyses:

S1	Agriculture, silviculture and fishery;
S2	Industry of intermediate goods;
S3	Industry of professional equipment;
S4	Industry of consumers equipment;
S5	Industry of transport equipment;
S6	Industry of consumption goods.

These sectors can be found in CNT with the French branch codes U01, U04, U05A-U05C U06. Sectors S3-S5 comprise the industry of investment goods. The manufacturing industry comprise the sectors S2-S6.

Each sector has a national account, in constant and current prices, that looks as:

Assets	Liabilities
Consumption	Production (= Value added + Intermediate goods)
Gross investments	Importations
Government spending	Commercial margin
Exportations	Taxes
Variations in stocks	

In the analyses, $Q^s \equiv$ production, $\Delta V \equiv$ variation in inventories and $Q^d \equiv Q^s - \Delta V$, all in constant prices.

The utilization rate, U, is calculated from quarterly (unadjusted) margins of the available physical capital stock capacity for 1976.I-1992.IV. To obtain a value for the stock of inventories a benchmark V_0 is used and $V_t = V_0 + \sum_{i=1}^{t} \Delta V_i$ is generated. The benchmark is the value of inventories in 1980, obtained from surveys on the individual firm level. Each firm in this survey is classified according to its main activity, the so called 'sector' classification. On the contrary, the data of the national accounts are divided into parts according to the different final products made. Each part is classified according to the type of product. Because of this so called 'branch' classification a translation had to be made from sectors to branches in order to use the benchmarks V_0 of the sector classification. As a consequence of the use of these branch inventory data, backlogs of ordered but not yet delivered goods are not included.

I.3.3 Calculation of physical capital stock series

It is assumed that capital is built stagewise according to Kydland and Prescott (1982), see chapter 2, section 2.3. To construct series that account for gestation lags it is here assumed that $J = 3$. This is close to Kydland and Prescott (1982), who use four quarters for macroeconomic capital series, and to Altug (1989), who uses four quarters and one quarter for macroeconomic structures and equipment series respectively, and to the analyses in chapter 3 and 4. For each sector the capital stock of 1970 is used as a benchmark (from FS and CNT) and $\kappa = 0.025$ (so $D_{t-1} = 0.025 K_{t-1}$). Gross investments are from CNT. The investments scheme is fixed at $\delta_1 = 1/6$, $\delta_2 = 2/6$, $\delta_3 = 3/6$, thus proportionally decreasing during the construction period. This investment scheme is chosen according to findings in chapter 4. For the initial quarter it is assumed that $S_{1,1970.I} = S_{2,1970.I} = S_{3,1970.I} = S_{4,1970.I} = I_{1970.I}$.

BIBLIOGRAPHY

Abel, A.B. (1983), 'Optimal investment under uncertainty', <u>American Economic Review</u>, 73, 228-233.

Abel, A.B. and O.J. Blanchard (1986), 'The present value of profits and cyclical movements in investment', <u>Econometrica</u>, 54, 249-273.

Abel, A.B. and O.J. Blanchard (1988), 'Investment and sales: some empirical evidence', in <u>Dynamic Econometric Modeling</u>, edited by W.A. Barnett, E.R. Berndt and H. White, Cambridge, Cambridge University Press, 269-296.

Alphen, J.H. and A.H.Q.M. Merkies (1976), 'Distributed lags in construction: An empirical study', <u>International Economic Review</u>, 17, 411-430.

Altug, S. (1989), 'Time-to-build and aggregate fluctuations: some new evidence', <u>International Economic Review</u>, 30, 889-920.

Bar-Ilan, A., A. Sulem and A. Zanello, 'Time-to-build and capacity choice', International Monetary Fund, Washington, D.C. 20431, USA, paper presented at European Economic Association conference in Helsinki, 1993.

Barron, J.M. and J. Bishop (1985), 'Extensive search, intensive search, and hiring costs: New evidence on employer hiring activity', <u>Economic Inquiry</u>, 23, 363-382.

Bentolila, S. and G. Bertola (1990), 'Firing costs and labour demand: How bad is Eurosclerosis?', <u>Review of Economic Studies</u>, 57, 381-402.

Berndt, E.R., M.A. Fuss and L. Waverman (1979), 'A dynamic model of costs of adjustment and interrelated factor demands, with an empirical application to energy demand in U.S. manufacturing, Working paper number 7925, University of Toronto, Canada.

Blanchard, O.J. (1983), 'The production and inventory behaviour of the American automobile industry', <u>Journal of Political Economy</u>, 91, 365-400.

Blinder, A. (1982), 'Inventories and sticky prices: More on the microfoundations of macroeconomics', <u>American Economic Review</u>, 72, 334-348.

Blinder, A. (1986), 'Can the production smoothing model of inventory behaviour be saved', <u>Quarterly Journal of Economics</u>, vol. CI, 431-453.

Brechling, F. (1975), <u>Investment and Employment Decisions</u>, Manchester University Press, Manchester.

Bresson, G., F. Kramarz and P. Sevestre (1993), 'Labor demand for heterogeneous workers with non linear asymmetric adjustment costs, An empirical analysis on French firms', Document de travail, INSEE, Paris.

Broer, D.P. (1987), Neoclassical Theory and Empirical Models of Aggregate Firm Behaviour, Kluwer Academic Publishers, Dordrecht.

Bruno, M. and J.D. Sachs (1985), Economics of Worldwide Stagflation, Harvard University Press, Cambridge, Massachusetts.

Burda, M.C. (1991), 'Monopolistic competition, costs of adjustment, and the behavior of European manufacturing employment', European Economic Review, 35, 61-79.

Cassing, S. and T. Kollintzas (1991), 'Recursive factor demand of production interrelations and endogenous cycling', International Economic Review, 32, 417-440.

Chirinko, R.S. (1993), 'Business fixed investment spending: Modeling strategies, empirical results, and policy implications', Journal of Economic Literature, 31, 1875-1911.

Christiano, L.J. (1988), 'Why does inventory investment fluctuate so much ?', Journalof Monetary Economics, 21, 247-280.

De la Croix, D. (1992), Union-firm Bargaining and Equilibrium Unemployment in Quantity Rationing Models, unpublished thesis, Catholic University of Louvain, Belgium.

Diewert, W.E. and T.J. Wales (1987), 'Flexible functional forms and global curvature conditions', Econometrica, 55, 43-68.

Dixit, A.K. and R.S. Pindyck (1994), Investment under Uncertainty, Princeton University Press, Princeton, New Jersey.

Dolado, J.J. (1987), 'An empirical study of the interrelationship between employment, price and inventory decisions in U.K. manufacturing', Discussion paper, Institute of Economics and Statistics, Oxford.

Dolado, J., J.W. Galbraith and A. Banerjee (1991), 'Estimating intertemporal quadratic adjustment cost models with integrated series', International Economic Review, 32, 919-936.

Durbin, J. (1970), 'Testing for serial correlation in least-squares regression when some of the regressors are lagged dependent variables', Econometrica, 38, 410-421.

Durlauf, S.N. and L.J. Maccini (1993), 'Measuring noise in inventory models', National Bureau of Economic Research working paper no. 4487, Cambridge, Massachusetts.

Eichenbaum, M. (1984), 'Rational expectations and the smoothing properties of inventories of finished goods', Journal of Monetary Economics, 14, 71-96.

Eichenbaum, M. (1989), 'Some empirical evidence on the production level and production cost smoothing models of inventory investment', American Economic Review, 79, 853-864.

Eisner, R. and R.H. Strotz (1963), 'Determinants of business investment', in Impacts of Monetary Policy, Commission on Money and Credit. Englewood Cliffs, New Jersey: Prentice-Hall, 60-337.

Eisner, R. (1974), 'Econometric studies of investment behavior: A comment', Economic Inquiry, I2, page 91-104.

Engle, R.F. (1982), 'Autoregressive Conditional Heteroscedasticity with Esitmates of the Variance of U.K. Inflations', Econometrica, 50, 987-1008.

Engle, R.F., D.F. Hendry and J.F. Richard (1983), 'Exogeneity', Econometrica, 51, 277-304.

Fuller, W.A. (1976), Introduction to Statistical Time Series, New York: John Wiley and Sons.

Gallant, A.R. (1987), Nonlinear Statistical Models, New York, Wiley.

Ginsburgh, V.A. (1971), 'A further note on the derivation of quarterly figures consistent with annual data', Applied Statistics, 1, 368-374.

Gordon, S. (1992), 'Costs of adjustment, the aggregation problem and investment', The Review of Economics and Statistics, 74, 422-429.

Gould, J.P. (1968), 'Adjustment costs in the theory of investment of the firm', Review of Economic Studies, 35, 47-55.

Granger, C.W.J. and T.H. Lee (1989), 'Investigation of production, sales and inventory relationships using multicointegration and non-symmetric error correction models', Journal of Applied Econometrics, 4, S145-S159.

Granger, C.W.J. and T.H. Lee (1990), 'Multicointegration', in Advances in Econometrics, Cointegration, Spurious Regressions, and Unit Roots, eds. T.B. Fomby and G.F. Rhodes, 8, 71-84.

Greenwood, J., Z. Hercowitz and G.W. Huffman (1988), 'Investment, capacity utilization, and the business cycle', The American Economic Review, 78, 402-417.

Gregoir, S. and G. Laroque (1992), 'La place des stocks dans les fluctuations conjoncturelles: Quelques élements de statistique descriptive', Annales d'Economie et de Statistique, 28, 39-63.

Hansen, L.P. (1982), 'Large sample properties of generalized method of moments estimators', Econometrica, 50, 1029-1054.

Hansen, L.P. and T.J. Sargent (1980a), Formulating and estimating dynamic linear rational expectations models, Journal of Economic Dynamics and Control, 2, 7-46.

Hansen, L.P. and T.J. Sargent (1980b), 'Linear rational expectations models for dynamically interrelated variables', in Rational expectations and econometric practice, edited by R.E. Lucas Jr. and T.J. Sargent, University of Minnesota Press, Minneapolis, MN, 127-136.

Hayashi, F. (1982), 'Tobin's marginal q and average q: A neoclassical interpretation', Econometrica, 50, 213-224.

Holt, C.C., F. Modigliani, F.F. Muth and H.A. Simon (1960), Planning Production,Inventories, and Work Force, Prentice Hall, Inc., Englewood Cliffs, N.J.

Hussey, R. (1992), 'Nonparametric evidence on asymmetry in business cycles using aggregate employment time series', Journal of Econometrics, 51, 217-231.

Jarque, C.M., and A.K. Bera (1980), 'Efficient tests for normality, homoscedasticity and serial independence of regression residuals', Economic letters, 6, 255-259.

Johansen, S. (1991), 'The role of the constant term in cointegration analysis of nonstationary variables', forthcoming in Econometric Reviews.

Johansen, S. and K. Juselius (1990), 'Maximum likelihood estimation and inference on cointegration - with applications to the demand for money', Oxford Bulletin of Economics and Statistics, 52, 169-210.

Jorgenson, D.W. (1963), 'Capital theory and investment behavior', American Economic Review, 53, 47-56.

Jorgenson, D.W. and J.A. Stephenson (1967), "Investment behavior and U.S. manufacturing, 1947-1960, Econometrica, 35, 169-220.

Jorgenson, D.W. (1971), 'Econometric studies of investment behavior: A survey', Journal of Economic Literature, 9, 1111-1147.

Jorgenson, D.W. and J.A. Stephenson (1967), 'The time structure of investment behavior in the United States manufacturing, 1947-1960, The Review of Economics and Statistics, 49, 16-27.

Kahn, J.A. (1990), 'The seasonal and cyclical behaviour of inventories', Working paper no. 223, University of Rochester, New York.

Kalecki, M. (1935), 'A macrodynamic theory of business cycles', Econometrica, 3, 327-344.

Keynes, J.M. (1936), The General Theory of Employment, Interest and Money, MacMillan, London.

King, R.G., C.I. Plosser and S.T. Rebelo (1988), 'Production, growth and business cycles: The basic neoclassical model', Journal of Monetary Economics, 21, 195-232.

Kolintzas, T. (1985), 'The symmetric linear rational expectations model', Econometrica, 53, 963-976.

Kramer, A. (1984), 'The new classical macroeconomics: Conversations with new classical economists and their opponents'.

Krane, S.D. (1993), 'Induced seasonality and production-smoothing models of inventory behavior', Journal of Econometrics, 55, 135-168.

Kuper, G.H. and B. Visser (1993), 'Investment theory: A survey', Research Memorandum 526, University of Groningen, The Netherlands.

Kydland, F.E., and E.C. Prescott (1982), 'Time to build and aggregate fluctuations', Econometrica, 50,1345-70.

Kydland, F.E. and E.C. Prescott (1988), 'The workweek of capital and its cyclical implications', Journal of Monetary Economics, 21, 343-360.

Lee, T.H. (1992), 'Stock-flow relationships in US housing construction', Oxford Bulletin of Economics and Statistics, 54, 419-430.

Licandro, O. (1990), Investment and the Stock Market in Quantity Rationing Models, unpublished thesis, Catholic University of Louvain, Belgium.

Lichtenberg, F.R. (1988), 'Estimation of the internal adjustment costs model using longitudinal establishment data', The Review of Economics and Statistics, 70, 421-430.

Lucas, R.E. Jr. (1967b), 'Adjustment costs and the theory of supply', The Journal of Political Economy, 75, 321-334.

Lucas, R.E. Jr. (1976), 'Econometric policy evaluation: a critique' in The Phillips Curve and Labor Markets, edited by K. Brunner and A.H. Meltzer, Carnegie-Rochester Conference Series on Public Policy, North-Holland, Amsterdam, 19-46.

Lucas, R.E. Jr. and E.C. Prescott (1971), 'Investment under uncertainty', Econometrica, 39, 659-681.

Lütkepohl, H. (1990), 'Asymptotic distributions of impulse response functions and forecast error variance decompositions of vector autoregressive models', The The Review of Economics and Statistics, 116-125.

Majd, S. and R.S. Pindyck (1987), 'Time to build, option value, and investment decisions', Journal of Financial Economics, 18, 7-27.

Malinvaud, E. (1989), 'Profitability and factor demands under uncertainty', De Economist, 137, 1-15.

Mayer, T. (1960), 'Plant and equipment lead times', The Journal of Business, 33, 127-132.

Mayer, T. and S. Sonenblum (1955), 'Lead times for fixed investment', The Review of Economics and Statistics, 37, 300-304.

Meese, R. (1980), 'Dynamic factor demand schedules for labor and capital under rational expectations', Journal of Econometrics, 14, 141-158.

Meijdam, L. (1991), Rational Disequilibrium Dynamics: A New-Classical Synthesis, unpublished thesis, University of Tilburg, The Netherlands.

Merkies, A.H.Q.M. and I.J. Steyn (1994), 'Modelling changing lag patterns in Dutch construction', Journal of Economic Dynamics and Control, 18, 499-509.

Mohnen, P.A., M.I. Nadiri and I.R. Prucha (1986), 'R&D, production structure and rates of return in the U.S., Japanese and German manufacturing sectors: A non-separable dynamic factor demand model', European Economic Review, 30, 749-771.

Morrison, C.J. and E.R. Berndt (1981), 'Short-run labor productivity in a dynamic model', Journal of Econometrics, 16, 339-365.

Mosconi, R. and C. Giannini (1992), 'Non-causality in cointegrated systems: representation estimation and testing', Oxford Bulletin of Economics and Statistics, 54, 399-417.

Motahar, E. (1992), 'Endogenous capital utilization and the q theory of investment', Economics Letters, 40, 71-75.

Mussa, M. (1977), 'External and internal adjustment costs and the theory of aggregate and firm investment', Econometrica, 44, 163-178.

Muth, J.F. (1961), 'Rational expectations and the theory of price movements', Econometrica, 29, 315-335.

Nadiri, M.I. and S. Rosen (1969), 'Interrelated factor demand functions', American Economic Review, 59, 457-471.

Neftçi, S. (1984), 'Are economic time series asymmetric over the business cycle ?', Journal of Political Economy, 92, 307-328.

Nerlove, M., D. Ross and D. Willson (1993), 'The importance of seasonality in inventory models', Journal of Econometrics, 55, 105-128.

Netherlands Central Bureau of Statistics, 'Monthly bulletin of construction statistics',various issues, Voorburg.

Netherlands Central Bureau of Statistics, 'Statistics on stocks of capital goods', various issues, Voorburg.

Nickell, S.J. (1975), 'A closer look at replacement investment', Journal of Economic Theory, 10, 54-88.

Nickell, S.J. (1978), The Investment Decisions of Firms, Cambridge University Press, Oxford.

Nickell, S.J. (1985), 'Error correction, partial adjustment and all that: An expository note', Oxford Bulletin of Economics and Statistics, 47, 119-129.

Nickell, S.J. (1986), 'Dynamic models of labour demand', in Handbook of Labor Economics, edited by O. Ashenfelter and R. Layard, Elsevier, Amsterdam, Vol. 1, 473-522.

Nickell, S. and J. Symons (1990), 'The real wage-employment relationship in the United States', Journal of Labor Economics, 8, 1-15.

Oi, W.Y. (1962), 'Labor as a quasi-fixed factor', Journal of Political Economy, 70, 538-555.

Ouliaris, S., J.Y. Park and P.C.B. Phillips (1989), 'Testing for a unit root in the presence of a maintained trend', in Advances in econometrics and modelling, eds. B. Raj, Dordrecht: Kluwer Academic Publishers, 7-28.

Palm, F.C., H.M.M. Peeters and G.A. Pfann (1993), 'Adjustment costs and time-to-build in factor demand in the U.S. manufacturing industry', Empirical Economics, 18, 639-671.

Park, J.A. (1984), 'Gestation Lags with Variable Plans: An Empirical Study of Aggregate Investment', Ph.D. dissertation, Carnegie-Mellon University.

Pesaran, M.H. and A.S. Deaton (1978), 'Testing non-nested nonlinear regression models', Econometrica, 46, 677-694.

Pfann, G.A. (1990), Stochastic Adjustment Models of Labour Demand, Springer-Verlag, Germany.

Pfann, G.A. and F.C. Palm (1993), 'Asymmetric adjustment costs in non-linear labour demand models for the Netherlands and UK manufacturing sectors', Review of Economic Studies, 60, 397-412.

Pindyck, R.S. (1991), 'Irreversibility, uncertainty, and investment', Journal of Economic Literature, 29, 1110-1148.

Pindyck, R.S. and J.J. Rotemberg (1983a), 'Dynamic factor demand under rational expectations', Scandinavian Journal of Economics, 85, 223-238.

Pindyck, R.S. and J.J. Rotemberg (1983b), 'Dynamic factor demands and the effects of energy price shocks', American Economic Review, 73, 1066-1079.

Plosser, C.I. (1989), 'Understanding real business cycles', Journal of Economic Perspectives, 3, 51-77.

Ramey, V. (1989), 'Inventories as factors of production and economic fluctuations', American Economic Review, 79, 338-354.

Ramey, V. (1991), 'Nonconvex costs and the behaviour of inventories', Journal of Political Economy, 99, 306-334.

Rossana R.J. (1993), 'The long-run implications of the production smoothing model of inventories: An empirical test', Journal of Applied Econometrics, 8, 295-306.

Rossi, E.R. (1988), 'Comparison of dynamic factor demand models', in Dynamic Econometric Modeling, edited by W.A. Barnett, E.R. Berndt and H. White, Cambridge, Cambridge University Press, 357-376.

Rouwenhorst, K.G. (1991), 'Time to build and aggregate fluctuations, Are consideration', Journal of Monetary Economics, 27, 241-254.

Sargent, T.J. (1978), 'Estimation of dynamic labor demand schedules under rational expectations', Journal of Political Economy, 86, 1009-1044.

Sargent, T.J. (1987), Macroeconomic Theory, Second edition, Academic Press, Inc.,San Diego, California.

Schaller, H. (1990), "A re-examination of the Q theory of investment using U.S. firm data", Journal of Applied Econometrics, 5, 309-325.

Schiantarelli, F. and D. Georgoutsos (1990), 'Monopolistic competition and the q theory of investment', European Economic Review, 34, 1061-1078.

Schultz, T.W. (1961), 'Investment in human capital', The American Economic Review, 51, 1-17.

Schwarz, G. (1978), 'Estimating the dimension of a model', Annals of Statistics, 6, 461-464.

Sensenbrenner, G. (1991), 'Aggregate investment, the stock market, and the Q model, Robust results for six OECD countries', European Economic Review, 35, 769-832.

Shapiro, M.D. (1986), 'The dynamic demand for capital and labour', Quarterly

Journal of Economics, 513-542.

Smolny, W. (1993), Dynamic Factor Demand in a Rationing Context: Theory and Estimation of a Macroeconomic Disequilibrium Model for the Federal Republic of Germany, Physica-Verlag, Springer-Verlag, Germany.

Solow, R.M. (1957), 'Technological progress and productivity change', The Review of Economics and Statistics, 39, 312-320.

Spence, M. (1973), 'Job market signaling', Quarterly Journal of Economics, 355-374.

Tauchen, G. (1986), 'Statistical properties of Generalized Method-of-Moments estimators of structural parameters obtained from financial market data', Journal of Business and Economic Statistics, 4, 397-416.

Taylor, J.B. (1982), 'The Swedish investment funds system as a stabilization policy rule', Brookings Papers on Economic Activity, 57-106.

Tobin, J. (1969), 'A general equilibrium approach to monetary theory', Journal of Money, Credit and Banking, 1, 15-29.

Toda, H.Y. and P.C.B. Phillips (1991), 'Vector autoregression and causality: a theoretical overview and simulation study', Cowles Foundation Discussion Paper No. 1001, Yale University.

Toda, H.Y. and P.C.B. Phillips (1993a), 'The spurious effect of unit roots on vector autoregressions, An analytical study', Journal of Econometrics, 59, 229-255.

Toda, H.Y. and P.C.B. Phillips (1993b), 'Vector autoregressions and causality', Econometrica, 61, 1367-1393.

Treadway, A.B. (1969), 'On rational entrepreneurial behaviour and the demand for investment', Review of Economic Studies, 36, 227-239.

Treadway, A.B. (1971), 'The rational multivariate flexible accelerator', Econometrica, 39, 845-855.

Urbain, J.P. (1993), Exogeneity in Error Correction Models, Springer-Verlag, Germany.

Uzawa, H. (1964), 'Optimal growth in a two-sector model of capital accumulation', Review of Economic Studies, 31, 1-24.

Vuong, Q.H. (1989), "Likelihood ratio tests for model selection and non-nested hypotheses", Econometrica, 57, 307-333.

Ward, M. (1976), "The measurement of capital", Organisation for Economic Co-operation and Development, Paris, France.

West, K.D. (1986a), 'A variance bounds test of the linear quadratic inventory model', Journal of Political Economy, 94, 374-401.

West, K.D. (1986b), 'Full- versus limited-information estimation of a rational-expectations model, Some Numerical Comparisons', Journal of Econometrics, 33, 367-385.

West, K.D. (1987), 'Order backlogs and production smoothing', National Bureau of

Economic Research working paper no. 2385, Cambridge, Massachusetts.

West, K.D. (1993), Inventory models, National Bureau of Economic Research technical working paper no. 143, Cambridge, MA.

West, K.D. and D.W. Wilcox (1993), Some evidence on finite sample behavior of an instrumental variables estimator of the linear quadratic inventory model, National Bureau of Economic Research technical paper no. 139, Cambridge, Massachusetts.

Wolfson, P. (1993), 'Compositional change, aggregation, and dynamic factor demand', Journal of Applied Econometrics, 8, 129-148.

AUTHOR INDEX

LIST OF SYMBOLS IN ECONOMETRIC ANALYSES

a	parameter in production function or restricted cost function
c	intercept
cov_t	covariance
e_t	residual
f_t	K_t, N_t or V_t
p_t	C_t^n, W_t^n, P_{mt}^n or Q_t^d
q_t (q_t^{marg}, q_t^{aver})	quotient of market value and replacement value of physical capital stock, Tobin's (marginal, average) q
r	rank of matrix Π in cointegration analyses; sample correlation coefficient
r_t	nominal interest rate
s	sample standard deviation
$\bar{x}$	sample mean
z_t	variable representing a production factor or a price
C	matrix with intercepts
C_t (C_t^s, C_t^e)	real investment price of (structures, equipment) capital good
C_t^n (C_t^{sn}, C_t^{en})	nominal investment price of (structures, equipment) capital good
D_t	depreciation at time $t+1$; matrix of exogenous variables in cointegration analyses
E	rational expectations sign
I_t (I_t^s, I_t^e)	gross (structures, equipment) investments in volumes
I_i	identity matrix with dimension i
J (J^s, J^e)	time-to-build, length of construction period (structures, equipment)
G_2	statistic in unit root analyses
K_t (K_t^s, K_t^e)	productive (structures, equipment) physical capital stock
K_t^*	productive capital stock utilized for production
L	delivery lag length; lag operator
L_{it}	criterium function in inventory analyses
N_t	$\equiv NP_t + NH_t$, labour, the average number of hours worked
NP_t	number of all employees
NH_t	average number of hours worked
$M_{(i)}$	parameter matrix in process of prices; parameter matrix in flexible accelerator model

M_t	materials and energy
O_i	square zero matrix with dimension i
P_t	$\equiv [C_t^s \ C_t^e \ W_t]'$, real factor price vector in chapter 3, appendix 4.A;
	$\equiv [C_t \ W_t]'$, real factor price vector in appendix 4.B
P_t^n	$\equiv [C_t^{sn}, C_t^{en}, W_t^n]'$, nominal factor price vector
P_{mt}^n	nominal price of materials (including energy)
P_t^q	price of product
Q_t, Q_t^s	production, supply of product
Q_t^d	sales, demand of product
R	parameter matrix in technology process
R_t	$\equiv P_t^q Q_t$, revenues
S_2	statistic in unit root analyses
$S_{j,t}$	physical capital stock project under construction j periods from completion
T	sample size
U_t	utilisation rate of physical capital stock
V_t	inventory stock
$V_{(i)t}$	criterium function in model
W_t	real hourly wage
W_t^n	nominal hourly wage
X_t	$\equiv [K_t^s \ K_t^e \ N_t]'$, vector of production factors in chapter 3, 4, appendix 4.B;
	$\equiv [K_t \ N_t]'$, vector of production factors in appendix 4.A;
	$\equiv [K_t^s \ N_t \ V_t]'$, vector of factors in chapter 5
X_t^d	$\equiv [K_{t+Js-1}^s \ K_{t+Je-1}^e \ N_t]'$, vector with decision variables
X_t^*	stationary solution for X_t
Y_t	$\equiv [I_t^s \ I_t^e \ N_t]'$
Z_t	vector containing production factors and/or real prices

f, g, h_i	functions
b, f	reduced form parameter
$B_{(ii)}, C_i, D, F_{(i)}, G_{(ii)}, M, M_i^*, \overline{M}, U_{(i)}$	reduced form matrices
$AC_t \ (IAC_t, EAC_t)$	(internal, external) adjustment costs
AVC_t	average variable costs
$EAAC_t \ (IAAC_t)$	external (internal) average adjustment costs
$EMAC_t \ (IMAC_t)$	external (internal) marginal adjustment costs
VC_t	variable costs
VC_t^-	variable costs minus external adjustment costs
TC_t	$\equiv AC_t + VC_t$, total costs

α	parameter or parameter vector in production function or restricted cost function; weighting matrix in cointegration analyses
α_s (α_d)	intercept in cointegration analyses in production (sales) equation
β	matrix in cointegration analyses containing the cointegration relationships; constant nominal discount factor
β_t	nominal discount factor
β_s (β_d)	parameter in cointegration analyses in production (sales) equation
γ	parameter in adjustment costs function
δ_j	parameter in time-to-build specification, value-put-in-place of capital project j periods from completion
$e_t^{(i)}$	disturbance
e_{fp}^i	'elasticity' or reaction of Δf by change in Δp in the short term (i=s), medium term (i=m) or long term (i=l)
ζ	asymmetry parameter in adjustment costs function
η	parameter in adjustment costs function in production smoothing model
η^s (η^e)	parameter in structures (equipment) investment price influencing equation
θ	parameter in objective function concerning inventories
κ (κ^s, κ^e)	constant (structures, equipment) depreciation rate
λ	vector of unobservable technology shocks
λ_{max}	test statistic in cointegration analyses
μ	parameter in process of prices
ν	parameter in unit root tests
ρ	parameter in process of technology shocks; (sample) correlation coefficient
σ^2	variance
τ	parameter associated with deterministic trends
$\hat{\tau}$	test statistic in unit root analyses
φ (φ^s, φ^e)	parameter in time-to-build specification, net increase in productive (structures, equipment) capital stock
ψ	parameter associated with nominal cost shocks in production smoothing model
ψ^s (ψ^e)	parameter in structures (equipment) investment price influencing model
ω	parameter associated with level of production in production smoothing model

A	parameter matrix in production function
Γ	parameter matrix in adjustment cost function
Γ$_i$	matrix in cointegration analyses
Σ (Σ^λ, Σ^p)	covariance matrix disturbance (technology equation, factor prices equation)
diag{ }	diagonal, i.e. elements in curled brackets are the diagonal elements
Δ	first difference operator
Δ_t^*	$\equiv V_t - \theta_0 - \theta_1 Q_t^d$, deviation of inventory stocks from sales
$\Delta_{j,t}$	$\equiv S_{j,t} - S_{j-1,t+1}$, change in current project under construction that is j periods from completion
Π	$\equiv \alpha\beta'$, parameter matrix in cointegration analyses
Ψ_{ii}	parameter matrix in impulse response functions
Ω_t	information set that includes variables up to and including period t

Subscript i refers to a number.
Subscript t refers to period t.

Vol. 325: P. Ferri, E. Greenberg, The Labor Market and Business Cycle Theories. X, 183 pages. 1989.

Vol. 326: Ch. Sauer, Alternative Theories of Output, Unemployment, and Inflation in Germany: 1960–1985. XIII, 206 pages. 1989.

Vol. 327: M. Tawada, Production Structure and International Trade. V, 132 pages. 1989.

Vol. 328: W. Güth, B. Kalkofen, Unique Solutions for Strategic Games. VII, 200 pages. 1989.

Vol. 329: G. Tillmann, Equity, Incentives, and Taxation. VI, 132 pages. 1989.

Vol. 330: P.M. Kort, Optimal Dynamic Investment Policies of a Value Maximizing Firm. VII, 185 pages. 1989.

Vol. 331: A. Lewandowski, A.P. Wierzbicki (Eds.), Aspiration Based Decision Support Systems. X, 400 pages. 1989.

Vol. 332: T.R. Gulledge, Jr., L.A. Litteral (Eds.), Cost Analysis Applications of Economics and Operations Research. Proceedings. VII, 422 pages. 1989.

Vol. 333: N. Dellaert, Production to Order. VII, 158 pages. 1989.

Vol. 334: H.-W. Lorenz, Nonlinear Dynamical Economics and Chaotic Motion. XI, 248 pages. 1989.

Vol. 335: A.G. Lockett, G. Islei (Eds.), Improving Decision Making in Organisations. Proceedings. IX, 606 pages. 1989.

Vol. 336: T. Puu, Nonlinear Economic Dynamics. VII, 119 pages. 1989.

Vol. 337: A. Lewandowski, I. Stanchev (Eds.), Methodology and Software for Interactive Decision Support. VIII, 309 pages. 1989.

Vol. 338: J.K. Ho, R.P. Sundarraj, DECOMP: an Implementation of Dantzig-Wolfe Decomposition for Linear Programming. VI, 206 pages.

Vol. 339: J. Terceiro Lomba, Estimation of Dynamic Econometric Models with Errors in Variables. VIII, 116 pages. 1990.

Vol. 340: T. Vasko, R. Ayres, L. Fontvieille (Eds.), Life Cycles and Long Waves. XIV, 293 pages. 1990.

Vol. 341: G.R. Uhlich, Descriptive Theories of Bargaining. IX, 165 pages. 1990.

Vol. 342: K. Okuguchi, F. Szidarovszky, The Theory of Oligopoly with Multi-Product Firms. V, 167 pages. 1990.

Vol. 343: C. Chiarella, The Elements of a Nonlinear Theory of Economic Dynamics. IX, 149 pages. 1990.

Vol. 344: K. Neumann, Stochastic Project Networks. XI, 237 pages. 1990.

Vol. 345: A. Cambini, E. Castagnoli, L. Martein, P Mazzoleni, S. Schaible (Eds.), Generalized Convexity and Fractional Programming with Economic Applications. Proceedings, 1988. VII, 361 pages. 1990.

Vol. 346: R. von Randow (Ed.), Integer Programming and Related Areas. A Classified Bibliography 1984–1987. XIII, 514 pages. 1990.

Vol. 347: D. Ríos Insua, Sensitivity Analysis in Multiobjective Decision Making. XI, 193 pages. 1990.

Vol. 348: H. Störmer, Binary Functions and their Applications. VIII, 151 pages. 1990.

Vol. 349: G.A. Pfann, Dynamic Modelling of Stochastic Demand for Manufacturing Employment. VI, 158 pages. 1990.

Vol. 350: W.-B. Zhang, Economic Dynamics. X, 232 pages. 1990.

Vol. 351: A. Lewandowski, V. Volkovich (Eds.), Multiobjective Problems of Mathematical Programming. Proceedings, 1988. VII, 315 pages. 1991.

Vol. 352: O. van Hilten, Optimal Firm Behaviour in the Context of Technological Progress and a Business Cycle. XII, 229 pages. 1991.

Vol. 353: G. Ricci (Ed.), Decision Processes in Economics. Proceedings, 1989. III, 209 pages 1991.

Vol. 354: M. Ivaldi, A Structural Analysis of Expectation Formation. XII, 230 pages. 1991.

Vol. 355: M. Salomon. Deterministic Lotsizing Models for Production Planning. VII, 158 pages. 1991.

Vol. 356: P. Korhonen, A. Lewandowski, J . Wallenius (Eds.), Multiple Criteria Decision Support. Proceedings, 1989. XII, 393 pages. 1991.

Vol. 357: P. Zörnig, Degeneracy Graphs and Simplex Cycling. XV, 194 pages. 1991.

Vol. 358: P. Knottnerus, Linear Models with Correlated Disturbances. VIII, 196 pages. 1991.

Vol. 359: E. de Jong, Exchange Rate Determination and Optimal Economic Policy Under Various Exchange Rate Regimes. VII, 270 pages. 1991.

Vol. 360: P. Stalder, Regime Translations, Spillovers and Buffer Stocks. VI, 193 pages . 1991.

Vol. 361: C. F. Daganzo, Logistics Systems Analysis. X, 321 pages. 1991.

Vol. 362: F. Gehrels, Essays In Macroeconomics of an Open Economy. VII, 183 pages. 1991.

Vol. 363: C. Puppe, Distorted Probabilities and Choice under Risk. VIII, 100 pages . 1991

Vol. 364: B. Horvath, Are Policy Variables Exogenous? XII, 162 pages. 1991.

Vol. 365: G. A. Heuer, U. Leopold-Wildburger. Balanced Silverman Games on General Discrete Sets. V, 140 pages. 1991.

Vol. 366: J. Gruber (Ed.), Econometric Decision Models. Proceedings, 1989. VIII, 636 pages. 1991.

Vol. 367: M. Grauer, D. B. Pressmar (Eds.), Parallel Computing and Mathematical Optimization. Proceedings. V, 208 pages. 1991.

Vol. 368: M. Fedrizzi, J. Kacprzyk, M. Roubens (Eds.), Interactive Fuzzy Optimization. VII, 216 pages. 1991.

Vol. 369: R. Koblo, The Visible Hand. VIII, 131 pages.1991.

Vol. 370: M. J. Beckmann, M. N. Gopalan, R. Subramanian (Eds.), Stochastic Processes and their Applications. Proceedings, 1990. XLI, 292 pages. 1991.

Vol. 371: A. Schmutzler, Flexibility and Adjustment to Information in Sequential Decision Problems. VIII, 198 pages. 1991.

Vol. 372: J. Esteban, The Social Viability of Money. X, 202 pages. 1991.

Vol. 373: A. Billot, Economic Theory of Fuzzy Equilibria. XIII, 164 pages. 1992.

Vol. 374: G. Pflug, U. Dieter (Eds.), Simulation and Optimization. Proceedings, 1990. X, 162 pages. 1992.

Vol. 375: S.-J. Chen, Ch.-L. Hwang, Fuzzy Multiple Attribute Decision Making. XII, 536 pages. 1992.

Vol. 376: K.-H. Jöckel, G. Rothe, W. Sendler (Eds.), Bootstrapping and Related Techniques. Proceedings, 1990. VIII, 247 pages. 1992.

Vol. 377: A. Villar, Operator Theorems with Applications to Distributive Problems and Equilibrium Models. XVI, 160 pages. 1992.

Vol. 378: W. Krabs, J. Zowe (Eds.), Modern Methods of Optimization. Proceedings, 1990. VIII, 348 pages. 1992.

Vol. 379: K. Marti (Ed.), Stochastic Optimization. Proceedings, 1990. VII, 182 pages. 1992.

Vol. 380: J. Odelstad, Invariance and Structural Dependence. XII, 245 pages. 1992.

Vol. 381: C. Giannini, Topics in Structural VAR Econometrics. XI, 131 pages. 1992.

Vol. 382: W. Oettli, D. Pallaschke (Eds.), Advances in Optimization. Proceedings, 1991. X, 527 pages. 1992.

Vol. 383: J. Vartiainen, Capital Accumulation in a Corporatist Economy. VII, 177 pages. 1992.

Vol. 384: A. Martina, Lectures on the Economic Theory of Taxation. XII, 313 pages. 1992.

Vol. 385: J. Gardeazabal, M. Regúlez, The Monetary Model of Exchange Rates and Cointegration. X, 194 pages. 1992.

Vol. 386: M. Desrochers, J.-M. Rousseau (Eds.), Computer-Aided Transit Scheduling. Proceedings, 1990. XIII, 432 pages. 1992.

Vol. 387: W. Gaertner, M. Klemisch-Ahlert, Social Choice and Bargaining Perspectives on Distributive Justice. VIII, 131 pages. 1992.

Vol. 388: D. Bartmann, M. J. Beckmann, Inventory Control. XV, 252 pages. 1992.

Vol. 389: B. Dutta, D. Mookherjee, T. Parthasarathy, T. Raghavan, D. Ray, S. Tijs (Eds.), Game Theory and Economic Applications. Proceedings, 1990. IX, 454 pages. 1992.

Vol. 390: G. Sorger, Minimum Impatience Theorem for Recursive Economic Models. X, 162 pages. 1992.

Vol. 391: C. Keser, Experimental Duopoly Markets with Demand Inertia. X, 150 pages. 1992.

Vol. 392: K. Frauendorfer, Stochastic Two-Stage Programming. VIII, 228 pages. 1992.

Vol. 393: B. Lucke, Price Stabilization on World Agricultural Markets. XI, 274 pages. 1992.

Vol. 394: Y.-J. Lai, C.-L. Hwang, Fuzzy Mathematical Programming. XIII, 301 pages. 1992.

Vol. 395: G. Haag, U. Mueller, K. G. Troitzsch (Eds.), Economic Evolution and Demographic Change. XVI, 409 pages. 1992.

Vol. 396: R. V. V. Vidal (Ed.), Applied Simulated Annealing. VIII, 358 pages. 1992.

Vol. 397: J. Wessels, A. P. Wierzbicki (Eds.), User-Oriented Methodology and Techniques of Decision Analysis and Support. Proceedings, 1991. XII, 295 pages. 1993.

Vol. 398: J.-P. Urbain, Exogeneity in Error Correction Models. XI, 189 pages. 1993.

Vol. 399: F. Gori, L. Geronazzo, M. Galeotti (Eds.), Nonlinear Dynamics in Economics and Social Sciences. Proceedings, 1991. VIII, 367 pages. 1993.

Vol. 400: H. Tanizaki, Nonlinear Filters. XII, 203 pages. 1993.

Vol. 401: K. Mosler, M. Scarsini, Stochastic Orders and Applications. V, 379 pages. 1993.

Vol. 402: A. van den Elzen, Adjustment Processes for Exchange Economies and Noncooperative Games. VII, 146 pages. 1993.

Vol. 403: G. Brennscheidt, Predictive Behavior. VI, 227 pages. 1993.

Vol. 404: Y.-J. Lai, Ch.-L. Hwang, Fuzzy Multiple Objective Decision Making. XIV, 475 pages. 1994.

Vol. 405: S. Komlósi, T. Rapcsák, S. Schaible (Eds.), Generalized Convexity. Proceedings, 1992. VIII, 404 pages. 1994.

Vol. 406: N. M. Hung, N. V. Quyen, Dynamic Timing Decisions Under Uncertainty. X, 194 pages. 1994.

Vol. 407: M. Ooms, Empirical Vector Autoregressive Modeling. XIII, 380 pages. 1994.

Vol. 408: K. Haase, Lotsizing and Scheduling for Production Planning. VIII, 118 pages. 1994.

Vol. 409: A. Sprecher, Resource-Constrained Project Scheduling. XII, 142 pages. 1994.

Vol. 410: R. Winkelmann, Count Data Models. XI, 213 pages. 1994.

Vol. 411: S. Dauzère-Péres, J.-B. Lasserre, An Integrated Approach in Production Planning and Scheduling. XVI, 137 pages. 1994.

Vol. 412: B. Kuon, Two-Person Bargaining Experiments with Incomplete Information. IX, 293 pages. 1994.

Vol. 413: R. Fiorito (Ed.), Inventory, Business Cycles and Monetary Transmission. VI, 287 pages. 1994.

Vol. 414: Y. Crama, A. Oerlemans, F. Spieksma, Production Planning in Automated Manufacturing. X, 210 pages. 1994.

Vol. 415: P. C. Nicola, Imperfect General Equilibrium. XI, 167 pages. 1994.

Vol. 416: H. S. J. Cesar, Control and Game Models of the Greenhouse Effect. XI, 225 pages. 1994.

Vol. 417: B. Ran, D. E. Boyce, Dynamic Urban Transportation Network Models. XV, 391 pages. 1994.

Vol. 418: P. Bogetoft, Non-Cooperative Planning Theory. XI, 309 pages. 1994.

Vol. 419: T. Maruyama, W. Takahashi (Eds.), Nonlinear and Convex Analysis in Economic Theory. VIII, 306 pages. 1995.

Vol. 420: M. Peeters, Time-To-Build. Interrelated Investment and Labour Demand Modelling. With Applications to Six OECD Countries. IX, 204 pages. 1995.

Vol. 421: C. Dang, Triangulations and Simplicial Methods. IX, 196 pages. 1995.